AGENDA FOR
EDUCATIONAL CHANGE

Edited by John Shortt
and Trevor Cooling

APOLLOS

Stapleford House Education Centre

APOLLOS (an imprint of Inter-Varsity Press),
38 De Montfort Street, Leicester LE1 7GP, England

© The Stapleford Project and Contributors, 1997

First published 1997

British Library Cataloguing in Publication Data
A catalogue record for this book is available from the British Library.

ISBN 0–85111–449–0

Set in 11 pt Garamond

Typeset in Great Britain by Stapleford House Education Centre

Printed in Great Britain by Clays Ltd, Bungay, Suffolk

*This book is dedicated to the Whitefield Institute
and particularly to its director, Dr David Cook.
Their interest over many years has helped to keep alight
the flame of Christian concern for education.*

ACKNOWLEDGMENTS

The editors would like to express their thanks to the many people who have contributed to the appearance of this book. David Cook, Ruth Deakin, Colin Duriez, Deborah Helme, Brian Hill, Ann Holt, Pam MacKenzie and Elmer Thiessen all kindly gave three days of their valuable time to plan the structure. Members of the annual Theory of Education Conference held at Stapleford House in January 1994 offered a host of ideas for topics to cover. David Pepper's wizardry on the computer and Heather Miller's persistence with the typing of the text ensured that we had a computer disk ready for the printer. Elaine Cooke, Ruth Cooper and Dianne McLaren in the Stapleford House office dealt with the many telephone calls, faxes and letters generated by the process of liaising with contributors. The Trustees of the Stapleford Project are to be thanked for funding the book. Without their support we could not have proceeded. Finally, the contributors showed great patience as we asked them for revisions of their chapters. They are to be congratulated on the professional way in which they fulfilled our many requests. To them particularly we are grateful. It is their hard work that created this book.

CONTENTS

PREFACE

An emerging community of thought

Over the past couple of decades in the UK and in other countries, evangelical Christians have been making a small but growing contribution to debate about the nature and aims of education. This has been achieved through academic journals such as *Spectrum* and the Australian *Journal of Christian Education* as well as through articles appearing in other journals and a number of books.

Although individual thinkers making this contribution come from countries as far apart as Canada and the USA, Australia, Great Britain and several countries on the European mainland, a very loose-knit and informal but definite community of thought can be seen to be emerging. It is part of a wider community of writers within the evangelical Christian tradition who share a concern to integrate their faith with their theoretical studies across the whole range of academic disciplines.

In sponsoring this present volume, the Stapleford Project was concerned to bring together a number of writers from this community to focus upon a particular contribution to the educational debate. The writers come from a range of disciplines, but the focus is upon educational issues, and the concern is to make an academically serious and distinctively Christian contribution to discussions about the nature and purpose of education.

Evangelical and transformationalist

There are two main characteristics which make this community of thought distinctive.

11

First, the theological tradition represented by the contributors to Parts 1 to 5 of this symposium is identified as evangelical. Each contribution is intended to offer a clear evangelical Christian grounding. Authors were invited to demonstrate how such a Christian theology makes a distinctive contribution to the subject matter.

'Evangelical' and its cognates do not lend themselves to exact and universally acceptable definition, but their uses do have what the philosopher Wittgenstein termed 'family resemblances'. In his major study of British evangelicalism (*Evangelicalism in Modern Britain*, Unwin Hyman, 1989, p. 3), David Bebbington identifies four such characteristics:

> ... conversionism, the belief that lives need to be changed;
> activism, the expression of the Gospel in effort; biblicism,
> a particular regard for the Bible; and what may be called
> crucicentrism, a stress on the sacrifice of Christ on the
> cross. Together they form a quadrilateral of priorities that
> is the basis of Evangelicalism.

The 'particular regard for the Bible' referred to here is in turn difficult to define precisely, but it is of central importance among these characteristics. Evangelicals hold that the Bible uniquely records God's special revelation to humankind ('special' as distinct from his 'general' revelation in nature, including human nature). In it are revealed by God truths not otherwise known, and it is held to be supremely authoritative in all matters of faith. Regarded as central among these divinely revealed truths are the deity of Christ, his death for sinners on the cross and his bodily resurrection, the need of personal response in repentance and faith in order to have an assurance of salvation, and a responsibility to be active in the proclamation in life and word of the good news of Christ.

The community of thought from which this symposium comes is characterized not only by its evangelical theology but also by a particular kind of approach to the integration of faith and learning in the various academic disciplines. Several of the chapters that follow provide a more detailed acount of this kind of approach, so I will outline it only briefly at this stage. It is often termed 'transformationalist', and it is contrasted with 'compatibilism' on the one hand and, on the other, 'reconstructionism'.

The compatibilist maintains the strict autonomy of the forms of human knowledge and understanding, so that basic theological beliefs cannot have any implications *within* non-theological areas. Nevertheless, the compatibilist claims, the different ways of understanding – including the theological – all fit together in a total view of reality in all its diverse aspects. At the other extreme (or the other end of the continuum along which these three integrative strategies are ranged) is the approach of the reconstructionalist. According to this, there is a total antithesis between Christian presuppositions and those of all alternative worldviews and life-views, such that talk of 'common ground' or 'common notions' is without meaning. The forms of knowledge have at their bases anti-Christian presuppositions and therefore need to be totally reconstructed on exclusively biblical assumptions.

Between these positions is that of the transformationalist strategy generally adopted by the contributors to this symposium. This strategy brings Christian presuppositions into relationship with those which are not exclusively Christian but rather are common to Christian and non-Christian. The concern is to bring about a transformation of a form of knowledge but, unlike the reconstructionalist, to do so from within and by making use of shared insights – but without ascribing to them the worldview-independent status they are given by the compatibilist.

Key themes

In January 1994, a group of eight Christian educationalists met for three days at Stapleford House Education Centre to discuss the nature and structure of this symposium. They discussed the overall purposes of such a volume, identified key themes and issues to be addressed and worked on the outline of a brief for the writers.

Four key themes were identified:

- The role of worldview (presuppositions) in knowing. The impossibility of neutrality. The balance between objectivity and subjectivity.

- The relationships between the constants of the Christian

13

faith and the need for creative response to a changing educational world.

- The importance of defining a vision for the sort of people and hence the sort of society we should be striving to create through education.

- The centrality of relationships and an ethic of love in any Christian vision for education.

The commentary at the beginning of each part of the book will seek to identify which of these themes are present and how they are dealt with by the writers. These commentaries will also seek to identify any other themes that emerge and run through the book. These themes will all be brought together in the concluding chapter, and particular attention will be given there to the nature and role of presuppositions.

Overall purposes

The educational scene is going through many upheavals at the present time. They are all happening against the backdrop of major changes in how knowledge is regarded in all the disciplines (changes that one contributor to this volume terms a 'modern Babel'). One of the purposes of the book is to be proactive rather than reactive. It is all too easy to keep revisiting the issues of the past or to assume that the future will be an extension of the present. One of our hopes for this book is that it will open up new issues as well as uncover new ways of dealing with those of the present, so that, even in a small way, it might be influential in shaping education into the next millennium and offer practical ways forward.

Although the general approach to be taken has been identified as evangelical in its theology and transformationalist in its faith-learning strategy, another purpose of the book is to celebrate the differences in the ways individual authors approach the issues they address. There is variety not only in the issues themselves and in the specialist areas from within which they are tackled, but also in the particular theological and philosophical perspectives which are brought to bear upon them (within the broadly evangelical and transformationalist limits defined earlier).

A third purpose – and by no means the least of them – is that the book should open up a wider debate by having a section where three scholars from outside the community of thought offer their comments on the main body of the contents. They were asked to respond in the light of their own educational concerns and worldviews. (As it turns out, the Islamic response is rather more of an outline of an Islamic approach to education than a detailed response to the earlier chapters.) In addition, another evangelical scholar was asked to reflect on the book in the light of this preface.

Whether, and to what extent, these purposes have been realized in the book is finally for the reader to decide. The editors and contributors would be very pleased to have any responses that readers would like to make. Please send them to us at Stapleford House Education Centre, Wesley Place, Stapleford, Nottingham, NG9 8DP (e-mail: actuk@hway.net).

John Shortt

THE CONTRIBUTORS

Professor Syed Ali Ashraf is General-Director of the Islamic Academy, Cambridge, and a member of the Faculty of Education, University of Cambridge. He is also the Founder-Rector of Darul Ihsan Private University in Dhaka, Bangladesh, and Director-General of the World Centre for Islamic Education, Makkah. He is the author or editor of a number of books and founder-editor of *Muslim Education Quarterly*.

Rev. Dr Jeff Astley is Director of the ecumenical North of England Institute for Christian Education and Honorary Lecturer in Theology and Education at the University of Durham. He has written or edited a number of texts on Christian education and religious education, including *The Philosophy of Christian Religious Education* (SPCK, 1994) and *Christian Theology and Religious Education* (with Leslie Francis, SPCK, 1996).

Dr Ian Barns is based at the Institute for Science and Technology Policy at Murdoch University, Western Australia, where he has responsibility for teaching and research in the areas of public theology, technology and ethics, and science and the media. He is also a member of the Social Responsibilities Commission of the General Synod of the Anglican Church in Australia.

Luke Bretherton is International Director of the Ethics Development Initiative, a CARE Trust project working with the church in Central and Eastern Europe. He is also engaged in part-time PhD research in Christian ethics at the University of London and is a member of Abundant, a group of Christians organizing arts events and nightclubs in London.

Dr Jonathan Chaplin is Tutor in Politics at Plater College in Oxford and a Visiting Tutor at Oxford University Department of Continuing Education. He has edited two books and published a number of articles on Christian political thought and pluralism, and is currently completing a book on the political thought of Herman Dooyeweerd.

Rev. Colin Chapman is Principal of Crowther Hall, Selly Oak, Birmingham. He worked for a number of years in the Middle East and has written a number of books and articles, several of which have been about Christianity and Islam.

Dr Trevor Cooling is Projects Officer for the Association of Christian Teachers and Director of the Stapleford Project, a curriculum project which has published over thirty books to support the teaching of Christianity in school Religious Education. He is also course leader for a range of distance learning courses validated by the University of Nottingham and sponsored by Stapleford House and St John's College Extension Studies. He is author of *A Christian Vision for State Education* (SPCK, 1994).

Dr Ruth Deakin is engaged in research in education at the University of Bristol. She is chairperson of the board of the European Educators' Christian Association (EurECA). She was formerly headteacher of Oak Hill Independent Christian School, Bristol, and Director of the Christian Schools Campaign.

Dr Ron Elsdon is Northern Ireland Regional Co-ordinator for Crosslinks, an evangelical Anglican mission agency. He formerly lectured in Geology at University College, Dublin, and he continues to lecture and write on subjects where science and faith converge, such as ecology and information technology.

Professor Brian V. Hill is Professor of Education at Murdoch University in Western Australia. He was formerly a high-school teacher and a Scripture Union Schools staff worker. He has also been variously president of the Australian Teachers' Christian Fellowship and the Australian Fellowship of Evangelical Students, and editor of *The Journal of Christian Education*. He has written over 200 articles and ten books.

Dr Stanton L. Jones is Provost of Wheaton College, Wheaton, Illinois, USA. He was formerly Chairman of the Psychology Department at Wheaton College and has recently been a Visiting Scholar with the University of Cambridge Faculty of Divinity. In addition to works cited in his chapter, he is co-author with his wife Brenna of *God's Design for Sex*, a five-volume series on sex education in the Christian family.

Dr Paul Marshall is Senior Member in Political Theory at the Institute for Christian Studies, Toronto, and a visiting Professor at Catholic University, Washington, DC. He is the author or editor of eight books and several hundred articles on the theme of religion and politics.

Dr John Shortt is Director of Stapleford House Education Centre and Editor of *Spectrum*. He is also Director of the Charis Project, a curriculum project producing Christian resources for promoting spiritual and moral development through the teaching of mathematics, English, modern foreign languages and science. He is a member of the board of the European Educators' Christian Association (EurECA). He was for seventeen years a secondary-school teacher in England and, briefly, in Somalia.

David Smith is pursuing postgraduate studies in philosophical theology and education at the Institute of Christian Studies, Toronto. He has taught modern languages in several schools in England and he is founding editor of *Language in God's World* and chair of the Association of Christian Teachers/Christian Schools' Trust working group for modern languages. He has been involved in in-service events for Christian teachers in the UK, USA, Canada and Australia.

Monica J. Taylor is a Senior Research Officer at the National Foundation for Educational Research in England and Wales and a Visiting Senior Research Fellow at University College of St Martin, Lancaster. She has undertaken research on multicultural anti-racist, religious, moral, and personal and social education for a range of sponsors, often with a pupil perspective. She has been Editor of the *Journal of Moral Education* for twenty years and a founder member and first Chair of the Values Education Council of the UK.

Dr Elmer J. Thiessen teaches philosophy at Medicine Hat College, Alberta, Canada. He has recently authored *Teaching for Commitment: Liberal Education, Indoctrination and Christian Nurture* (Gracewing, 1993), and is presently working on a book on religious schools in a pluralist democracy. He has also published a number of articles on education and served as a guest editor of a special issue of *Ethics in Education* on the ethics of religiously based schools.

Richard Wilkins is General Secretary of the Association of Christian Teachers. He was formerly a teacher of history and religious education.

PART 1

INTRODUCTION:
BEYOND YESTERDAY

COMMENTARY

In his introductory chapter, David Smith calls for a fundamental reassessment of the relationship between faith, knowledge and the curriculum.

The curriculum is much more than a collection of subjects and quite other than a set of sets of facts to be learned. As the secular humanist vision loses its hold, the curriculum comes to be seen as 'the purveyor of a coherent or incoherent worldview, a way of understanding and being in the world'. As he develops this point, David Smith has much to say on the first of our four key themes – that of the role of worldviews. A worldview embodies not only a way of understanding life in the world but also a vision for it. Spirituality, he says, following some Reformed writers, is an active orientation of the whole person, a positive or negative response to the call of God which determines our ultimate point of commitment. This makes our worldviews and spiritualities 'religious' in the sense that our lives are 'oriented around that which is our operative god'. Mr Smith therefore depicts worldviews as rather more than the narrowly intellectual sets of basic beliefs that they are sometimes held to be. Rather, they are a matter of whole-person responses which include, but are by no means limited to, the cognitive as a central component.

The second of our key themes has to do with how Christians can hold the timeless truths of their faith and, at the same time, respond creatively to the changing educational scene. David Smith counters any suggestion that this is simply a matter of logical deduction from biblical premises to educational conclusions. He calls for a recognition of the complexity of the task as we move to and fro between our study of the Bible and our understanding and experience of our situation. We need to 'indwell the biblical narrative' so that we can create a curriculum story which comports well with the biblical story. Here Mr Smith refers to an analogy of Tom Wright's which talks of actors in a play trying to produce the unscripted final act in a way that is faithful to the first four, which had been written down by the playwright. Elmer Thiessen's chapter in Part 4 will deal further with this and with alternative ways of describing the relationship between basic Christian beliefs and the curriculum.

Implicit in David Smith's account is a view of human nature and a vision for the sort of people and society education should be concerned to develop (the third of our key themes). This involves seeing people as basically religious. We have an orientation towards or away from God and a need to develop an integrated worldview and life-view. Mr Smith's vision is for an education which contributes to 'community grounded in love and compassionate justice'. It follows from this that relationships and an ethic of love (our fourth theme) are central to this vision, although these are not matters that he deals with in any detail.

A related theme does break through in David Smith's account. It is that of the effects that not only our limitations as finite beings, but also the sinfulness of our tendencies to orient ourselves away from God, have upon our thinking, our reasoning and our knowing – what is sometimes referred to as 'the noetic effects of sin'. Mr Smith, in his account of the complex hermeneutical task of relating the Bible's teachings to educational practice, is very concerned to emphasize the ongoing struggle within us all between 'faithful and unfaithful patterns of thought'. He therefore cautions us against easy answers and triumphalism and calls for openness to correction, humility and even brokenness. Transformation of ourselves, our worldviews and our curricula is a gradual process and a hard work of faith.

1

Facing the challenge of educational change

David Smith

The accelerating demise of the Enlightenment project, with its trust in impartial reason, requires a fundamental reassessment of liberal education and of the relationship between faith, knowledge and the curriculum. A curriculum is more than a collection of 'facts' - it offers a guided tour rather than an aerial photograph, a 'horizon of possibility' for our students. The persons involved in education are spiritually responsive beings, and this aspect is more interwoven with the rest of their personhood than has traditionally been recognized. Christians have an important contribution to make to a reformulation of the educational agenda; such a contribution must be mindful of the complexity and provisionality of Christian understandings of both the Bible and the world.

Yesterday all our troubles seemed so far away. Yesterday, schools were for teaching the facts, and religion could be neatly excluded from the world of 'knowledge' by being kept boxed in a slot called 'religious education' or excluded from public education altogether. Yesterday, learners knew how to behave in school and in the community, and moral values were uncontroversial. Yesterday, Christian values could moral values were uncontroversial. Yesterday, Christian values could be assumed, while other faiths could be studied in much the same manner as other planets – distant, fascinating, undemanding (certainly not asking for their own schools!). Yesterday, reason, science and technology promised to solve all of our problems, given time.

Today our troubles seem to be here to stay. A sense of crisis has become a stable factor in western education as it gropes for adequate responses to a 'multi-racial, ethnically diverse, two-sex society that is struggling to keep things from falling apart at a historical moment when the clouds of nuclear as well as ecological disaster loom large' (Martin 1993: 125). Postmodern reactions against the rationalist tradition, an increasingly public pluralism of faiths and values, growing religious dissatisfaction with liberal solutions – these factors among others complicate the struggle profoundly. Believing in yesterday (an approach which evidences more gullibility than is warranted) will not suffice as we face the challenges of our educational tomorrow.

The challenge of responsible knowing

During a quiet part of a lesson, a thirteen-year-old student raises her hand. 'Sir, how can the Bible be true, what with the way we get taught history?' It is a French lesson. The follow-up question is: 'Sir, are you afraid of dying?' Despite the familiar compartmentalization of the curriculum, here is an individual groping for a sense of the whole, of how the pieces of the world presented by the curriculum are to be assembled. Here, too, is an individual with an ill-defined sense that the way the 'facts' are narrated in one curriculum area is at odds with the faith presented in another. And the 'facts' must be right, mustn't they?

Once upon a time, an unconditional faith in the facts might have been a plausible resolution of the tension. The rationalist tradition stemming from the Enlightenment dreamed of a knowledge independent of particular human knowers. Reason was the sure guide and sole authority which would guarantee the objective truth of our knowledge, locating it in a neutral, impartial, universal realm. Rational discussion became in the western world a matter of 'appeal to principles undeniable by any rational person and therefore independent of all those social and cultural particularities which the

25

Enlightenment thinkers took to be the mere accidental clothing of reason in particular times and places' (MacIntyre 1988: 6). This vision harboured a 'prejudice against prejudices' (Gadamer 1989: 272); faith, since it was personal, particular, contestable and thus threatening to 'pure reason', was to be kept safely apart from knowledge and pruned to keep it in line with reason's proclamations.

Such convictions have had a profound formative influence on western education. The ideal of incontestable, value-free knowledge has coloured much of the debate concerning neutrality and indoctrination, and promoted a resistance to suggestions that the voice of Christian faith may have something substantial to say about curriculum. The quest has been for 'a form of education knowing no limits other than those necessarily imposed by the nature of rational knowledge and thereby itself developing in man the final court of appeal in all human affairs' (Hirst 1974: 43); its authority was to be 'the objective necessity for accepting the conclusions of reason' (Hirst 1981: 92).

The Enlightenment sermon is now interrupted by a growing (if discordant) chorus of philosophical hecklers. As the years slip by, we are no nearer to universal agreement among rational people. The embeddedness of our knowing and perceiving in our human, embodied, located, gendered, selves is increasingly apparent, and it is no longer such a huge step to extend this embeddedness to our believing or unbelieving selves. Developments in various fields (not least the philosophy of science) have punctured positivism irreparably, and as the role of our worldviews in our knowing has become increasingly visible, faith has disconcertingly reappeared at the heart of our knowledge. As Michael Polanyi (1958: 266) puts it:

> We must now recognise belief once more as the source of
> all knowledge. Tacit assent and intellectual passions, the
> sharing of an idiom and of a cultural heritage, affiliation
> to a like-minded community: such are the impulses which
> shape our vision of the nature of things on which we rely
> for our mastery of things. No intelligence, however critical
> or original, can operate outside such a fiduciary framework.

In educational philosophy, even Paul Hirst, a key architect of liberal rationalist education, has joined the chorus in referring to 'the untenable view of reason as a disengaged, spectatorial capacity', noting that 'if our naturally given capacities of reason are exercised from the very start in inextricable involvement in our exerting our other given capacities, then the resulting achievements will of their nature be complex in character' (Hirst 1993: 190). This complexity defuses liberal rationalist rhetoric. If reason is universal and impartial, then the only alternative to accepting its deliverances is irrationality and dogmatism – a point not missed by liberal educators – but if reason partakes of the complexity and diversity of embodied human person-hood then alternative stances are not so easily dismissed. The plot thickens yet further if the complexity runs deeper than Paul Hirst suggests, our thinking and knowing being intertwined with our basic commitments, beliefs and ways of orienting ourselves in the world.

These considerations are of central relevance to the school curric-ulum. As long as knowledge is conceived as a value-free mirror-image of reality for which no-one need take personal responsibility, then the curriculum is simply a matter of selection and logical arrangement. This view has become decreasingly plausible as the relevance of issues such as class, gender and ethnicity for curriculum has been explored, and vitriolic debates over the 'right' content and shape of the curriculum have raged. If the knowledge that makes up the curric-ulum is someone's knowledge, an interpretation of the world framed by faith, then the hotly contested question becomes that of which vision of the world is to be promoted. In facing this question, the arrangement of the knowledge presented (or omitted) becomes at least as significant as the truth value of the individual 'facts'.

The design of a curriculum is not simply a matter of the juxtaposition of a series of facts; it includes psychological, develop-mental, ethical, social, pedagogical, economic, aesthetic, spiritual and other considerations. It is a creative response to a specific educational situation in which ideas and information drawn from and embedded in a surrounding culture are woven into a meaningful and selective whole by responsible human agents. This material will itself be in varying degrees contestable, reflecting worldview commitments (for examples from the natural sciences, still popularly supposed to be a haven of objectivity despite contrary developments in the philosophy of science; see Jones 1995: 138–140). What educates, however, is not only the 'facts' listed in the syllabus but the way they are organized and sequenced, the connections made, the implicit messages, the exclusions and silences, the methods used which call upon learners to be active or passive, competitive or co-operative, committed or disinterested, passionate or dispassionate (*cf.* Palmer 1983). A curriculum thus becomes the purveyor of a coherent or incoherent worldview, a way of understanding and being in the world. For most of the time, worldviews 'are that through which, not at which, a society or an individual normally looks' (Wright 1992: 125), and a curricular worldview may go largely unperceived until it is challenged in some way, its particularity concealed by its familiar air of normality.

Turning to concrete examples, history organized in such a way as to suggest linear progress towards modern western civilization, or to exclude the perspectives of, as opposed to mere mention of, the poor or the ethnically other, or to exclude any sense of pattern or meaning, teaches much more than a series of 'facts'. These additional lessons may in fact have a much longer-lasting impact. My doubts about many current course materials in modern languages are not a matter of whether it is true, for instance, that Germans go shopping and eat pizza, but rather of the pervasiveness of a consumer orientation and the range of human experience (including any kind of faith) typically excluded (see Smith 1994). A curriculum in which religious belief is either excluded altogether or confined within a special compartment and denied any import for the rest of curriculum (where the 'real world' is dealt with) teaches an Enlightenment lesson which many Christians have learned all too well. Moreover, as Cooling (1994) has shown in some detail, religious education itself may take place within a horizon which, in its emphasis on rational autonomy, makes committed faith seem inherently implausible.

All of this suggests that a curriculum is far more a guided tour than an aerial photograph of reality, and that the tour guides carry much more responsibility for the shape of that tour than is sometimes acknowledged. As Simon comments (1992: 56):

Education is implicated in the production, accessibility, and legitimization of the language and images that give our relations with our social and material world a particular intelligibility. This means that educational practice is a power relation that participates in both enabling and constraining what is understood as knowledge and truth. When we teach we are always implicated in the construction

of a horizon of possibility for ourselves, our students and
our communities.

A preoccupation with what 'works' or with the accumulation of true
propositions misses this dimension of curriculum, in which a vision
for, as well as of, our life in the world is communicated.

Failure to give due weight to this 'horizon of possibility' has
contributed to myopia concerning the relevance of faith for the
curriculum. The question of a Christian curriculum is not the somewhat facile question of whether individual facts in each curriculum
area can be deduced from the Bible; it is the question of whether
Christians are prepared to take responsibility for developing their
vision for and understanding of the world.

This responsibility runs deeper than evangelicals have sometimes
implied. Christian thought also is informed by a cultural, historical
and intellectual context. It does not stand outside the struggles and
influences which characterize human attempts to know truly, or the
realities of a human learning process. The fear of the LORD is a good
start (Proverbs 1:7), but the process of making every thought obedient
to Christ (2 Corinthians 10:5) is no more characterized by instant-
aneous perfection than any other aspect of sanctification; it too must
be worked out with fear and trembling. Sin and distortion are found
in the church as well as in the world.

Any attempt to relate the Scriptures to our human tasks and
callings (such as education) involves an effort to understand the Bible
in relation to an effort to understand the situation in which we live
and work. The burgeoning literature on hermeneutics makes clear
that neither of these efforts is a simple, contextless reading of what is
there; they both take place within the complex of expectations,
experiences, questions and influences which characterizes all of our
knowing; in short, within the horizon of a worldview. Moreover, the
movement is not simply from the Bible to our situation. The two
efforts to understand interact with and influence each other; our ways
of reading the Bible contribute to the worldview through which we
interpret our situation, while our understanding and experience of
our situation will help to condition the kinds of questions and
expectations which we bring to the Bible (cf. Olthuis 1985).

Attempts at Christian thinking are, then, also 'of their nature
complex in character', reflecting growth in or failure of understanding

and an ongoing struggle between faithful and unfaithful patterns of thought (*cf.* Klapwijk 1991). Relating scriptural truth to education is not, then, a safely mechanical process of linear deduction by which the security of scriptural authority can be simply transferred to Christian educational contributions. The Bible is not a divine encyclopedia offering information on all subjects. While some specific requirements and prohibitions and some broad areas of permission can be found in Scripture, these taken alone will leave a truncated sense of the Bible's authority in education. Also needed is a sense of how we are invited to indwell the biblical narrative, allowing its 'horizon of possibility' to become ours and to shape the way we look at and live in the world. As Christians seek to work out their faith in an educational arena they are not on a production line, assembling identical products from a detailed blueprint. They are more like actors given a play to perform whose last act is not scripted, exerting all their capacities to produce a final act which is faithful to the first four (Wright 1991; 1992: 140–144; *cf.* also Elmer Thiessen's comments on this in chapter 10 below). Their aim in education will be that the story told by the curriculum, the worldview conveyed by its choice and organization of content and methods, should fit well with the contours of the biblical story. This will involve active appropriation and creative response, a responsible working out of the orientation provided by the Scriptures in ongoing humility and openness to correction. (For a more detailed discussion see Smith 1995.)

The alternative to this process is capitulation to the apparent givenness of dominant educational paradigms and practices. This route can seem less risky, but it amounts to abdication of responsibility. If knowledge and belief are intimately intertwined, then honesty demands that a threadbare show of neutrality give way to a responsible rooting of educational contributions in an openly confessed faith.[1]

The challenge of responsive persons

Discussions of the nature of knowledge have clear connections to shifting beliefs concerning the persons (learners, teachers, philosophers) who know. Ironically, progress in this area has raised some of the contemporary difficulty. If questions such as gender, ethnicity and faith are not accidental trappings surrounding a uniform rational core, then our personhood is much more interwoven and diverse than traditional accounts have often perceived. Given that education must be faithful not only to the nature of the knowledge which it seeks to convey but also to the human persons which it seeks to educate (or employs to do the educating), such shifts must be taken seriously. The question of the human person in education is discussed at greater length by Stanton Jones in chapter 6, so here I will focus on one current issue where the problems of pluralism are particularly evident, that of spiritual development.

Since the 1988 Education Reform Act, British educators have been required to cater for spiritual development across the curriculum. An agreed definition of spiritual development is, however, still not available. Any working definition adopted faces the challenging task of being helpful to schools in which children from a variety of both religious and non-religious backgrounds are educated. Since spirituality is understood and experienced differently even within a given religion, the challenge is considerable. The danger arises of being so impressed by this diversity (especially against a background of appeal to neutrality in education) that a 'lowest common denominator' approach, in which the spiritual is reduced to the aesthetic or the cognitive, will dilute the potential for helpful curricular progress (*cf.* Hill 1989). Can Christian understandings of spirituality make a contribution?

Theological developments have paralleled philosophical shifts in pursuing a more integrated vision of the person. The historical tendency to view the spirit as an immaterial substance operating in relative isolation from a less important material body has given way, in discussions of biblical texts, to an emphasis on the psychosomatic unity of the person. The biblical 'soul' is seen to be 'the totality of human nature caught up in love and wonder ... stressing the totality of life and, at the heart of it, man as a being capable of spiritual responses to God' (Carey 1977: 28). The 'spirit' may be similarly described: 'The *ruach* – breath, wind, or spirit – can act to prompt or motivate the person, while the *lebb* – heart – represents the feeling aspects of the person and his tendencies to action. The effect of either or both is to urge the central focus of the person in a certain direction' (Anderson 1969: 176).

Reformed writers in particular have focused on spirituality as an active orientation of the whole person, and on a view of the person as fundamentally one who responds to God's words of call and promise – not just in the behaviourist sense of conditioned reaction, but in the sense of heart response, of worship, commitment and service or idolatry, disobedience and rejection (*cf.* Geertsema 1993: 142-152). All of us, overtly religious or not, are both responding positively or negatively to the call of God to and in his creation, and orienting our lives around that which is our operative god, which has our trust as our ultimate point of commitment. This means that

> ... the religious way of being in the world and the 'religious' point of view is an ordinary, unavoidable way of human functioning which everyone experiences and expresses ... the quest for certainty is a common human experience, as inescapable a part of living as thinking and feeling. Belief is as natural as speech, confession as common as digestion, commitment as human as contentment (Olthuis 1978: 5).

Spirituality is a whole-person response to a call which originates outside the self and becomes 'the dynamic which leads and guides us in all the affairs of life' (Olthuis 1978: 7). It may be viewed as 'our self-conscious awareness and nurturing of the interconnectedness of all aspects of human life and the rest of existence with the existential boundary issues of life, as we are empowered or inspired to do so by a motivating dynamic or spirit' (Hart 1997).

How can this Reformed notion of spirituality as response help in a common educational setting? Here an approach to faith development taken by James Olthuis might be helpful. Olthuis contends that all people have to answer four sets of questions as they live out their lives. These are:

> Questions of being and security: Is there 'something' and not 'nothing'? Why? What, who, where is the heart of reality? And how can I be grounded securely in the ground of being? Do I have a right to be? How can I/we face the terror of non-being?
>
> Questions of trust and meaning: Is the 'something' to be trusted? To what and whom can I finally entrust myself

totally? Can I trust that my fundamental needs will be met and my life filled with meaning? How can I/we resolve our experiences of abandonment and deprivation?

Questions of power and freedom: What is the ultimate source of power and freedom? Can I, and how can I, enjoy and responsibly deal with my freedom and power as an independent agent of action and intention? In relation to others and to God? How can I deal with my/our experiences of powerlessness, violence, and bondage?

Questions of love and purpose: What is the final purpose and meaning of life? How can I experience fulfilment and integration? How can I reach out in intimacy, justice, and love to others, be connected with all the creatures of the world and with God? How can I/we overcome our pretence to self-sufficiency and/or our servile dependencies, and with open hearts freely give of ourselves to God and neighbour? (Olthuis 1985: 500).

It will be evident that all people (including those who would delete the references to God) must respond in some way to these questions. There is a great variety of responses, the differences being both individual (reflecting individual uniqueness and experience) and communal (patterned by such broader forces as social and cultural influences and specific faith traditions). Responses include the cognitive, but also every other aspect of our lives, affecting our economy, our sexuality, our language behaviour, our leisure, our emotions, our relationship to our environment, our art, our historical choices, our technology. They are not separately religious, but form a basic aspect of being human.

Such a view of spirituality clearly affects the whole curriculum. It is by no means strange today to assert, for instance, that questions of economy or technology are bound up with issues of trust, power and purpose. My questioning French student mentioned above could sense links between her history syllabus and security in the face of death. Spiritual development might accordingly be approached as a cross-curricular consideration of diverse human responses to these basic questions. These would be presented not simply as theologies, creeds or philosophies, but as actually enfleshed in different historical contexts, geographical locations, scientific developments, cultural expressions, artistic productions, with an eye to both individual and communal response. This is more than an expansion of religious education. It should be combined with an awareness that the various subject-matters delivered in the curriculum are also human responses to the questions posed by our world, and not disinterested, disembodied, neutral bodies of knowledge.

Ironically, such an awareness may do more to evade indoctrination than claims to disinterested knowledge (*cf.* Degenhardt 1990; Badley 1996). An awareness of the radical divergence and committed nature of human response could be facilitated, moving us beyond liberal education's fiction of what all reasonable people believe. School would be a place where various responses can be explored and where the rooting of the exploration in committed faiths is not denied. The fact that this exploration will often be weighted towards the cognitive in an educational environment should not be confused with an identification of the cognitive with the spiritual; students' responses to the questions posed through their education will ultimately have to be embodied in the various dimensions of life patterns lived. For many subject areas this requires new approaches – confessionally based schools and curriculum projects such as the Charis Project[2] can play an important role in developing and exploring these. This should be welcomed; the concept of cross-curricular spiritual development may be most fruitful precisely if it challenges and modifies existing practices and worldviews, provoking them to adjust to the education of spiritually responsive persons.

Beyond yesterday

The approach outlined here implies a stance towards today's problem of pluralism in beliefs and values which is itself shaped by specific commitments. This is not in itself exceptional. No attempt to encompass plurality in society either theoretically or practically is neutral or value-free; all models of pluralism have their ultimate horizons against which the plurality is described and limits are set (Mouw and Griffioen 1993; Thomas 1994). A thorough relativism would involve a 'rather quick retreat into silence' (Mouw and Griffioen

1993: 10) and the end of concern for truth or justice. For liberal education, the favoured horizon has been the ideal of a common commitment to the rational life achieved through education for rational autonomy and a downplaying of other commitments. This solution lacks credibility not only philosophically but practically; that it has alienated rather than accommodated faith communities is suggested by the growing popularity of home education and private confessionally based schools, and by current demands by Christians, Muslims and Jews for such schooling to receive government support. By seeking to banish ultimate convictions from the public realm (including, and by means of, education) and to redefine them as private preferences, secular liberalism both violates the nature of those commitments and seeks to replace them with its own vision, the particularity of which it denies (*cf.* Hulmes 1989). As the emperor's state of undress becomes increasingly evident, a more appropriate set of clothes is needed for tomorrow.

I have suggested that an essential step beyond the continuing hangover from the Enlightenment party is to reaffirm faith and commitment as profound dimensions of being human and vital elements in our visions of and for the world. The Christian faith, like other faiths, is more than a bundle of private preferences. It seeks, often brokenly, to articulate the claim of a living God to loving rule over every aspect of human existence, public and private. Our position in relation to that claim is a basic feature of our life, and any solution to the problems of pluralism which tramples over this feature of our humanity will generate injustice. The question must then be shifted from how faith commitments can be suppressed to how they can be honoured and to which faith commitments can bring life to society, growing the fruit of wholeness in place of sterility and decay.

This question will not be adequately answered by easy words, or by a triumphalist opposition between correct Christian under-standings and false non-Christian ones. The interwovenness of faith commitments with personal experience and cultural patterns makes the task of discerning what is faithful in the church's walk of faith and what is rebellious in the cultural expressions of other faiths far from straightforward. With the tares and the wheat so entangled, over-enthusiasm before the harvest is ill advised (*cf.* Matthew 13:24–25).

Evangelical Christians, themselves deeply influenced by the posi-tivist heritage, have much ground to recover in developing a Christian mind and Christian approaches to curriculum (*cf.* Noll 1994). There is a great deal of necessary work here which has simply not been done in recent times. Teachers in general are not well prepared to explore the spiritual dimension of education. In my experience, many in the United Kingdom still have minimal awareness of their present obligations in that area, let alone any clear vision of how those obligations might be approached. Communicating and envisioning for a way forward here is in itself a considerable task. The church also has ground to recover in living out the plausibility of a vision of community grounded in love and compassionate justice. If Christian educators are to present the challenge of the gospel to the educational world, there are challenges for them to face up to first. Nostalgia can be comforting, but if our yesterdays have indeed lighted fools then Christians in education must set their pilgrim faces towards tomorrow, trusting that in seeking to express Christian love and truth in the educational world they are responding to the yearnings of God and are heirs to the promise of his presence.

NOTES

1   Given the rushes of vertigo which can be experienced when the rationalist rug is tugged at the corners, it should perhaps be noted here that this does not imply irrationality, relativism or constructivism. To emphasize the role of worldviews as windows through which we look on and communicate about the world is not the same as denying that there is any givenness about the world on which we all look, that one worldview might provide a more true and life-giving view than another, or that those holding different worldviews will be capable of communicating with, influencing or even co-operating with each other. It is rather a question of emphasizing our responsibility for our believing and our knowing. As Polanyi comments (1958: 268), 'innocently we had trusted that we could be relieved of all personal responsibility for our beliefs by objective criteria of validity – and our own critical powers have shattered this hope'.

2   The Charis Project has been developing resources for addressing spiritual and moral development in various curriculum areas including English, French, German and mathematics. For more information, contact Dr John Shortt, Charis Project Director, Stapleford House Education Centre, Wesley Place, Stapleford, Nottingham NG9 8DP, UK.

BIBLIOGRAPHY

Anderson, William E. (1969), 'Education and the Biblical Concept of a Person', *Journal of Christian Education* 12/3: 170-184.

Badley, Ken (1996), 'Indoctrination and Assimilation in Plural Settings', in James H. Olthuis (ed.), *Towards an Ethics of Difference: Negotiations towards Community in a Pluralistic Society* (Washington: University Press of America), chapter 5.

Barrow, Robin, and White, Patricia (eds.) (1993), *Beyond Liberal Education: Essays in Honour of Paul H. Hirst* (London: Routledge).

Carey, George (1977), *I Believe in Man* (London: Hodder and Stoughton).

Cooling, Trevor (1994), *A Christian Vision for State Education: Reflections on the Theology of Education* (London: SPCK).

Degenhardt, M. A. B. (1990), 'The "Ethics of Belief" and Education in Science and Morals', in Leslie Francis and Adrian Thatcher (eds.), *Christian Perspectives for Education* (Leominster: Gracewing): 214-230.

Gadamer, Hans-Georg (1989), *Truth and Method*, 2nd revised edition (New York: Crossroad).

Geertsema, Hendrik (1993), 'Homo Respondens: On the Historical Nature of Human Reason', *Philosophia Reformata* 58: 120-152.

Hart, Hendrik (forthcoming, 1997), 'Conceptual Understanding and Knowing Other-wise: Reflections on Rationality and Spirituality in Philosophy', in James H. Olthuis (ed.), *Knowing Other-wise, Epistemology/ Ethics/ Spirituality* (Fordham: Fordham University Press), chapter 1.

Hill, Brian V. (1989), ' "Spiritual Development" in the Education Reform Act: A Source of Acrimony, Apathy or Accord?' *British Journal of Educational Studies* 37/2: 169-182.

Hirst, Paul H. (1974), *Knowledge and the Curriculum: A Collection of Philosophical Papers* (London: Routledge and Kegan Paul).

—— (1981), 'Education, Catechesis and the Church School', *British Journal of Religious Education* 3/3: 85-93.

—— (1993), 'Knowledge, Education and Practices', in Barrow and White 1993: 184-199.

Hulmes, Edward (1989), Education and Cultural Diversity (London: Longman).

Jones, Arthur (1995), 'Common Schools: A Christian Reflection on the Issues', *Spectrum* 27/2: 125-144.

Klapwijk, Jacob (1991), 'Epilogue: The Idea of Transformational Philosophy', in Jacob Klapwijk, Sander Griffioen and Gerben Groenewoud (eds.), *Bringing into Captivity Every Thought: Capita Selecta in the History of Christian Evaluations of Non-Christian Philosophy* (Lanham: University Press of America): 241-266.

MacIntyre, Alasdair (1988), *Whose Justice, Which Rationality?* (London: Duckworth).

Martin, Jane Roland, 'Curriculum and the Mirror of Knowledge', in Barrow and White 1993: 107-128.

Mouw, Richard J., and Griffioen, Sander (1993), *Pluralisms and Horizons: An Essay in Christian Public Philosophy* (Grand Rapids: Eerdmans).

Noll, Mark A. (1994), *The Scandal of the Evangelical Mind* (Leicester: IVP).

Olthuis, James H. (1978), *Models of Humanity in Theology and Psychology* (Toronto: Institute for Christian Studies).

—— (1985), 'Faith Development in the Adult Life Span', *Studies in Religion* 14/4: 497-509.

—— (1985b), 'On Worldviews', *Christian Scholars Review* 14/2: 153-164.

Palmer (1983), *To Know as We are Known: A Spirituality of Education* (San Francisco: Harper & Row).

Polanyi, Michael (1958), *Personal Knowledge: Towards a Post-Critical Philosophy* (London: Routledge and Kegan Paul).

Simon, Roger I. (1992), *Teaching Against the Grain: Texts for a Pedagogy of Possibility* (Toronto: OISE Press).

Smith, David (1994) (with ACT Modern Languages Working Party), *Teaching Modern Languages: A Fresh Approach to the National Curriculum* (St Albans: Association of Christian Teachers).

—— (1995), 'Christian Thinking in Education Reconsidered', *Spectrum* 27/1: 9-24.

Thomas, Owen C. (1994), 'Religious Plurality and Contemporary Philosophy: A Critical Survey', *Harvard Theological Review* 87/2: 197-213.

Wright, N. T. (1991), 'How Can the Bible be Authoritative?', *Vox Evangelica* 21: 7-32.

—— (1992), *The New Testament and the People of God* (London: SPCK).

PART 2

BEYOND THE
LIBERAL SOCIETY

COMMENTARY

The purpose of this part is to examine the deficiencies of some liberal models of society and education and to consider two approaches to education, that of common schooling and that of structural pluralism, in the light of the changing agenda in education.

Paul Marshall leads off with an account of liberalism, and its claim to deal justly with the plurality of worldviews and ways of life. Its central emphasis on freedom leads liberals to claim a universal tolerance. This, it believes, allows all to be free to live out their own ways of life with as little hindrance as possible, and requires that no view is imposed on others. The state, it claims, is neutral – not least in its educational provision – in the face of all competing worldviews. Dr Marshall argues that, far from leading to an open society, liberalism is actually opposed to plurality and the diversity that it claims to protect. This is because individualism and the fundamental value placed on autonomous choice are imposed on communities which may have other fundamental values. The effect is that their values become privatized as the communities themselves are constrained to become liberal associations.

Nor is the situation very different with postmodernism – which Paul Marshall claims to be generally just another, albeit more radical, form of liberalism. Although it claims to reject liberalism, postmodernism emphasizes even more the equal status of diverse worldviews and brings with it the same privatizing and trivializing tendencies as far as other fundamental values and beliefs are concerned. Because it is often religious values and beliefs that are privatized and trivialized, the effect is that societies in general and education in particular are secularized.

How then should Christians respond? How should they seek to influence the public realm? Jonathan Chaplin describes four main and often overlapping kinds of strategy that Christians adopt in relation to public policy. It is interesting to compare his classification with the threefold one mentioned in the preface, and described more fully in chapter 10. Both his 'traditionalist' and 'liberationist' classes seem to have elements of reconstructionalism about them; his 'liberal' category seems clearly compatibilist; while that of the fourth in his list, which he himself advocates, is undoubtedly transformationalist or, as he terms it, 'transformationist'.

The situation to which Christians need to respond with such a transforming strategy is one of pluralities of various kinds, but, most importantly, it is characterized by 'directional plurality'. This plurality of visions of the good life 'must surely be seen as the result of the fall'. In this respect, it differs from the other pluralities – those of associations and organizations and of the customs of different cultural traditions. These kinds are good and enriching and to be advocated, Chaplin says, whereas directional plurality follows from humanity's sinful rebellion and is to be tolerated rather than celebrated. The two most dominant worldviews in the western world in recent centuries have been secular liberal humanism and Christianity, but there are signs now of the emergence of a 'directional vacuum'.

Chaplin argues from what he takes to be a Christian view of the nature of faith (a free response to what is seen as divine revelation) and of the purpose of the state (to establish public justice) to the conclusion that different directional visions should be treated equitably in as many areas of public policy as possible. There are limits to this pluralism, this toleration of diverse directional pluralities, limits which are set by a Christian (and therefore non-neutral and contestable) conception of fundamental, or God-given, human rights. The object is to seek agreement through a 'dialogue of conviction', but, in a democracy, some compromise may be necessary. When that is no longer possible, the defence of a fundamental principle may even require civil disobedience.

What does this mean for education and schooling? Trevor Cooling comes to the defence of common schools as being desirable in addition to, but not instead of, separate faith-based schools. But if, as David Smith said in the introductory chapter, curriculum inevitably purveys a worldview, which worldview should that of common schools impart?

41

If, as Paul Marshall claims, that of secular liberal humanism is what is generally imposed, Christians and others will naturally find this objectionable. But if Christianity is imposed, non-Christians will also have grounds for objection (and, following Jonathan Chaplin's emphasis on the voluntary nature of faith, Christians might share some of them!). Dr Cooling considers a structural pluralism of state-supported schools, based on the beliefs and values of different communities, to be an acceptable response to this situation. He questions, however, the assumption that we should have *either* common schools *or* structural pluralism but not both existing alongside each other in the system.

Trevor Cooling finds the way the notion of 'primary culture' is used against common schooling to be quite problematic. The development of a coherent worldview is not necessarily hindered by exposure to the influence of ways of life different from that of the home and its parental primary culture. There is a problem of definition and demarcation of primary cultures, and, he adds, there may even be a tendency to an un-Christian form of relativism which loses sight of the fact that there is ultimately one truth for all.

This does not leave everything as it is in the common school system, however. Dr Cooling is a transformationalist and he wants to see a negotiation of frameworks of values in order to create institutions which promote both 'reflective understanding of the relationship between belief and knowledge and ... civic values'. Common schools should not be 'religion-free zones'. On the other hand, the systematic nurture of a child's primary culture and the formation of faith are the responsibilities of parents and of communities, such as local churches, and cannot be those of common schools in a plural society. This is not to say that what common schools do provide is not important, and, since they are the best way of providing for the educational needs of the majority of children, they should have the support and active presence of Christians. Trevor Cooling's underlying appeal is to a Christian view of basic rights to religious liberty. This means that, due to the unavailability of the ideal in our fallen world, with its child labour and its refugee camps, the *best* way is a state-financed system of (transformed) common schools, and faith-based schools where parents want to set up and run them.

There are undoubted resonances between Jonathan Chaplin's and Trevor Cooling's proposals in their appeals to Christian values on freedom and justice and a Christian view of God-given basic rights, and in their advocacies of a less-than-ideal way as the best for our fallen and directionally plural world. An emphasis on the same values is present also in the final chapter in Part 2. In this, Ruth Deakin develops a theological rationale for structural pluralism as a way of affirming 'the freedom of individuals and communities to subscribe to different worldviews and ways of life'. Human beings are made in God's image and, whether or not they acknowledge it, they are responsible to him for the ways in which they organize themselves and their communities. They are made for relationships with each other for which 'the persons-in-relations model of the Trinity legitimates relations of love and equality rather than domination and subjection'. Dr Deakin therefore appeals explicitly to the Christian doctrines of the Trinity and of creation as a basis for her proposals for education. There also seems to be an implicit appeal to that of the fall in her references to the tension between God's suffering presence in human history and hope for the future he promises (again a finding of the best way in the real situation in the light of the ideal?).

Dr Deakin is also a self-confessed transformationalist, seeking educational policies which are consistent with a Christian vision. These should provide for 'the free expression of differing worldviews in schools within a common framework'. Schools should be explicit about their communal belief systems and how their school visions and values flow from them. The diversity that results is, she says, something to be 'celebrated as a healthy expression of a diverse society which seeks to act fairly towards all of its member communities'. (This is a more positive note than Jonathan Chaplin's toleration of directional plurality.) Dr Deakin seems to make no provision for the kind of common school argued for by Trevor Cooling, but, at the end of her chapter, there is an important counter to any tendency towards a fixed structure of relatively isolated and static schools. This is to be found in her emphasis on the needs of individual teachers to be value-critical and, at the same time, openly committed to their own worldviews.

The theme of worldviews and their influence recurs in these four chapters. Their 'directional' role is brought to the fore by Jonathan Chaplin. Freedom and justice feature prominently as characteristics of the kind of society which we should seek to create. Particular basic Christian doctrines – the Trinity, creation and the fall – are made use of in the framing of proposals for education policy. The centrality of relationships and its theological base in the Trinity are particularly to the fore in Ruth Deakin's chapter. The other two key themes – of interplay between Christian constants and educational situations and of a Christian vision for people and society – are also present in these chapters. They underlie what is being said and are implicit throughout rather than explicitly dealt with. Transformationalism is the common strategy, although the conclusions reached are not identical.

2

Liberalism, pluralism and education

Paul Marshall

Western societies are marked by a plurality in which there are people with importantly different beliefs and ways of life, differences which cannot easily be reconciled. Contemporary liberalism claims to be the answer to dealing justly with such plurality. Whether in its traditional or postmodern form, however, liberalism's preoccupation with individual choice undercuts the very diversity it claims to protect. It marginalizes traditional and minority communities, and religious belief, and it tends to produce a society of homogeneous individualists. It should not be seen as a means of reconciling differences but as one more difference with which we need to contend.

Introduction

While there are remnants of socialism and traditional conservatism in western countries, and some resurgence of a more Fascist outlook, the dominant ethos is liberal. The prevailing vocabulary emphasizes rights, self-esteem, self-fulfilment, autonomy and, above all, individual choice. Hence debate largely concerns the degree and type of government involvement most likely to enhance individual freedom. Postmodernism, while making a splash in the academy and in cultural circles, usually only reinforces these tendencies in the political sphere.

Liberal democratic societies face problems of pluralism, and liberalism claims a unique ability to cope with this through a stress on individuality, freedom and openness. I will argue, however, that liberalism tends to quash differences, especially in education, and pushes for a homogeneous secular society. But, before proceeding further, I need to say a little more about what is meant by liberalism and pluralism.

Liberalism and pluralism

The current philosophical view of what constitutes a situation of pluralism is that it is one in which there exist different philosophical views which cannot be reconciled with one another by means of something more basic. Some refer in this context to 'incommensurable ideological communities', a typification that can serve us politically and sociologically as well. It suggests that a situation of social pluralism is one in which there is the co-existence of peoples having importantly different beliefs and ways of life whose differences are for practical purposes incommensurate. As I am concerned with education, I will not address whether on epistemological or other grounds the current differences could in principle be resolved. We face a situation where no ready resolution is in sight and where education policies must somehow deal with the current fact of differences. I shall proceed on the basis that in most western societies we face the fact of plurality and I shall focus on responses to it.

Liberalism is both a political theory and a political movement, and the two often do not hang together well. Its roots can be traced to certain developments in the early modern era, notably (a) the appearance of independent men (or families) due to urbanization and the growth of a market economy, leading to a stress on autonomy and freedom; (b) the attempt to found the state on a non-religious basis due to the problem of the religious wars of the sixteenth and seventeenth centuries; and (c) the growth of Enlightenment philosophies leading to anti-dogmatism and a belief in the autonomy of reason from belief (Hall 1987; Arblaster 1984: 12).

Since then, liberalism, and liberal parties, have had a convoluted history. Originally it was a European and American movement which did not wish to be conservative in that it wanted to move ahead, though not as fast as the radicals. Depending on the relative power of competing radical or conservative movements, liberalism has appeared in different guises. In Europe, 'liberal' means a conservative individualist, one who resists more revolutionary socialist or social-democratic pressures. Raymond Aron and Friedrich von Hayek were such liberals, that is, free-market conservatives. In America the word 'liberal' means 'progressive', as there is no socialism against which it can be defined. Liberalism, in its nineteenth-century heyday, was anti-clerical, but in modern Europe it often fuses with Christian Democracy.

The political creed of liberalism has also varied over time. Much modern liberalism, however, claims that it has, or is, no creed. This feature is certainly not universal: indeed, where liberalism has a strong opponent, its presence as a position becomes much clearer. But, in the latter twentieth century, where liberalism is ascendent or dominant, its claim to be no claim comes to the fore. This claim is made because the principal feature of liberalism is something like 'a set of beliefs which proceed from the central assumption that man's essence is his freedom and, therefore, that what chiefly concerns us in this life is to shape the world as we want it' (Grant 1969: 114). This stress on freedom leads liberals to emphasize that they do not wish to impose their way of life on anyone else, but desire that all should be free to live out their own ways of life with the least hindrance. Hence liberalism claims to be a neutral philosophy. For Ronald Dworkin, the liberal state 'must be neutral on ... the question of the good life ... political decisions must be, so far as possible, independent of any particular conception of the good life, or of what gives values to life' (Dworkin 1985: 191; Ackerman 1980: 11). This view manifests itself in the common liberal piety that says, 'You can't impose your beliefs on others.'

Hence liberalism now appears as a variable political attitude that stresses some or all of the following: individuality, freedom, autonomy, rights, the separation of religion and politics, reason, tolerance, the non-imposition of belief, and decent progressiveness. It is doubtful that these disparate elements yield any coherent view but, like most political movements, it can usually manage without coherence (Voegelin 1974: 506).

Liberalism against plurality

Given liberalism's stress on neutrality and openness, liberals see themselves as exponents of pluralism *par excellence*. They wish to provide the political and educational setting in which each individual can pursue his or her own freely chosen life, where no view is imposed on another, and where the state is neutral between all competing particular value claims. Such a view, however, can lead not to an open society but to the imposition of individualism and autonomy on all, replacing a diverse society with a homogeneous liberal one. In order to illustrate how this can happen, I shall consider some examples taken from liberal theory in order to show its inner logic, and then I shall try to illustrate the effects through some examples.

To illustrate the closure of society induced by liberalism it is useful to consider Robert Nozick's *Anarchy, State and Utopia*.[1] This book is the most libertarian of contemporary works in political theory. What liberal theorists like Rawls or Dworkin might forbid, Nozick allows. Consequently, if even Nozick's ideas lead to closure in society, then our criticism is likely to apply *a fortiori* to other liberal writers.

Nozick emphasizes the wide diversity of people in the world. He provides a partial list: 'Wittgenstein, Elizabeth Taylor, Bertrand Russell, Thomas Merton, Yogi Berra ... the Lubavitcher Rebbe, Picasso, Moses, Einstein, Hugh Hefner, Socrates, Henry Ford ... Peter Kropotkin, you and your parents. Is there really one kind of life which is best for each of these people?' (Nozick 1974: 312). Given this rich diversity, he exhorts us to develop a society whose hallmark is not what is supposedly best for everyone, but one which respects the right of each person to live in his or her own way. Unlike many liberals, Nozick is aware that ways of life are communal and that a healthy society is composed of communities, not individuals. His society is not intended to be a community itself but only a framework in which many communities can co-exist. The communities themselves can exclude, discriminate, or be authoritarian. They can be anything their members choose. But choice is the key: each member must choose to be in a particular community, and must be able to choose to leave.

The illiberality of communities is not an affront to liberalism because the only people in them are those who choose to be in, and who are under no compulsion to stay. The overall society retains a liberal character because it is composed of voluntary communities.

This stress on voluntariness, however, is not as benign as it might appear (Orwin 1984). This is because, for free will to be real, it must be an *informed* will. Each person must be aware of his or her options and so must be informed about the alternatives. Each must also be continually aware of his or her right to leave, so that each community must remind its members that they can go at any time.[2] The result is that commitment to the community must portray itself and become perceived, not as a necessary moral commitment, but merely as one among many possible moral options open to the individual. In the end a claimed moral right to choose overrides the moral right of any community to claim (and, hence, honestly to believe) that it holds the truth. The priority of choice undercuts the ability of a community to shape its members and succeeding generations so that they will uphold the truth.

Consider, for example, an Amish community. Such non-violent Christian communities, common in the eastern United States, refuse electricity and cars, and live a simple, agrarian life wherein children are shielded from the outer world and raised into the mores of the community. Let us suppose that all members of the community, in particular those of school age, had to be advised (and therefore sufficiently educated and informed for the advice to mean something) that they are free to leave at any time, and that the community will respect this right and will not insist that, morally, communal solidarity comes before individual will. In this case, whatever such a community may have become, it is no longer an Amish community in its heart, and it will soon cease to be one in its practices. It will be forced to deny that which it holds most dear: that it is not simply another individual option among America's ways of life, but struggles to follow a way of life commanded by God. While they will not try physically to compel anyone to join or remain within their way, they cannot treat it as simply another option which is morally secondary to human choice. The Amish themselves realize this fact and have fought diligently and successfully against liberal educators in order to focus their children's education on those things required for life within the community.[3]

The Amish are a striking example, but the same strain affects any community that holds its beliefs to be true. It would have to inform its members that its beliefs are not the most fundamental thing of all. Communities thus become half-minded and thus half-hearted. As Orwin points out, they become communities founded on prior respect for individual choice and hence become mirror images of the larger liberal society.[4] They are not left free, but are constrained to become liberal associations.

Nozick is laudably genuine in his desire that people should be legally free to live in different ways. He wants a society in which different commitments can live alongside one another. But this is done only by pushing each community towards 'half measures for the half-hearted, dilettantism on a grand scale' (Orwin 1984: 7). The result is similar to Canadian George Grant's depiction of liberal society:

> As for pluralism, differences ... are able to exist only in private activities: how we eat, how we mate, how we practice ceremonies. Some like pizza, some like steaks; some like girls, some like boys; some like synagogue, some like the mass. But we all do it in churches, motels, restaurants, indistinguishable from the Atlantic to the Pacific (Grant 1969: 26).

Postmodernism

Postmodernity is a notoriously slippery concept, but one of its most persistent themes is a reluctance to find unity amid the diversity of the world. It is postmodern in that it rejects modernity's preoccupation with science and reason as the sources of reliable knowledge and, hence, of unity. The result is a preoccupation with difference and diversity. While there are certainly useful postmodern insights into the effects of communications technology, when the cloud of words has cleared, its current contributions to political debate appear to be a redoubled emphasis on the incommensurability of viewpoints, openness to other people, cultures and viewpoints, and the equal status of diverse views. Hence, in most of its forms, it merely repeats, and radicalizes, the liberal claim to protect diversity. Philosophers such as John Rawls have managed to retain their liberalism while switching from a neo-Kantian position (wherein liberalism is seen as a position that conforms to the nature of human reason) to postmodern views (wherein liberalism is seen only as the current opinion of a majority of Americans) (Rawls 1971, 1993). Similarly, many postmoderns (such as Richard Rorty) hold on to some Enlightenment views, either out of nostalgia for a dream of reason that they had previously treasured, or else in hope that if we abandon and deconstruct our aspirations for commonly agreed metaphysics, language and political structures, we will end up in a primitive state of equality with the future open before us. This position is remarkably akin to seventeenth- and eighteenth-century schemes of politics as arising out of an agreement (a 'social contract') between equals in a 'state of nature'. In this respect too, postmodernism shows itself to be akin to the liberalism it often professes to reject.

In addition, the characteristic postmodern stress on 'recognition' (appreciation) of the other suffers from internal tensions between its demands both for equality and for difference. Charles Taylor points out that the modern call for 'recognition' is a child of the older concept of 'honour'. But honour was the mark of one who was outstanding, the one who stood above the rest. To give 'recognition' to all would be like the modern practice of giving everyone medals, or 'A' grades, to show how outstanding everyone is. But where everyone is outstanding, no-one is. 'Recognition' tries to combine this stress on honour, now transmuted as distinctness, with a view of equality between persons and cultures and viewpoints. A stress on equal dignity, however, highlights what is thought to be universally the same in each, while a stress on difference highlights the distinctness of each from everyone else. These two modes of politics, both based on the notion of equal respect, are in conflict and, as Charles Taylor says,

> The reproach the first makes to the second is just that it violates the principle of nondiscrimination. The reproach the second makes to the first is that it negates identity by forcing people into a homogeneous mould that is untrue to them (Taylor 1992: 38, 43).

The sceptical trait of postmodernity runs into similar problems. In the post-Reformation debates on religious freedom, those influenced by scepticism held that in important areas we cannot know the truth, or that we would always have uncertainty.[5] But this leaves open the question of areas where we think we do know the truth, unless we are disposed to think that we do not know the truth about anything. And it also became clear that scepticism could lead to repression just as much as, or perhaps more than, freedom.

For instance, if we believe that something cannot really be known, then, rather than leaving the matter open to a debate that is bound to be futile, why not simply impose an answer for the sake of civil peace (Marshall 1994)? Uncertainty might lead to a call not for the authorities but for the dissenters to forbear: should they not just shut up, or be shut up, if they persist in pushing unknowable speculations that disrupt the social order? A sceptical view can lead to the state's imposing a view without even necessarily making any claim that it is the true one. It merely imposes a uniformity that is philosophically or theologically arbitrary but politically useful (Locke 1967). In debates about what to do in matters on which the Bible is silent (such as the vestments to be worn by priests and ministers), a frequent, and successful, strategy was to demand conformity to a common practice rather than to allow individual or congregational choice. Often such matters were explicitly referred to as 'things indifferent'. Indifference and uncertainty can override conscience as well as support it.

Richard Tuck points out that many sceptics were advocates of religious repression. Hugo Grotius thought no-one 'was entitled to enforce more extensively specified religious opinions upon another merely because of their conviction that those opinions were correct; but neither were they entitled to resist the imposition of religious ceremonies and dogmas by the state if it believed that it was necessary to do so for political reasons' (Tuck 1988: 30-31). Indeed Tuck describes a 'combination of respect for the arguments of the sceptic ... and support for a potentially intolerant state' as 'standard'.

Whether pragmatists, sceptics or relativists revert to their authoritarian past or manage to hold on to their present liberal predilections, we should not put too much faith in their ability to deal justly with our diversity.

The effects in education

The dynamics of liberalism are comparable to some current practices in state schools. In many schools the liberal ideal is followed by, in theory, exposing each child in a full, fair and balanced way to the options that exist, exhorting them to give serious consideration to these options, and then perhaps to make a serious commitment to one of them (Swann 1985, chapter 6, paragraphs 1.4; 2.5; chapter 8, I, paragraph 2.11). This approach is applied only in certain parts of the curriculum; it is not done in physics or mathematics, or in matters of creation and evolution. But it is frequently applied in politics, ethics and religion. What children actually learn from this approach is not that one religion supposedly set before them is true, but that no religion has a compelling claim to be treated as true (Thiessen 1991). Hence children learn implicitly that each religion has a claim as good as any other, so that what is paramount is the priority of their own individual choice. They are placed at the centre of the moral universe. In so far as this education works, the pupil has become trained in the dogmatics of liberalism.

Alasdair MacIntyre highlights a similar phenomenon in the development of the modern university. He points out that preliberal universities required religious conformity from their teachers so that they were in principle embodying a particular tradition of enquiry. Later, either religious tests were gradually abolished or else universities were founded that did not have such tests. The result was not, however, that universities became places where alternative points of view were elaborated and debated. Instead, questions about points of view and their influence in shaping the university tended to be ignored or even excluded. Appointed teachers presented what they taught as if there were indeed shared standards of rationality, accepted by all teachers and accessible to all students. Universities became institutions committed to upholding a fictitious objectivity (MacIntyre 1988: 399).

Consequently the student usually meets 'an apparent inconclusiveness in all argument outside the natural sciences, an inconclusiveness which seems to abandon him or her to his or her prerational preferences. So the student characteristically emerges from a liberal education with a set of skills, a set of preferences and little else ...' (MacIntyre 1988: 400). In so far as liberalism does shape the modern university, the result is not contending views of rationality but the assertion of neutral rationality in some areas (notably the natural sciences) combined with a pastiche in the humanities which trivializes choice, and, more particularly, the object of that choice.

Conclusion

Liberal patterns of exclusion exist throughout the world and affect minorities, religious groups, national groups, language groups and aboriginal peoples (Van Dyke 1982). The picture that emerges is that liberalism and liberal education are not neutral with respect to different ways of life. Rather, they undermine distinctive and traditional communities and replace them with a uniform regime of individual choices (Weaver 1985; Schouls 1989). The great liberal philosopher John Rawls takes a relatively sanguine view of the ways of life that are destroyed in this process:

> A well-ordered society [*i.e.* a society conforming to Rawls' criteria of justice] defines a fair background within which ways of life have a reasonable opportunity to establish themselves. If a conception of the good is unable to endure and gain adherents under conditions of equal freedom and mutual toleration, one must question whether it is viable conception of the good and whether its passing is to be regretted (Rawls 1975: 549).

As MacIntyre notes, liberal principles are 'not neutral with respect to rival conflicting theories of the human good. Where they are in force they impose a particular conception of the good life ... upon those who willingly or unwillingly accept the liberal procedures and the liberal terms of debate' (MacIntyre 1988: 344–345)

Liberalism often undercuts the very differences, especially religious differences, that it is intended to protect. In our present context we need to emphasize that the liberal option, with its incorporated individualism and secularism, is not merely a means of dealing with differences, but is *yet one more difference* concerning public and private life. It has to be brought alongside, not above. We need to bring our differences into the political and educational arenas. Diverse religious commitments must not be driven out of the schools in the name of a spurious tolerance or unity: they must be allowed to shape our curriculum and pedagogy.

NOTES

1 The following material is derived from Marshall (1994a).
2 Clifford Orwin refers to this as a kind of 'Miranda rule for enthusiasts' (1984: 8). I am indebted to Orwin's insightful discussion of Nozick's 'utopias'. The Miranda rule refers to the requirement that American law officers must advise people under arrest of their rights.
3 Their right to do so was fought by liberals but finally established in the celebrated US Supreme Court case of *Wisconsin v. Yoder*, 1972.
4 This is why the Islamic Academy in Cambridge and the Islamic Cultural Centre in London said they preferred the 1944 Education Act, with its provision for solely Christian teaching, to the 'diversity' recommendations of the 1985 Swann Report. See also Sandel (1982) and George (1993: 135–136).
5 This ranged from Dutch Remonstrants such as Arminius to Polish Socinians such as their namesake, Faustus Socinus. It included influential figures such as Grotius and Coonhert in the Netherlands, John Locke, John Milton and Jeremy Taylor in England, Bodin and Bayle in France and, later, Wolff and Thomasius in the German states.

BIBLIOGRAPHY

Ackerman, Bruce (1980), *Social Justice in the Liberal State* (New Haven: Yale University Press).

Arblaster, Anthony (1984), *The Rise and Decline of Western Liberalism* (Oxford: Blackwell).

Dworkin, Ronald (1985), 'Liberalism', in his *A Matter of Principle* (Cambridge, MA: Harvard University Press).

George, Robert (1993), *Making Men Moral* (Oxford: Clarendon).

Grant, George (1969), *Technology and Empire* (Toronto: Anansi).

Hall, John (1987), *Liberalism* (London: Paladin).

Locke, John (1961), *An Essay Concerning Human Understanding*, ed. J. Yolton, 2 vols. (London: Dent).

——— (1967), *Two Tracts on Government*, ed. Philip Abrams (Cambridge: Cambridge University Press).

MacIntyre, Alasdair (1988), *Whose Justice? Which Rationality?* (London: Duckworth).

Marshall, Paul (1994a), 'Human Rights and Religious Toleration' at Conference on Religion and Human Rights, Emory University, Atlanta, GA.

——— (1994b), 'Liberalism, Pluralism and Christianity: A Reconceptualization', in P. Marshall and J. Chaplin (eds.), *Politics and Christian Vision* (Lanham: University Press of America): 143–162.

Nozick, Robert (1974), *Anarchy, State and Utopia* (New York: Basic Books).

Orwin, Clifford (1984), 'Robert Nozick's Liberal Utopia', paper presented to the Annual Meeting of the Canadian Political Science Association, Guelph, Ontario.

Rawls, John (1971), *A Theory of Justice* (Cambridge: Harvard University Press).

—— (1975), 'Fairness to Goodness', *Philosophical Review* 84: 536–554.

—— (1993), *Political Liberalism* (New York: Columbia University Press).

Sandel, Michael (1982), *Liberalism and the Limits of Justice* (Cambridge: Cambridge University Press).

Schouls, Tim (1989), *Liberal Democracy and Canada's Aboriginal Peoples*, MPhil thesis, Institute for Christian Studies, Toronto.

Swann, Lord (1985), *Education for All: The Report of the Committee of Inquiry into the Education of Children from Ethnic Minority Groups* (The 'Swann Report') (London: HMSO).

Taylor, Charles (1992), *Multiculturalism and the Politics of Recognition* (Princeton: Princeton University Press).

Thiessen, Elmer (1991), *Teaching for Commitment* (Montreal and Kingston: McGill-Queen's University Press).

Tuck, Richard (1988), 'Scepticism and Toleration in the Seventeenth Century', in Susan Mendus (ed.), *Justifying Toleration: Conceptual and Historical Perspectives* (Cambridge: Cambridge University Press): 21–35.

Van Dyke, Vernon (1982), 'Collective Entities and Moral Rights: Problems in Liberal-Democratic Thought', *Journal of Politics* 44: 21–44.

Voegelin, Eric (1974), 'Liberalism and Its History', *Review of Politics* 37: 504–520.

Weaver, Sally (1985), 'Federal Difficulties with Aboriginal Rights Demands', in M. Boldt and D. Long (eds.), *The Quest for Justice: Aboriginal Peoples and Aboriginal Rights* (Toronto: University of Toronto Press): 139–147.

3

Christians and the public realm[1]

Jonathan Chaplin

This chapter addresses problems encountered when Christians seek to influence public policy in a secular, plural society. It opens by distinguishing four trends currently present in Christian political public action - traditionalist, liberal, liberationist and transformationist - noting thereby the existence of plurality within the Christian community. It then discusses the specific dilemmas thrown up for Christian political action by religious ('directional') plurality in contemporary society, and proposes an authentically Christian case for the toleration of directional plurality. The argument rests on distinctively Christian conceptions of the nature of faith and the nature of the state. Finally, the problem of the limits of tolerable directional plurality is dealt with by appealing to a Christian conception of human rights.

Introduction:
Christian attitudes to the public realm

Few Christians today dispute the legitimacy and necessity of Christians' seeking to influence the public realm by engaging in political activity. Equally, few can fail to observe that there remain sharp disagreements over the appropriate ends and means of such activity. There are more politically active Christians now than there have been for a generation, yet there is no greater evidence of Christian consensus on policy or strategy. The purpose of this chapter is to consider how, in a late-modern or postmodern society characterized by increasing religious, moral and cultural fragmentation, Christians can best seek to shape public policy.[2]

Let me first identify a matter on which there is unanimity among Christians, namely the responsibility of those in public life to maintain the highest standards of personal, professional and political integrity. In Britain, concern over falling standards, heightened by a series of well-publicized lapses, recently prompted the Government to establish the 'Nolan Committee' on standards in public life, which reported in 1995 (Nolan 1995). Chaired by Lord Nolan, a senior judge and, as it happens, a practising Roman Catholic, the committee formulated seven key principles – selflessness, integrity, objectivity, accountability, openness, honesty and leadership – to guide those in public life, the content (if not the detailed implementation) of which must surely command universal Christian endorsement. Such principles are intended to apply to elected politicians and all public officials, as well as to office-holders in publicly funded institutions such as universities and common schools. An explicit moral foundation for this kind of principle, and broader political and constitutional ones, was robustly restated by Pope John Paul II in his recent encyclical letter, *Veritatis Splendor*:

> In the political sphere, it must be noted that truthfulness in the relations between those governing and those governed, openness in public administration, impartiality in the service of the body politic, respect for the rights of political adversaries, safeguarding the rights of the accused against summary trials and convictions, the just and honest use of public funds, the rejection of equivocal or illicit means in order to gain, preserve or increase power at any cost – all these are principles which are rooted in, and in fact derive their singular urgency from, the transcendent value of the person and the objective moral demands of the functioning of states (John Paul II 1993: 150).[3]

In most liberal democracies these principles are widely endorsed in public rhetoric (even if practice often falls woefully short of principle), but where they are fragile or even absent – in the new eastern European democracies and many developing countries, for example – establishing such standards throughout public life must surely be an especially urgent priority for politically active Christians. Without them the political process will remain wracked and paralysed by corruption and simply will not deliver effective public policies at all.

Christians may agree on all this, but frequently disagree on the content of public policy. In Britain, as in other countries where Christians are now politically engaged, Christians increasingly speak with a 'scattered voice' (Skillen 1990; cf. Atherton 1992; Chaplin [ed.] 1992; Gay 1991; Smith 1989; Wogaman 1988). Simplifying greatly, at least four broad (and often overlapping) tendencies, not all present in every country, can be distinguished: a 'traditionalist' tendency which views the objective of influencing public policy as defending or even restoring what is supposedly the traditionally Christian character of the nation; a 'liberal' tendency which affirms the value of Christian political activity but recoils at the suggestion of a distinctively Christian contribution to public policy; a 'liberationist' tendency which claims that the gospel is radically at variance with mainstream political options, but often finds natural allies in sections of the secular political left; and a 'transformationist' tendency which purports to be able to bring an authentically Christian perspective to bear within the public policy process, while renouncing the idea that the Christian faith or Christian institutions can claim a privileged status within that process denied to other faiths.[4] This fourth position, which I share, will be elaborated later in this chapter.

The situation is further complicated by the fact that none of these tendencies line up straightforwardly with any particular ideological preference. Particular individuals or organizations often exhibit more than one tendency. For example, some find it possible to advocate traditionalist educational, family or church–state stances while remaining agnostically liberal, or even committedly transformationist, on the economy. And, of special relevance for this book, evangelical Christians are to be found in all tendencies. In Britain there are evangelical traditionalists whose conception of the British national character they seek to defend bears an uncanny resemblance to the mores of Victorian evangelicalism. Self-proclaimed evangelical transformationists are now to be found among both neo-conservatives and democratic socialists (*cf.* Chaplin [ed.] 1992). And there are evangelicals displaying impeccably orthodox doctrinal credentials who see no trace of a contradiction in espousing a thoroughly 'liberal' position (in the sense defined above) on the question of political involvement. Analysing this cacophony is beyond the scope of this chapter. I mention it simply to illustrate the obstacles facing any attempt to win support among Christians, even those from the same theological stable, for any proposed public policy reform, whether in education or any other sector. Christian attempts to shape public policy in a plural society must first reckon with plurality within the Christian community.

The political problem of pluralism

Before proceeding further, some clarity about the meaning of 'pluralism' is essential. Mouw and Griffioen helpfully distinguish between three senses of 'pluralism' (Mouw and Griffioen 1993: 15–18; *cf.* also Skillen 1994: 83–95; McCarthy *et al.* 1981). 'Associational' pluralism refers to the plurality of associations, institutions or organizations populating any modern, differentiated society – family, school, corporation, union, *etc.* 'Contextual' pluralism denotes the plurality of customs, mores or practices by which we distinguish between different cultural traditions.[5] The term 'directional' pluralism, by contrast, refers to 'the diversity of visions of the good life that give direction to people's lives' (Mouw and Griffioen 1993: 16). What we are dealing with here are contending fundamental beliefs about the world and the practices flowing from those beliefs. Associational, contextual and directional pluralism are typically all simultaneously present in any particular society, and they are interwoven in complex ways. Directional visions, for example, are not disembodied beliefs but are necessarily manifested through particular associations or cultural contexts.

It is important to note, too, that each of these three senses of 'pluralism' can be intended in either a descriptive sense (henceforth *plurality*) or a normative sense (henceforth *pluralism*). There is no doubt that, descriptively, associational, contextual and directional plurality are important features of contemporary society, though the extent to which each is actually present in any given society is open to debate. Different people will, however, evaluate these states of affairs differently in a normative sense. Arguably, from a Christian standpoint both associational and contextual plurality can be seen as consequences of the human development of the social potentials of the created order, and, as such, intrinsically good and enriching (*cf.* McCarthy *et al.* 1981; Skillen and McCarthy [eds.] 1991). Christians, then, should advocate both associational and contextual pluralism. Directional plurality, however, must surely be seen as the result of the fall (*cf.* Mouw and Griffioen 1993: 87-109). Radical differences in ultimate beliefs about the world follow from humanity's rebellion against the Truth. In contrast to many secular liberal and postmodern thinkers, Christians should not celebrate or advocate such plurality as if it were a healthy, normative state of affairs. But where directional plurality exists as a social fact, they must respond to it in an authentically Christian way.

I now want to explore the special dilemmas thrown up for a transformationist approach to public policy by the fact of directional plurality. A plural society is one characterized by the presence of a diversity of directional visions, each displaying distinctive beliefs and practices. The dilemma of a plural society is not the mere diversity of such directional visions, but the fact that at least some of these are seriously at odds with each other, that their beliefs and practices are, at least at some points, incompatible. But for the problem to matter politically and thus to have implications for public policy, some of these incompatible beliefs or practices must impinge upon the ordering of the public realm. Directional plurality will generate specifically political problems whenever the political community (the state) imposes on its members (as it often does) legal or other obligations or constraints which conflict with those arising from their adherence to a directional vision. Such problems will become acute when the political community is, or is perceived to be, dominated by one particular directional vision. This, as Paul Marshall shows in chapter 2, is the case with the dominant directional vision of the West, namely secular liberal humanism (*cf.* Chaplin 1993; Marshall 1989; Mouw and Griffioen 1993: 20-48; Parekh 1990; Greenawalt 1988; Mendus 1989).

There is an obvious sense in which western societies are directionally plural. For example, there are in the UK about 1 million Muslims, probably over 0.25 million Jews, Sikhs and Hindus, and a growing number of Rastafarians. In addition there are dozens of other minority cultural or religious groups, including, for example, adherents to the so-called 'new religious movements', New Age philosophy and so on. It is these kinds of groups which people typically have in mind when they speak of a 'plural' or 'multicultural', society.

But this is only the most recent manifestation of an increasing directional diversity in western society. It is often assumed that these new arrivals to our society entered what was a directionally homogeneous home culture, and that western societies like Britain were directionally unified until such groups arrived with their 'alien' customs. But this is seriously misleading, since (again simplifying greatly) for the last two centuries most western societies have been not mono-directional but bi-directional. These two directions have been Christianity and secular liberal humanism, though of course each has displayed great diversity and each has profoundly influenced the other. Roughly speaking, Christianity was dominant in public culture until around the eighteenth century, but by the middle of the nineteenth, secular liberal humanism had largely superseded it as the leading cultural force - a point which advocates of both the 'traditionalist' and the 'liberal' tendencies seem unable to grasp. Today, the situation is very different. Secular liberal humanism is still dominant, but its spiritual foundations are rapidly crumbling, and Christianity, though still influential, is now perhaps the largest of a variety of minority visions, whose adherents watch uneasily as a directional vacuum emerges, uncertain how to react.

A Christian case for pluralism in public policy

I now want to propose a transformationist perspective on Christian political involvement in a plural society. This will involve arguing that a Christian political theory both generates a principled defence of the toleration of directional plurality, and identifies the acceptable limits of such plurality.[6] I rest my argument on two ideas with deep roots in Scripture and Christian tradition: the nature of faith, and the purpose of the state.

The nature of faith
The first point here is simply that faith - a person's basic spiritual

direction - cannot and should not be coerced. It is in the nature of faith that it must be a free response to (what is taken to be) revelation. While it is possible to coerce people into making confessions, these are spiritually valueless and unauthentic. This necessarily implies that all attempts in history to coerce people into accepting the Christian faith, from Constantine onwards, have been illegitimate, and that the 'Christian capital' we have inherited in Britain and that others may have inherited in their own countries, and which Christian tradition-alists are keen to preserve, is at least partly the result of illegitimate coercion by our Christian forebears - a point which should instil in us today an appropriate modesty.

This view of the nature of faith is, of course, a specifically Christian view; other religions may have different views of the legitimacy of religious coercion. Here Christians will often find themselves in political alliance (if not philosophical agreement) with secular liberals. But there is a crucial second point about the nature of faith which puts us at odds with many secular liberals, and this is that faith has comprehensive implications requiring expression in all areas of life. Authentic (as opposed to privatized) faith must come to expression in all dimensions of human existence, including the public and political. Further, on this Christian view of the scope of faith, this is also true of every other faith, even if that faith has a privatized, and thus defective, conception of itself. There is an Islamic view not only of headscarves, but also of banking. There is a distinctively Hindu cultic practice, but also a Hindu view of social reform. The New Age movement offers techniques not only of contemplation, but also of corporate management. The same applies to all faith directions, including secular faiths like liberal humanism, each of which generates distinctive ethical, social, economic and political stances. Thus, in a directionally plural society there will be *rival comprehensive* visions of life whose adherents, if consistent, will regard themselves as obliged to contend over many areas of social life. If Christians believe in a faith with comprehensive implications and if they claim the right to live out such implications, they must be prepared to allow others the right to live out the comprehensive implications of theirs too, as far as is possible within the necessary limits of democratic government and public law. To deny to rival faiths the legitimacy of their claim to a right to express their faith in manifold ways in the public as well as the private realm, is to be religiously (directionally) intolerant, to restrain people in the exercise of what they take to be their most fundamental obligations. I shall shortly discuss the question of the necessary limits to the acceptable scope of such toleration. But if it is true that the choice is not a simplistic one between tolerance and intolerance, it is also true that a Christian view of faith leads us to hold that tolerance is to be preferred wherever possible. Our starting-point should be the presumption of a general right to the expression of directional liberty within the public realm.

The purpose of the state

The second ground on which I want to argue for a Christian political ethic of directional pluralism is the nature and purpose of the state. It can be argued that the purpose of political authority, as this emerges through the Scriptures and Christian tradition, can be summarized as the *establishment of justice in the public realm of society*.[7] Public justice implies a just adjudication among all the legitimate rights and duties within a society, in so far as these have public consequences. On a Christian view, the state is not a mere broker of contending interests or simply an enforcer of (any) order, but is under a divine mandate to establish an order of public justice. Nor is the content of our rights and duties – the content of justice – determined by our subjective preferences (as in utilitarianism), by our contracts (as in natural-rights liberalism), or by abstract universal principles of rationality (as in Kantian liberalism). Rather, this content is determined by what is in accordance with the Creator's law, which calls all things, including social and political things, to their assigned purpose within the structure of creation as a whole.

The purpose of the state, then, is to secure justice within the public realm. This purpose also circumscribes the state's legitimate authority. In a contemporary context we might conclude, for example, that the state is not competent to appoint the leaders of trade unions or political parties, but it is competent to ensure that principles of natural justice are adhered to when such appointments are made, for the right to natural justice is a right belonging to all citizens and so is a public right. It might also be argued that the state lacks the competence to determine the content of the school curriculum (raising serious questions about the British Government's imposition of a 'national' curriculum in all publicly funded schools). One of the most important limits on the competence of the state arises from the right to the choice of basic spiritual direction (*i.e.* the right to religious liberty). The state is simply not authorized to require its citizens to adopt any particular faith or prevent them adopting one (*cf.* Skillen 1994; Murray 1993: 145–146, 152–153; Guinness 1991, 1993). Indeed, the apostle Paul appeals to his rights as a Roman citizen as a way of protecting his right to religious liberty (Acts 16:37).

I have described the purpose of the state as involving 'just adjudication' among legitimate rights and duties within society. This involves both 'negative' and 'positive' adjudication. Negatively, the state must protect persons and communities against intrusions into their legitimate sphere of free action. Today this requires, among other things, the continuing protection of religious liberty, the freedom to adhere to, and to change, one's religious belief, to practice religious worship unhindered, and to be protected against religious discrimination in the distribution of civil rights, jobs or public services (*cf.* Poulter 1990; Lustgarten 1983). But if what I said above regarding the comprehensive character of faith is correct, then these 'negative' rights to religious liberty are not sufficient. Beyond negative rights, 'positive' adjudication by the state is required. This implies, importantly, the principle that, as far as possible, different directional visions be treated equitably in as many areas of public policy as possible (*cf.* Lynch 1990: 37).

A particularly pertinent example of this is the public funding of Islamic or other kinds of 'confessional' school on the same basis as state schools. Part of the argument here is a straightforward appeal against fiscal injustice (*cf.* Skillen 1994: 125–136; McCarthy *et al.* 1981, 1982). Muslims who wish to live out the implications of their faith in the schooling of their children have to pay twice for it, once through general taxation and a second time through their school fees. The same situation faces the newer, independent 'confessional' Christian schools. Not to fund such schools is not simply to be indifferent or neutral, but to discriminate against such minority religious groups. This conclusion should be accepted by Christians *irrespective* of their own views of the educational or other merits of 'confessional' Christian schools. Even if we decline to send our own children to such schools, we should not endorse depriving other parents of the right to do so. I said earlier that a Christian case for tolerating directional plurality does not involve actively promoting non-Christian faiths. Funding Islamic schools is not doing this, but merely distributing public revenues equitably. Of course, doing justice to such groups will assist them in the practice of their religion, but it would be wholly improper to argue that justice should be done only towards those with whose religious objectives we agree. Similar arguments could, in principle, be made across the whole range of activities which flow from one's faith - education, business, banking, healthcare, sexual relations, the arts and so forth. Since faith generates implications in all of these areas, it would appear that believers have legitimate interests in all those areas, interests which have a *prima facie* case for protection by the state. Christians cannot consistently advance a claim that the state should grant them the liberty to follow their conscience in hospitals, businesses, unions, schools, and so on, unless they are also prepared to recognize the validity of a similar claim from those of other faiths.[8]

This, then, is a possible Christian case for acknowledging and dealing justly with directional plurality in public policy. A further clarification is in order at this point. My case for doing justice to directional plurality is a normative one. It should not be thought, however, that I am therefore advocating directional pluralism after all; I am defending only the political toleration of the fact of directional plurality. In fact, my argument regarding the limited authority of the state and the presumption of directional liberty is really a specific application of a normative associational pluralism. Such pluralism holds that diverse associations - families, churches, schools, states and so on - each possess distinct spheres of authority and responsibility which reciprocally circumscribe one another and which ought to be respected in public policy. Another way of stating my position, then, is to say that political associations (states) ought not to violate the directional freedoms proper to any of these other kinds of association (or, of course, to individual citizens). Properly understood, therefore, a normative case for associational pluralism will already contain an argument for the political toleration of directional plurality.

I noted above that the assumptions about the nature of faith on which my argument rests may be contested by others (such as some secular liberals). Similarly, the assumptions I make about the purpose of the state can be contested. Some (including some Christians) will reject the concept of public justice outlined above and advocate instead various forms of political monism (in which the rights of other associations are seen as concessions from the supreme authority of the state) or religious or moral paternalism (in which the state is thought to have a duty to impose a particular religion or morality upon its citizens). There is no way of avoiding these fundamental disputes about the very nature of the political community. A vital point, however, is that when Christians aim to persuade others of their view of the purpose of the state, they are seeking a *limited political*, not a *comprehensive religious* consensus, an agreement not over ultimate directions but over the proper authority of one particular institution, the state, which we all need to come to terms with if we are to enjoy the freedom to live out our ultimate beliefs.

To do this, Christians need to be able to engage in what Skillen terms 'differentiated moral discourse', requiring the ability to differentiate between the different kinds of moral and structural norms appropriate to different kinds of institution (Skillen 1994: 66ff.). Differentiated moral discourse would, for example, distinguish the ecclesiastical norm of confessional unity from the political norm of legal unity (the requirement to have a single legal system), or the kind of moral loyalty appropriate to a family from the civic unity valid for a national political community; states do not need and should not seek either confessional unity or unity on the ultimate foundations of morality.

A similar concern motivates Guinness's notion of 'chartered pluralism', which he defines as 'a vision of religious liberty in public life that, across the deep religious differences of a pluralistic society, guarantees and sustains religious liberty for all by forging a substantive agreement ... over three things ... rights, responsibilities and respect' among different religious visions. This would be a 'principled' pluralism, one avoiding the pitfalls of relativism, interest-group liberalism or empty proceduralism, yet firmly committed to a limited public agreement on the mutual recognition of religious rights (Guinness 1991: 43–44; *cf.* Guinness 1993; Hunter and Guinness [eds.] 1990). Chartered pluralism would allow even radically monotheist faiths like Christianity 'to balance the twin demands of theological integrity and civil unity' (1991: 45). Actually, the term 'balance' here suggests that these two demands stand in tension. The burden of the case I have been presenting is, rather, that it is precisely our theological integrity which calls for a civil unity (*i.e.* political agreement) on the issue of respecting religious plurality. Skillen integrates the two in this way: 'Part of the way government should honor God ... is to uphold public justice for all citizens by protecting their consciences and the jurisdictional independence of ecclesiastical institutions ...' (1994: 72). There is no guarantee that even such limited political agreement will be forthcoming or indefinitely sustainable, but Christians and others must devote all their resources to realizing and upholding it wherever possible.

The limits of pluralism

To conclude, I must deal with a question raised earlier but not adequately addressed, namely the limits of acceptable directional plurality within a single polity. In the first place, the scope for tolerating such directional plurality is limited by the necessary requirements of the structure of the state (*cf.* Lynch 1990: 37). There are certain functions which necessarily fall to the state and which in principle cannot be plural: legislation, defence, diplomacy, monetary policy and so on. This is not to say that a governing political party motivated by a particular directional vision would not implement these functions in a distinctive way; a monetary or judicial policy modelled on Islam would probably turn out rather different from one inspired by secular liberalism or Christian democracy. But in the case of each of these functions there can only be one authoritative centre of policy decision. Adherents of directional (and some other) visions concentrated in a particular geographical area may have a case for devolution or autonomy, but this would not remove the need for a central institutional structure. The state, especially in its federal form, can accommodate a degree of legal plurality. The American states operate with different sentencing policies, and even such a highly unitary and centralized state as the UK has retained a distinct legal system in Scotland. A less clear-cut issue is whether particular religious groups should be permitted distinct systems of personal or family law, such as exist in a number of Commonwealth countries. The Union of Muslim Organizations in the UK and Ireland lobbied unsuccessfully for such a system during the 1970s. The main objection was that certain aspects of Muslim family law were deemed to conflict with provisions in various international codes of human rights, especially those protecting the equality of women (Poulter 1990: 21-22; some Muslims, however, might dispute this interpretation of Islamic law).

Serious concerns for the status of women also lie behind many people's hesitations about funding Islamic schools.

There are no obvious solutions to these particular issues, but a piecemeal approach is likely to generate glaring inconsistencies which will make winning public support for a Christian view even more difficult than it already is. Some general criterion is required if Christians are to deal with this and other issues of the limits of directional plurality in a consistent manner. I said earlier that not only the grounds for allowing directional plurality but also the limits on it ought to reflect a Christian view of the state. I also said that what Christians should regard as a legitimate legal right or duty should be determined according to an authentically Christian conception of justice. For a Christian view to be consistent, the limits to directional plurality must also be set by Christian criteria. What seems necessary here is a distinctively Christian conception of fundamental human rights (*cf.* Marshall 1983, 1994). While we must allow people freedom of conscience in all areas of life, we cannot stand by when their consciences lead them to violate what, from our viewpoint, are fundamental rights. Obviously there will be disagreement among Christians on precisely when fundamental rights are at stake, and if so, in what ways the state and the law should safeguard them, but the following examples may illustrate the point. Christians may not wish to outlaw the ritual slaughter of animals, but they should obviously outlaw wife-burning and slavery, and, arguably, female circumcision, however well-supported these may be by religious arguments. While rights to euthanasia and abortion may be viewed by some as essential ethical implications of their secular humanist faith, many Christians would argue that such practices must be legally prohibited, or, at least, be placed under strict legal limits. Most Christians would not seek to make homosexual intercourse illegal, but many would oppose placing homosexual unions on the same legal footing as heterosexual marriage, even though this will inevitably be experienced by some as discriminatory.

The issue is yet more complex. It must be frankly recognized that there can be no neutral definition of what counts as a human right. So we should not necessarily expect adherents of rival faiths (and here I include supposedly secular faiths) to accept a Christian definition of the limits of acceptable directional plurality. In a directionally plural society there will be contending, often incompatible, definitions of these limits. Whose version is to prevail? In at least some areas of law and public policy, it will be impossible to reconcile different versions. Many Christians, for example, would not be satisfied simply for Christian hospitals to have the liberty not to practise euthanasia. Since from their Christian standpoint life is a human right, they will want to curtail euthanasia everywhere. Not to try to do so would, from that point of view, be an abject retreat from public responsibility. Precisely the same point applies in the case of practices such as racial abuse, or economic exploitation. Both of these are, from a Christian viewpoint, violations of God-given human rights. Such rights are, however, also to some degree recognized by the prevailing secular mainstream (or parts of it), so Christians will often simply be adding their weight to an existing consensus or campaign. On these two issues, Christians will inevitably appear intolerant to racists and libertarian capitalists, but then so will secular liberals, socialists and others with whom they find themselves in alliance at these points. In a democracy, however, Christians may not be able to ensure that human rights, as they define them, are adequately protected. This necessarily implies the acceptance of political (as distinct from moral or religious) compromise. In a democracy all directional visions can claim an equal right to press their claims on the state through the representative process. The outcome in any particular case should reflect the relative levels of political support for rival proposals, though of course even the most representative democratic system will often be distorted by powerful sectional interests, inefficient legislatures, bureaucratic folly, public ignorance and other factors. But however representative the system, there may be - indeed have been - times when Christians, or advocates of other directional visions, will feel compelled to engage in civil disobedience or other illegal acts in order to defend a fundamental principle. No political or constitutional procedure can guarantee that this will never be necessary, though Christians should be among the most scrupulous in seeking to avoid it if possible.

My final point is to note the sobering possibility that, under the persisting corrosive effects of late modernity or postmodernity, the very moral foundations of democratic and constitutional government, such as those enunciated by Pope John Paul II and cited above (see p. 58), may begin to disappear (*cf.* note 3). In the face of this, what should Christians do? The first thing is to recognize that there is no *political* solution to such acute directional fragmentation. Once a culture loses its most fundamental moral and spiritual orientations, the state is powerless to rebuild them. The only solution to this problem, from a Christian viewpoint, is, literally, 'evangelical': the proclamation and demonstration of the truth of the gospel. This is not incompatible with a genuinely open dialogue with those of other faiths; indeed, a readiness to contend for one's own faith is a presupposition of taking others' faith with full seriousness.[9] Out of such a dialogue of conviction – which should be proceeding anyway irrespective of its possible political benefits – may emerge a far greater consensus on how to live together politically than any of us might have thought possible in a fragmenting culture.

NOTES

1 I am grateful to John Shortt, to an anonymous reader, and to my colleague Nicholas Townsend, for their valuable critical comments on this chapter. Any remaining deficiencies are, of course, my responsibility.

2 It should be noted that what is termed 'public policy' is not the whole of the 'public realm' referred to in the title; the social space we call the public realm is broader and less easily circumscribed than the sphere of public policy (cf. Mouw and Griffioen 1993: 80). The noun 'public' refers to an arena of social interactions embracing, in principle, anyone or everyone within a local, national or international society. 'Public policy' is a product of one specific public institution, the political community or state, which makes up only one part of the public realm. Certainly everything done by the state has a public character, but not everything having a public character is part of the state, even though it may shape, and be shaped by, what the state does.

3 The encyclical continues with a salutary warning: 'When these principles are not observed, the very basis of political coexistence is weakened, and the life of society itself is gradually jeopardized, threatened, and doomed to decay ... the risk of an alliance between democracy and ethical relativism ... would remove any sure moral reference point from political and social life, and on a deeper level make the acknowledgement of truth impossible' (1993: 151–152).

4 A discussion of an American version of the traditionalist position is found in Smith (ed.) 1989, Part III. Elements of the position are also found in Neuhaus 1984, and, from a more popular, and British, standpoint, in Holloway 1987. Liberal and liberationist positions are discussed in Wogaman 1988, chapters 4, 6; Forrester 1988; Preston 1994,

Part I. Recent statements of the transformationist position include Marshall 1986; Skillen 1994; Townsend and Ashcroft 1994; Alton 1991. I would also include the last century of official Catholic social teaching as a version of the transformationist position (*cf.*, e.g., Walsh and Davies [eds.] 1991).

5 It may be noted that the relationship between 'culture' in this sense, and 'nation', is a complex one. Some distinct cultures are specific to a single nation, others straddle many nations, and many nations are multicultural. Similarly, nations can be multi-directional. Further, nations are to be distinguished from states. The problem I will be concerned with is the presence of a plurality of directions within the same state (rather than the same nation). For valuable Christian reflections on nationhood, *cf.* Townsend 1995; Storrar 1990, Part 2; Maritain 1951, chapter 1.

6 Similar arguments are elaborated more fully in the following: Skillen 1994; McCarthy *et al.* 1981, 1982; Smith (ed.) 1989, especially Part II ('Principled Pluralism'); Guinness 1991, 1993; Murray 1993.

7 For a brief summary of biblical support for this position, *cf.* Chaplin 1994; *cf.* also Marshall 1986: 39–65; Mott 1993: 58–73; Smith (ed.) 1989; Townsend and Ashford 1994; for more classical references, *cf.* O'Donovan 1986: 127–130; Maritain 1951; Brunner 1945; Murray 1993.

8 My argument here tends to support what is known as the 'consociational' model of public policy found in varying forms in continental countries such as Germany, Belgium, Austria and the Netherlands (*cf.* McCarthy *et al.* 1982: 107–123; Fogarty 1957). There it has come to be associated with the development of parallel Christian institutions in education, unions, healthcare, broadcasting and so on. The state has for many decades treated these more or less equitably in various areas of public policy, notably in the distribution of public funding. The only significant realization of this approach in the UK is in the funding of denominational schools and colleges, although this falls a good way short of continental practice. I suggest that UK Christians might profitably explore how the consociational model could be applied more widely here.

9 Mouw and Griffioen propose an approach termed 'dialogical theocentrism', one which affirms the transcendent truth of God while acknowledging that insights into that truth can be discerned through dialogue with those of other faiths (Mouw and Griffioen 1993: 101–109). Two fine statements of such an approach are Newbigin 1989, and Middleton and Walsh 1995.

BIBLIOGRAPHY

Alison, M., and Edwards, D. (eds.) (1990), *Christianity and Conservatism*

(London: Hodder and Stoughton).

Alton, D. (1991), *Faith in Britain* (London: Hodder and Stoughton).

Atherton, J. (1992), *Christianity and the Market: Christian Social Thought for Our Times* (London: SPCK).

Bonino, J. M. (1983), *Toward a Christian Political Ethics* (London: SCM).

Brunner, E. (1945), *Justice and the Social Order* (London: Lutterworth).

Chaplin, J. P. (1987), 'Church and Politics', *Third Way* (June): 27–30.

—— (1993), 'How Much Cultural and Religious Pluralism Can Liberalism Tolerate?' in J. Horton (ed.), *Liberalism, Multiculturalism and Toleration* (London: Macmillan): 32–49.

—— (1994), 'Government', in D. J. Atkinson *et al.* (eds.), *New Dictionary of Christian Ethics and Pastoral Theology* (Leicester: IVP).

—— (ed.) (1992), *Politics and the Parties* (Leicester: IVP).

—— and Marshall, P. (eds.) (1994), *Political Theory and Christian Vision* (Lanham, NY: University Press of America).

Commission for Racial Equality (1990), *Britain: A Plural Society* (London: CRE).

Cooling, T. (1994), *A Christian Vision for State Education: Reflections on the Theology of Education* (London: SPCK).

Fogarty, M. (1957), *Christian Democracy in Western Europe* (London: Routledge and Kegan Paul).

Forrester, D. B. (1988), *Theology and Politics* (Oxford: Blackwell).

Gay, C. M. (1991), *With Liberty and Justice for Whom? The Recent Evangelical Debate over Capitalism* (Grand Rapids: Eerdmans).

Greenawalt, K. (1988), *Religious Convictions and Political Choice* (New York: Oxford University Press).

Guinness, O. (1991), 'Tribespeople, Idiots or Citizens? Religious Liberty and the Reforging of the American Public Philosophy', *Spectrum* 23/1: 29–50.

—— (1993), *The American Hour: A Time of Reckoning and the Once and Future Role of Faith* (New York: Free Press).

Holloway, D. (1987), *A Nation Under God* (Eastbourne: Kingsway).

Hunter, J. D., and Guinness, O. (eds.) (1990), *Articles of Faith, Articles of Peace: The Religious Liberty Clauses and the American Public Philosophy* (Washington: Brookings).

John Paul II (1993), *Veritatis Splendor* (London: Catholic Truth Society).

Jones, P. (1989), 'The Ideal of the Neutral State', in R. E. Goodin and A. Reeve (eds.), *Liberal Neutrality* (London: Routledge): 9–38.

Kymlicka, W. (1989), *Liberalism, Community, and Culture* (Oxford: Clarendon).

Lustgarten, L. S. (1983), 'Liberty in a Culturally Plural Society', in A. Phillips Griffiths (ed.), *Of Liberty* (Royal Institute of Philosophy Lecture Series 15, Cambridge: Cambridge University Press): 91–107.

Lynch, J. (1990), 'Cultural Pluralism, Structural Pluralism and the United

Kingdom', in Commission for Racial Equality (1990): 29-43.

McCarthy, R. M., Oppewal, D., Peterson, W., and Spykman, G. (1981), *Society, State and Schools: A Case for Structural and Confessional Pluralism* (Grand Rapids: Eerdmans).

―― *et al.* (1982), *Disestablishment a Second Time: Genuine Pluralism for American Schools* (Grand Rapids: Christian University Press).

Maritain, J. (1951), *Man and the State* (Chicago: Chicago University Press).

Marshall, P. (1983), *Human Rights Theories in Christian Perspective* (Toronto: Institute for Christian Studies).

―― (1986), *Thine is the Kingdom: A Biblical Perspective on Government and Politics Today* (Basingstoke: Marshalls).

―― (1989), 'Liberalism, Pluralism and Christianity: A Reconceptualiza-tion', *Fides et Historia*, XXI/3: 4-17.

―― (1994), 'Universal Human Rights and the Role of the State' (paper presented at the conference 'Sovereignty at the Crossroads? International Morality and the Search for a New World Order', Calvin College, Grand Rapids, Michigan, 30 September-1 October).

Mendus, S. (1989), *Toleration and the Limits of Liberalism* (London: Macmillan).

Middleton, R. J., and Walsh, B. J. (1995), *Truth is Stranger Than It Used to Be: Biblical Faith in a Postmodern Age* (London: SPCK).

Mouw, R. J., and Griffioen, S. (1993), *Pluralisms and Horizons: An Essay in Christian Public Philosophy* (Grand Rapids: Eerdmans).

Mott, S. C. (1993), *A Christian Perspective on Political Thought* (New York: Oxford University Press).

Murray, J. C. (1993), *Religious Liberty: Catholic Struggles with Pluralism*, ed. J. Leon Hooper (Louisville, KY: Westminster/John Knox).

Neuhaus, R. J. (1984), *The Naked Public Square: Religion and Democracy in America* (Grand Rapids: Eerdmans).

Newbigin, L. (1989), *The Gospel in a Pluralist Society* (London: SPCK).

Nolan, Lord (1995), *Standards in Public Life: First Report of the Committee on Standards in Public Life* (London: HMSO).

O'Donovan, O. M. T. (1986), *Resurrection and Moral Order: An Outline of Evangelical Ethics* (Leicester: IVP).

Parekh, B. (1990), 'Britain and the Social Logic of Pluralism', in Commission for Racial Equality (1990): 58-78.

Poulter, S. (1990), 'Cultural Pluralism and Its Limits: A Legal Perspective', in Commission for Racial Equality (1990): 3-28.

Preston, R. H. (1994), *Confusions in Social Ethics: Problems for Geneva and Rome* (London: SCM).

Skillen, J. W. (1990), *The Scattered Voice: Christians at Odds in the Public Square* (Grand Rapids: Zondervan).

―― (1994), *Recharging the American Experiment: Principled Pluralism for*

Genuine Civic Community (Grand Rapids: Baker).

—— and McCarthy, R. M. (eds.) (1991), *Political Order and the Plural Structure of Society* (Atlanta, GA: Scholars).

Smith, G. S. (ed.) (1989), *God and Politics: Four Views of the Reformation of Civil Government* (Phillipsburg, NJ: Presbyterian and Reformed).

Storrar, W. (1990), *Scottish Identity: A Christian Vision* (Edinburgh: Handsell).

Townsend, C., and Ashcroft, J. (1994), *Political Christians in a Plural Society: A New Strategy for a Biblical Contribution* (Cambridge: Jubilee Policy Group).

Townsend, N. (1995), 'A Race Apart?' *Third Way* (March): 18-21.

Walsh, M., and Davies, B. (eds.) (1991), *Proclaiming Justice and Peace: One Hundred Years of Catholic Social Teaching* (London: Cafod/Collins).

Wogaman, J. P. W. (1988), *Christian Perspectives on Politics* (London: SCM).

4

In defence of the common school

Trevor Cooling

The policy of providing common schools for all children is currently being seriously questioned. In particular the theory of knowledge on which they are based is regarded by many as inadequate. Some Christians are therefore suggesting they be replaced by a system of different schools based on the beliefs of the parents. Accepting the criticisms, this chapter, however, questions whether the rejection of common schools is in fact the best way forward for Christians. Some difficulties with the alternative are discussed alongside suggested modification of the rationale for common schools which capitalizes on developments in the theory of knowledge.

Most western democracies have built their educational systems on the concept of the common school. By a 'common school' is meant an institution that can serve the needs of all students irrespective of their own background by providing a common education which is appropriate for all. *One nation, one people, one school* has been the overriding political justification for this policy. Many, however, are now arguing that the concept of the common school is in disarray and that a new way of thinking about educational provision by the state is needed (*e.g.* Crittenden 1988; Holmes 1992; Halstead 1994). Evangelical

Christians have been among the most vocal proponents of change (*e.g.* McCarthy *et al.* 1981; Deakin 1989; Thiessen 1994; Jones 1995). Whether or not Christians should support a policy of common-school provision is hotly debated.

Educationalists have, in the past, rested the case for the common school on one main foundation, namely the Enlightenment idea that human beings share common knowledge which is independent of disputed beliefs. Knowledge is considered to have universal authority, whereas belief is a matter of personal choice. Science is the supposed paradigm of knowledge, religion the paradigm of disputed belief. Common schools are justified on the grounds that through them this undisputed, neutral knowledge is passed on to pupils, thereby inducting them into public rationality. In relation to disputed beliefs, the ideal is that pupils should choose for themselves so that indoctrination is avoided.

This Enlightenment foundation, however, has been eroded by developments in the theory of knowledge (*e.g.* Hart 1995). Many educationalists would now agree with the statement that 'culture is a window not a cell' (Feinberg 1995: 204), meaning that we learn through our beliefs rather than independently of them. Even Paul Hirst, once a guru of the Enlightenment model, now questions its validity (1993). Some Christians are therefore arguing, rightly in my opinion, that all knowledge is religious in the sense that we cannot know anything without holding fundamental beliefs about the nature of reality.

It is for this reason that some commentators are now saying that the common school is a redundant concept, because it is parasitic on the Enlightenment model of knowledge and the idea that schools can be neutral. They argue that some framework of beliefs has to be assumed if we are going to be able to teach anything. The key question in a plural society is 'Whose?' The major objection to common schools in our current context is that it is the beliefs of humanistic liberalism that are being imposed on everyone else. Evangelical Christians and others find this objectionable and protest against it as an infringement of their religious liberty. Non-Christians, in turn, find any attempt to reinstate Christianity as the assumed belief system objectionable. It seems that whatever beliefs are assumed, imposition is inevitable. So it is argued that common schools represent an inappropriate invasion by the state of the domain of religious nurture which is the rightful province of parents. The major challenge is to develop a model of educational provision which accommodates our new understanding of the intimate relation between knowledge and belief without offending religious liberty.

The only way forward for common schools which does not entail imposition may seem to be to find some minimal set of beliefs upon which it is in fact possible to obtain agreement. A major criticism of these 'low-doctrine schools', however, is that they provide a low-value education (Holmes 1992). Education should offer youngsters a vision for life. Common schools deprive everyone equally of a high set of binding beliefs and values on which to base their lives.

These considerations have led some Christians to campaign for a model of state educational provision usually called 'structural plural-ism' (e.g. McCarthy et al. 1981). In this, the state funds a variety of schools based on the beliefs and values of the different communities that comprise the nation. No one ideology is imposed on all and the paternalism of state control of education is banished. Parents and communities are free to set up 'high-doctrine' schools, which reflect the beliefs of their primary culture. Such a system protects religious liberties because no community is denied access to the sort of education that it deems right and proper for its children. This system is already well established in Denmark and Australia, is the subject of continuing debate in Canada, and is the aspiration of many Christians in countries like France and the USA where religion is constitutionally barred from having a presence in common schools.

I find the criticisms of the Enlightenment model of knowledge and of the neutral school convincing (Cooling 1994). I therefore happily embrace the principles behind structural pluralism. Where I wish to differ, however, is in the assumption made by some that continuing support for the principle of the common school is inconsistent with the structural pluralist view of knowledge and the concern for religious liberty (Thiessen 1995; Jones 1995). In this chapter I will question this assumption in two ways. First, I shall suggest that there are weaknesses in a fundamental concept deployed by those who reject the common school. Secondly, I shall propose some modifications that are necessary to transform the concept of the common school if the justified criticisms of the current Enlighten-ment rationale are to be met.

Difficulties with a fundamental concept

A fundamental concept for those who reject common schools is that of primary culture. Thiessen defines this as follows:

> Every child inherits a language and a host of attitudes,
> values and beliefs ... the validity of which they do not
> normally question and, in the ordinary course of events, are
> not prepared to question (1993: 169–170).

Thiessen's case is that gaining knowledge is dependent on the possession of a primary culture. So some form of nurture in belief is an essential and inescapable element in acquiring knowledge, and therefore in education. Such views are anathema to many liberals, who believe that children should choose their own primary culture and who would therefore level the charge of indoctrination against Thiessen. Accepting the new understanding of knowledge described earlier, however, his arguments are convincing (Cooling 1994). Here, I wish only to question Thiessen's further conclusion that establishing that nurture within a primary culture is an integral aspect of education *entails* the rejection of a common-school policy because children should be nurtured in the primary culture of their parents *in school*. I shall do this by suggesting some difficulties that emerge from the way he develops the notion of primary culture.

One of his main assumptions about the nature of a child's primary culture seems to be that it is a clearly identifiable phenomenon that can be equated with one set of pre-packaged beliefs. Thus a child can be correctly 'classified' according to the various belief systems that can be found in the world at large. Children will therefore be educated as Christians or Muslims or humanists or Buddhists according to the group to which their parents belong. There are a number of difficulties with this approach.

First, extensive ethnographic research among children from a number of distinctive religious communities has suggested that such children in fact display *multiple cultural competence* (Jackson 1995). By this it is meant that children, in the development of their beliefs, are not confined to one discrete culture determined by their parental background, but rather come to their own system of meaning through interaction with the different belief systems they meet in the various

79

contexts they inhabit in their daily lives. These will include their family, their religious community, the television programmes they watch, their peer group, their school, and the books and magazines they read. This system of meaning is, of course, influenced to varying degrees by these different influences and it is certainly true that the influence of parental beliefs is often the strongest. It is also true that there will probably be one framework which will provide the main integrating structure for the child's thinking. It is incorrect, however, to suggest that children can learn *only* if they are taught *exclusively* from within one coherent belief framework or that they will be seduced from the parental framework if they encounter a different framework in school, both of which seem to be assumptions made by critics of common schools. Rather, it appears that experience of a variety of influences actually helps the development of a coherent primary culture.

It is of course true that Christian parents will want to ensure that their children's *primary* focus of loyalty in integrating their knowledge and values is Christian and they will be rightly concerned about any attempt by the common school to undermine this. What I am disputing is the idea that if Christian beliefs are not the *only* influence in a child's schooling, then some other belief system will automatically take their place. I am questioning the assumption that a fully Christian primary culture can develop only if a child attends a school which consistently reflects its parental primary culture. It is the either/or scenario, which suggests that a coherent primary culture can be developed only in substantial isolation from other influences, that I am challenging.

Secondly, there does seem to be a very real question as to where the line between one primary culture and another is to be drawn. Clearly there are fundamental differences of great substance between Christians, so we cannot really talk about *one* Christian primary culture. Even if we talk about an *evangelical* Christian primary culture we still have problems. Do we mean the charismatic or Reformed version, for example? The point is that there seems to be a problem in identifying the difference between primary and secondary cultural differences. This matters a lot if our ideal is that each child should be educated from within its *own primary culture*. The rigid application of the argument from primary culture will clearly lead to considerable fragmentation of educational provision and consequent isolation of children from each other.

Thirdly, I suggest that the notion of primary culture that I am criticizing is in danger of endorsing a form of relativism which is actually inconsistent with evangelical Christian beliefs. This form insists that different belief systems are incommensurable, that each of us inhabits a different world from people in other communities, that each of these worlds is valid and that there is no one truth to which all human beings are accountable irrespective of their culture or upbringing (Runzo 1986). Although many evangelical Christians accept that beliefs influence people's understanding of the world and that, in a fallen world, pluralism is therefore inevitable, they also believe that there is *one* God to whom all human beings are answerable and that there is *one* gospel which is good news for all people irrespective of their primary culture. Part of the evangelical credo is, in the midst of pluralism, to proclaim this gospel truth.

The reason I suggest that the use of the argument from primary culture is in danger of endorsing this form of relativism is the insistence that the existence of different primary cultures should be *affirmed and supported* by abolishing common schools and educating every child in a school based on the primary culture of its parents. Certainly religious and other forms of pluralism are a fact of life in modern societies. It is right and proper to accept this pluralism by not infringing people's religious liberty through the structures of public education. It is one thing, however, to insist that common schools should not impose a particular belief system in the cause of religious liberty. It is quite another for Christians to go as far as *protecting and sustaining* religious pluralism by creating educational structures which *guarantee its propagation* through abolishing the common school in favour of a system where every child is educated in the beliefs of its parents, be they Muslim, atheist, Christian or whatever. The common school is at least an institutional affirmation of the idea that there is ultimately one truth for all. A form of structural pluralism with no common schools seems to endorse a very different message and set in institutional concrete belief systems which Christians believe to be erroneous. So I am suggesting that by seemingly walking away from the notion of one truth to which all are accountable by adopting too rigid an understanding of the concept of primary culture in the way we structure public education, we are in danger of walking away from evangelical Christianity.

The transformation of the common school

So far I have been arguing that the structural pluralist view of knowledge does not entail the rejection of common schools as long as a less rigid understanding of primary culture is adopted. Doing this makes the concept of a common school coherent because it is recognized that a consistently Christian primary culture can develop even where children experience a variety of influences *as long as the parental primary culture is strong.*

I would also wish to argue that not only is the common school a coherent idea, but it is something that Christians should actually endorse. I do not have the space to argue the point in detail here, but my reasons can be summarized as follows.

1. Common schools offer a context in which Christians can be active in promoting co-operation and harmony between people of different communities. We should never assume that a Bosnia could not develop in Britain (Guinness 1991).

2. Common schools offer a context in which Christians can be active in promoting the good of other people as part of their evangelistic concern to incarnate the gospel (Fung 1992).

3. More explicitly, common schools offer a context in which the gospel story can be told to children of many different communities in a way that would not be possible in a system where schools are exclusively based on a variety of primary cultures.

4. Common schools offer a context in which Christians can seek to shape public life by involvement in a sphere of activity which impacts on the lives of most citizens.

Having said this, I do not wish to suggest that common schools are the ultimate ideal. There are dangers in seeking to establish ideals. An example will illustrate the point. I recently saw a television news report about child labour in Bangladesh. Pressure from western customers has resulted in the practice being made illegal. There are fewer children being exploited in sweat shops. Unfortunately there are also many families who are now poverty-stricken because the children who were the main breadwinners have lost their jobs. The ideal of removing exploitation of child labour is laudable. But simply introducing this 'good' reform without consideration of the consequences in this particular context was short-sighted. A more appropriate strategy might have been to accept the practice of child labour as necessary *in this context*, but to seek to reform it to make it less exploitative. The most Christian strategy possible in a given situation is not necessarily the ideal one.

From my perspective the theoretical ideal is that children receive a Christian education. To pursue this through legislation now, however, would entail either violating the religious liberties of other communities by imposing a Christian framework in state schools, or the setting up of schools based on other belief frameworks if these basic religious liberties are not to be violated. What is the ideal, namely offering a Christian education, will, in both these instances, have less than welcome consequences. Supporting common schools and ensuring an active Christian presence in the education of as many children as possible through them seems to me to be the best possible policy in our current circumstances.

If Christians are to support a policy of common schools, changes to the way people currently think about them are certainly necessary if the insights of the structural pluralist view of knowledge and the importance of respecting religious liberty are to be honoured.

First, we have to get away from the idea that the only possible scenario is a power struggle between various belief systems for the control of the common school. This is based on the either/or conception that if a school is not governed by my values it will be governed by someone else's values that I will not like. An alternative is to negotiate a framework of values that creates a learning institution with specific functions which are different from those carried out in a community of faith. If belief systems do overlap with each other in their concerns and interests, then such negotiation will be possible. Certainly Jackson's work on multiple cultural competence, referred to earlier, supports the idea that negotiation and interaction with other belief frameworks is an integral part of developing a coherent belief system.

Secondly, we have to accept that common schools cannot have the responsibility for the systematic nurture of a child's primary culture. That, I suggest, is an inappropriate activity for a state school in a plural society and is the primary responsibility of parents. Based on the new theory of knowledge discussed earlier, an appropriate function for common schools is that they are places where children learn to reflect on the relationship between belief and knowledge. They should come to a greater understanding of their own beliefs and an appreciation of other people's beliefs while facing up to their responsibility to explore the world and discover the truth to which all are ultimately responsible. People from many different backgrounds can then embark on a learning enterprise together, which will enable them to understand themselves and their fellow citizens better. This is both an essential educational activity and an important skill to develop for functioning as a responsible citizen in society. It is not, however, formation of the person in the way common schools, certainly in Britain, have traditionally seen their role. Rather, it is a much more limited activity which is appropriate to the common school in a plural society. In this context the responsibility for faith formation must rest with parents and faith communities.

These two points may seem to fall foul of Holmes's (1992) criticism that such low-doctrine schools offer low-value education. I suggest that this is to underestimate the importance of what common schools can offer. Promoting reflective understanding of the relationship between belief and knowledge and promoting civic values are very important activities. I concede that they are, in the final analysis, less important activities than faith formation. But that does not make them 'low-doctrine' activities which offer children no commitment for life. Rather, it means that the 'doctrine' that common schools are based on is a different type of high doctrine from the high-doctrine activities characteristic of faith communities.

An analogy may help. Aid workers in refugee camps often engage in activities with very limited goals. The situation they face may mean that, for example, they can do little more than erect plastic sheeting to offer some shelter even though, given different circumstances, they would wish to provide much better housing. Even though erecting plastic sheeting is an activity reflecting a low vision of human good, it is still a most important, indeed fully Christian, activity to be undertaking in those particular circumstances. In relation to common schools, I am suggesting that what might be termed 'low-doctrine' activities (because they are not what Christians would be pursuing in more ideal circumstances) could still be very important and in other ways reflect a high doctrine in those circumstances.

An important implication of my argument concerning the limited goals that common schools can fulfil is that Christian communities have to take their responsibility for the high-doctrine educational activity of religious nurture much more seriously than is currently the case. We cannot expect the Government to do it for us in its common schools.

In conclusion, it seems to me that a mixed economy of state educational provision is probably the most satisfactory way forward. On the one hand, I suggest that Christians should go on supporting the concept of the common school as the best way of providing for the educational needs of the majority of children. We should, however, be active in seeking to reform these from being either religion-free zones, as in the American or French conception, or places where a form of humanism is propagated in the name of Enlightenment rationality, as has happened in British schools. The transformed concept would be based on the acceptance of the intimate relations that exist between knowledge and religious belief and would recognize the pluralism that therefore exists. The school curriculum would encourage the exploration of this relationship and would respect the faith background of each child. The values of the school would be based on the importance placed on this mutual exploration and on the need for individuals from different communities to develop strategies for living and working alongside each other in their common civic life as citizens. At the same time the common school should affirm the importance of the pursuit of truth by requiring pupils to face the challenge presented to their own way of thinking by that of other people. Certainly, we can reasonably expect that all pupils ought to hear the basic Christian message.

Of course, not all parents will be satisfied with this type of education and will want something that reflects their own religious tradition much more distinctively. I suggest that, as a basic tenet of religious liberty, such parents ought to have the freedom to set up and run their own schools. And by freedom I do mean some financial freedom so that state funding should be forthcoming, at least to a degree, on condition that such schools do not threaten the stability of society or the welfare of the students. The existence of such schools is also a constant reminder to the common schools that religious belief and knowledge cannot be divorced from each other.

In conclusion, I have suggested that the common school is something that Christians should support even though it cannot offer a distinctively Christian education. Certainly the likelihood is that common schools will be the major providers of education for the foreseeable future, and we should therefore be seeking to reform them to ensure the possibility of Christian witness, to bring their rationale into line with developments in the theory of knowledge and to undermine those who wish to abuse them by imposing versions of humanism in the name of rationality. There is no doubt that common schools have their inherent faults, but, compared to those that would be perpetuated by their abolition, they can be lived with.

BIBLIOGRAPHY

Cooling, Trevor (1994), *A Christian Vision for State Education: Reflections on the Theology of Education* (London: SPCK).

Crittenden, Brian (1988), *Parents, the State and the Right to Educate* (Melbourne: Melbourne University Press).

Deakin, Ruth (1989), *Christian Schools: The Case for Public Funding* (Bristol: Regius).

Feinberg, Walter (1995), 'Liberalism and the Aims of Multicultural Education', *Journal of Philosophy of Education* 29/2: 203-216.

Fung, Raymond (1992), *The Isaiah Agenda: An Ecumenical Strategy for Congregational Evangelism* (Geneva: WCC Publications).

Guinness, Os (1991), 'Tribespeople, Idiots or Citizens? Religious Liberty and the Reforging of the American Public Philosophy', *Spectrum* 23/1: 29-50.

Halstead, Mark (1994), *Parental Choice and Education* (London: Kogan Page).

Hart, Trevor (1995), *Faith Thinking: The Dynamics of Christian Theology* (London: SPCK).

Hirst, Paul (1993), 'Education, Knowledge and Practices', in *Beyond Liberal Education: Essays in Honour of Paul H. Hirst*, ed. R. Barrow and P. White (London: Routledge).

Holmes, Mark (1992), *Education Policy for the Pluralist Democracy: The Common School, Choice and Diversity* (Lewes: Falmer).

Jackson, Robert (1995), 'From Community to Classroom', address given at the Professional Council for RE Annual Conference, 10 April.

Jones, Arthur (1995), 'Common Schools: A Christian Reflection on the Issues', *Spectrum* 27/2: 125-144.

McCarthy, R. M., Oppewal, D., Peterson, W., and Spykman, G. (1981), *Society, State and Schools: A Case for Structural and Confessional Pluralism* (Grand Rapids: Eerdmans).

Runzo, Joseph (1986), *Reason, Relativism and God* (Basingstoke: Macmillan).

Thiessen, Elmer (1993), *Teaching for Commitment* (Leominster: Gracewing).

—— (1994), 'Who Has the Right to Educate?' *Spectrum* 26/2: 141-155.

—— (1995), Review article on *A Christian Vision for State Education, Spectrum* 27/2: 145-152.

5

Exploring structural and confessional pluralism

Ruth Deakin

This chapter explores an understanding of structural and confessional pluralism in western education systems which does justice to the normative tasks of each of the partners involved in schooling, and also affirms the freedom of individuals and communities to subscribe to differing worldviews and ways of life. It shows how this framework is consistent with theological traditions within the historic Christian faith, particularly a trinitarian doctrine of God and a canonical doctrine of creation. As well as seeking education policies which are consistent with this vision, teachers need to develop ethical practice which is critical, reflective and driven by moral vision.

Reform and innovation have been characteristic of education policy in western democracies during the last fifteen years. These societies are grappling with the profound changes which accompany the shift to a condition of postmodernity. The expanding global marketplace, the broader and faster dissemination of information, the loss of scientific certainty and of a universalizing belief system, as well as the changing nature of production, are all factors which contribute to pressures and demands faced by today's teachers. Against this backcloth a central ethical question becomes: 'Whose vision should schools be serving?' The issue of the control of education and the quest for a socially just distribution of power moves to centre stage.

Christian faith and education

I will begin by suggesting a way of understanding a Christian doctrine of God which can inform an approach to the ethics of educational provision, and can illuminate issues of human hope and liberation which are central to the task of education. Nelson (1987) refers to three differing approaches which Christians might use to understand the relationship between their theology and academic discipline or profession. The first is the compatibilist approach, which assumes that academic knowledge is independent of faith. The second is the reconstructionalist approach, where all intellectual activity is based on theological presuppositions and there are two mutually incompatible and contrasting frameworks for knowledge, one of which depends on the authority of God expressed in propositional form in Scripture and the other of which depends entirely on human reason. Finally there is the transformationalist approach which affirms the belief that all knowledge is value-laden and that Christian belief has a distinctive role in shaping human knowledge, but also that there are distinctive features of the disciplines which are givens, and can be shared with other belief systems. For example, knowledge of mathematical laws is shared by people who might operate with significantly different belief systems or worldviews.

It is this transformationalist approach which I will seek to explore in more detail in order to provide a theological basis for a particular understanding of justice in educational provision. It is appropriate to use this framework to explore the issues from a British perspective. This is because the compatibilist approach has been dominant in education over the last fifty years, fitting well as it does with the now weakening positivistic orientation of the field. Also, perhaps as a reaction to this, there is evidence of a reconstructionalist approach to education by Christians in Britain, particularly in the new Christian-schools movement. Given that Britain has been the home of Christendom, with its established church and close structural links between church and state, there is potential for a deeply polarized and isolated Christian community as far as education is concerned because, with the renewal of evangelical Christianity over the last two decades, it is all too easy for Christians to assume a reconstructionalist position and for that to become entwined with a particular traditional right-wing political philosophy. A transformationalist perspective offers a means of dialogue with other positions which shows the relevance of Christian theology for all of culture, and may therefore offer new ways of understanding a complex issue. In my view a transformationalist approach will lead to a more authentic interaction with our culture, and more scope for the fulfilment of the great commission which is at the heart of the Christian gospel.

Christian praxis

The doctrine of the Trinity has been developed by theologians such as Jürgen Moltmann (1967, 1972, 1974) to take more seriously the historical and future-orientated nature of God's presence in human history in the cross and resurrection. God is not only the transcendent Self beyond history, but also the one who promises to act within history. Revelation of God is found by human beings in the tension between reflection on the Christian story within human history, and hope for the future in relation to God's promises for the world. Three consequences of this understanding of God are, first, that God is affected by passionate concern that involves vulnerability to human suffering; secondly, that the unity of God is the unity of persons in relationship to each other, and that unity is defined in terms of love which can open itself up to and include the world within itself; and, thirdly, that the persons-in-relation model of the Trinity legitimates relations of love and equality rather than domination and subjection because of the nature of the revelation of God and human participation in relationship with God.

Since God is present and knowable in the ordinary tasks of humanity, rather than being 'altogether other', the whole of reality becomes a sacrament, a place where God is present, which calls for a response from the follower of Christ. The knowledge of God is not only knowledge of a set of propositional truths but it is also a dialectical relationship between promise, history and fulfilment which is engaged in by agents of change who are drawn into expectant trust. This is a praxis-orientated way of understanding Christian engagement with society and culture. It combines theory with practice, and knowing with doing.

This has implications for the structure and the direction of education. The freedom of faith in Christ calls for political freedom, and it urges people on towards liberating actions because it makes them aware of suffering in human situations of exploitation, oppression, alienation and captivity. The heart of the Christian gospel is an encounter with the love of God which finds new possibility for life in the event of an unconditional love which liberates human beings to be all that God intended them to be in creation. For example, the refusal of a local education authority to provide statutory support for children with special needs who are being educated outside of the maintained sector is a form of oppression, to which people motivated by a Christian vision would respond with liberating action. A more subtle form of oppression is the emphasis by educational bureaucrats on basic need in the supply of school places, which is calculated purely by numbers, rather than by parental demand which should take into account the statutory requirement that as far as possible children are educated in accordance with the wishes of their parents.

Justice and structure: structural pluralism

Christian liberation, however, is not liberation for liberation's sake and, without addressing the matter of what we are seeking liberation from and liberation to, there is the danger of simply replacing one set of oppressions for another.

The question of the structure of educational provision therefore needs to be explored from a Christian perspective if we are to promote educational structures which enable and empower human liberation consistent with a Christian vision. While Moltmann's interpretation of Christian praxis can shed light on the direction and goals of education, a thorough understanding and exploration of the doctrine of creation is necessary to understand more deeply questions of structure. Protestant theology following the Reformation reoriented Christians towards their divine vocation in the world, and emphasized that the entire world and all that is in it is created by, points towards, and can be used to give honour to God (Marshall 1994). Human beings are made in the image of God, and as such possess not only an intrinsic dignity, but also a responsibility to God for their vocation and task in life and for the ways in which they organize themselves and their communities. There is, therefore, a created reality which exists independently of human knowledge. Human beings are engaged in a process of reproducing or transforming the ensemble of structures, practices and conventions which constitutes society. The social conditions in which this activity takes place are relationships of various kinds; between people and each other, their products, activities, nature and themselves (Bhaskar 1989). For human beings who have an awareness of God, an additional relationship which forms part of these social conditions is that between people and God.

From this perspective, society is differentiated not by the arbitrary self-expression and self-creation of autonomous individuals, but by the evident created reality which is upheld by the providence of God. God the Creator is also the order-giver and the norm-giver in both the natural and social world. Human activity can be consistent with those norms or differentiated from them; it can be loving or unloving, freedom-giving or exploitative, and so on.

The plurality of agents and agencies which participate in a sphere such as schooling each have a particular God-given responsibility and task and require political freedom within which to fulfil that task. When looking at the structures of education and the distribution of power between the participants in schooling – parents, children, teachers, governors, central government, local government, business and communities – it is important to ask questions concerning the God-given responsibilities and rights of the participants and to seek for educational provision which best enables each to fulfil their mandate without oppressing, exploiting or alienating the others. Justice in this sense can be understood as enabling right relationships to take place, and power is facilitative rather than coercive.

Rights and responsibilities

The rights and responsibilities of parents, their children and government will be discussed as examples. Each partner in education has a normative but limited role in schooling. A structurally pluralist framework will protect the rights of each participant as well as empower them to fulfil their responsibilities (McCarthy *et al.* 1981; Skillen 1992).

The rights of parents to have their children educated in accordance with their own religious and philosophical convictions is well argued, enshrined in human-rights documents and, in policy terms, currently expressed in the rhetoric of parental choice, which forms part of the wider educational reform context. From a theological perspective too, it can be argued that raising children is the vocation or the normative task of parents, given in creation, and any other societal agency which impedes them in that task is oppressive or unjust. The refusal of the British Government, so far, to fund new confessional schools is an example of oppression, where parents are disempowered in this way.

Children too, however, have God-given rights and responsibilities to learn and to grow. Where a child is unable to fulfil this task because its parents, or its school, is failing in some way, then it is oppressed, and liberating action is called for. Children are particularly vulnerable to oppression because they are not often powerful enough to help themselves. Liberating praxis in schools will encourage agencies which support families and at times intervene on behalf of children at risk.

The government has a legitimate role in the task of education and forms an important partner in the process, but it is going beyond its mandate if it restricts the rights and freedoms of families and communities. The normative task of the state is the securing of public justice – the fair and equitable treatment of all citizens in a setting which honours the independence of families and of schools. Thus the state can enforce policies which protect equal opportunities and equal access, or which protect certain standards within education. Indeed, the creation of a common framework for education can be seen as part of the God-given task of the state. The common framework in Britain today is extensive, including a national curriculum, health and safety legislation, instruments and articles of government, financial frameworks and accountability structures and equal-opportunity legislation. The state also has responsibility for encouraging conditions for healthy economic growth, which clearly requires an educated and vocationally oriented population.

Justice and neutrality: confessional pluralism

The debate about the relationships between the partners in the process of education is further complicated by the existence of multiple belief systems which co-exist in contemporary western society. Hargreaves describes the contemporary western education system as being characterized by a shift from a culture of certainty to a culture of uncertainty:

> The collapse of singular political ideologies, the diminishing credibility of knowledge bases and the declining certainty attached to scientific expertise have far-reaching ramifications for the changing world of education ... (1994: 57).

He goes on to argue that the crisis of educational and social purpose in the postmodern age is a crisis which still awaits resolution.

The liberal model of education, with its ideal of rational autonomy, has had as its central concern the avoidance of 'indoctrination'. This form of education is generally defined as providing experiences which are ordered in such a way that learners come to accept views only on the basis of reasons which seem valid to them as individuals. This view has been under increasing criticism from both post-structuralist and Habermasian views of education, which claim that reasons are embedded in a theoretical context and cannot be assessed outside of a historical/biographical horizon. Young puts the point succinctly when he says:

> Criticism always presupposes a schema, background, world-view, *Vorhabe*, or tradition ... Put crudely, in order to be critical you must first be indoctrinated (1995: 13).

Tradition, culture and learning

The beliefs, values and ideas which shape observable educational practice in schools are an important part of the learning process, and need to be made explicit and coherent. They enable learners to find meaning in their learning and provide a framework from which learners can be critical and grow, while understanding themselves as learners in a concrete socio-historical setting. Cultural deprivation occurs when children are estranged from their tradition and roots and do not have a sense of their own story and place in the wider family and community. Many learning skills are developed automatically in the child's primary culture, and can be critically developed as children respond from their own experience and sense of self to new ideas, worldviews and challenges.

In a multicultural and multifaith society, characterized as it is by diversity of belief systems and human aspirations, uniformity in schooling systems is inappropriate and oppressive. Religious neutrality within the liberal ideal is neutrality only as long as we are prepared to believe in the liberal ideal, which discriminates against those whose belief system is different from the dominant one. Confessional pluralism which allows the free expression of differing worldviews in schools within a common framework is an expression of liberation in education.

The question then is: how can we structure a schooling system which celebrates difference and also empowers the plurality of agents and agencies to fulfil their responsibilities and which protects their rights, especially the rights of the less powerful?

The school as a community

Schools as institutions are complex places which can be understood from a variety of perspectives. Hodgkinson (1991) suggests that schools are best understood as 'communities' and that the model of a family (*Gemeinschaft*) is perhaps a more appropriate one for schools than a bureaucracy, since it brings with it concepts of care, equity, tolerance and a tacit basis of faith in human nature which he suggests produces an organizational climate most compatible with the fullest possible psychological functioning. Communities are notoriously difficult to define, but I suggest that there are at least three necessary elements: a territorial element, a functional element and a relational element. The school functions in a particular location; its function is the education of its pupils, and the people who participate in the task of schooling are bound together by shared beliefs, values and goals. When schools are silent about their worldviews and beliefs, domination and oppression of minorities can result. When schools

94

are explicit about them, healthy debate, diversity and respect for others are facilitated.

Moral vision and leadership

Research suggests that effective schools have effective educational leaders. Effective leadership requires a number of components to be present, but without vision, or moral leadership, it will not be effective; indeed, it may not even be described as leadership. Moral leadership provides a cumulative focus and meaning for symbolic, human, instructional and administrative leadership. In the context of the self-managing school, an institutional form which is now widely and uncritically incorporated into western schooling systems, the importance of a clear educational vision within the school itself increases.

Educational vision and values are not arbitrarily selected, however, but are always rooted into a wider belief system, or set of ideas, or ideology. Ideology in the Marxist tradition is often seen as 'false consciousness' and is generally pejorative. Pratte presents an analysis of ideology which is essentially benign, in that he acknowledges the possibilities (which always exist) that ideologies can be used to manipulate and exploit, but suggests that in fact an ideology is

> ... part of a continuum of experience, of how individuals seek to account for, comprehend and organise action on a number of problematic issues found in the social order ... it expresses a particular range of beliefs , an organisation of empirical data, and an interpretation of these as applied to certain human endeavours (1977: 59).

An ideology can be described as a communally held worldview. Worldviews are not static in relation to social institutions, but rather they are dialectical, with practice and experience shaping the theory and the theory shaping the practice.

A substantial research project undertaken in North America (Bryk *et al.* 1993) sought to understand why Catholic high schools simultaneously manage to achieve relatively high levels of student learning, distribute this learning more equitably with regard to race, gender and class than in the public sector, and sustain high levels of teacher commitment and student engagement. The conclusions were that key factors in this effectiveness were a delimited technical core curriculum, a communal organization, school-based governance and an inspirational ideology.

It is not only important for ethical leadership but also educationally desirable that all schools are explicit about their communal belief system and how their school vision and values flow from it. Whether a school's natural or historical ideological roots are secular liberal, Christian, Jewish, Steiner or Muslim, it is helpful that they are made explicit, owned and shared by the school community, and that the diversity which develops as a result is celebrated as a healthy expression of a diverse society which seeks to act fairly towards all of its member communities.

From theory to practice

In policy terms the situation is more complex. The communitarian ideas developed here, which assume that children come from families and distinctive backgrounds with bonds of ideology and community which form a natural basis for education, are clearly at odds with the previously dominant liberal view, where children are individuals who are best educated together in a common school. In practical terms, all western democracies offer some choice and, as Holmes puts it, 'the question becomes not one of a common school or choice, but of which choices, under what conditions and developed by whom?' (1994: 68). Walford (1994) argues that parental choice as promoted by the British Government since 1979 actually becomes school choice of families, and socially disadvantaged families end up, not only with no choice, but with the weakest schools, or 'sink schools'.

Political, ideological and economic discourse

A more complex reading of the influences which shape schools is therefore necessary, and will help to identify ways in which individuals can resist and sometimes reshape what goes on in schools in order to protect the relative autonomy of the key actors, or to enable each to fulfil their normative tasks. This is because every societal institution

– the state, the family, the school – is made up of individuals, and these individuals are subject to powerful societal and cultural discourses which inform their individual and institutional behaviour and thus their direction. In other words the working worldview of decision-makers in education is often one which has key elements which are not consistent with liberation as defined here, but which are dominated by other interests. Also, each individual decision-maker's worldview is powerfully influenced by his or her own personal story and interests. These worldviews find expression in the language of discourse.

The state's role is particularly important to understand, since it is entwined with ideological, political and economic interests which are often hidden, but which nevertheless powerfully influence the activity of the state and mould individuals into a way of life which suits the state's interests. The educational state apparatus comprises those teachers, administrators and institutions which are publicly funded and certified. The control of education is achieved by the state at a number of levels; the legal constitution of the school, the bureaucracy of education, technocratic control and institutional corporation.

In practice today, simply in terms of timetabling of subjects, the humanities and the expressive arts have less time and therefore less status than science and technology, reflecting the interests of the state. The influence of bureaucracy in school planning and management is far reaching, and often debilitating for individuals and schools who do not want to accept the *status quo*, or who want to innovate and change. In a culture which itself is individualistic and materialist in its orientation, and where schools are not used to dealing with questions of value and belief, these influences need to be recognized and resisted if human liberation is our goal.

A discourse of difference

Given that there are powerful discourses which shape western education systems, it is important for the sake of justice, or right relationships which enable the fullest possibilities for human liberation, that individuals and communities are able to critique these influences and to resist and alter them. Habermas claims that there are three anthropologically deep-seated human interests: a technical interest in the control of objectified processes; a historical and hermeneutical interest in inter-subjective understanding; and an emancipatory interest in autonomy and responsibility. He suggests that these lead to differing types of rationality, and that western culture is often dominated by technical rationality, but all three are needed in ethical decision-making. This framework is useful from a Christian perspective, although a Christian understanding of emancipation would be distinct from the promissory notes offered by Freud and Marx (Outhwaite 1994).

Addressing these issues at a policy level is important, although messy and slow. It is not adequate simply to structure schools to be self-managing, or to empower teachers to take more responsibility for decisions, or to empower parents to choose schools, or even to enable new religious schools to come into the state sector, or to impose school planning systems designed to support the disadvantaged. We also need to discover ways in which teachers can 'develop the ability to survive the vicissitudes of planned and unplanned change while growing and developing' which Fullan (1994: 5) says is the core of productive educational change.

I suggest that, to be ethical, schools should focus primarily on the interests of their pupils because the primary, God-given task of the school is the education of its pupils. The term 'ethical' here means the normative action which should guide leaders in education and which will produce the maximum self-determination for individuals, whilst fostering an understanding of the interdependent nature of human life. It is consistent with the understanding of justice (developed earlier) which enables right relationships to take place. In Moltmann's terms, this means actions which respect the dignity and freedom of each individual, made in the image of God, and which foster respectful and open relationships that are facilitative rather than exploitative.

There are three main implications of my argument which are relevant to teachers in schools. First, to be ethical or to do justice, teachers need, in addition to technical, personal and instructional competencies, a rigorous and critical understanding of the role of ideology in schools. Second, they need an open and coherent commitment to a belief system, with a clearly articulated educational vision; and they need a commitment to critical reflection and professional growth. Third, given the nature of the powerful discourses which shape schools and individuals, teachers need moral courage, or the ability to stand up for what they believe in, rather than simply to accept the *status quo* or uncritically to incorporate externally imposed changes.

In this chapter, I have explored the question of the control of education, examining the role of the various agents and agencies which participate in schooling as well as wider and more diffuse societal influences. I have offered an analysis of rights and responsibilities in education which is rooted in a view of the person, knowledge and reality which is consistent with orthodox Christianity, using both the critical social-transformational model for understanding Christian theology and culture, as well as drawing on the doctrine of creation which has been developed by the Reformed tradition. I have argued for the need for confessional pluralism, with a concomitant view of the structurally diverse and limited role of the various partners in education. This, however, is not enough to promote human liberation. Teachers also need to be value-critical, to be prepared to be open and committed to their own educational worldview, to be prepared to reflect critically upon their own praxis and to grow as professionals, as well as to display moral courage.

BIBLIOGRAPHY

Bhaskar, R. (1989), *Reclaiming Reality* (London: Verso).

Bryk, A., Lee, V., and Holland, P. (1993), *Catholic Schools and the Common Good* (London: Harvard University Press).

Fullan, M. (1994), *Change Forces* (London: Falmer).

Habermas, J. (1984), *The Theory of Communicative Action*, trans. T. McCarthy (Boston: Beacon).

Hargreaves, A. (1994), *Changing Teachers, Changing Times* (London: Cassell).

Hodgkinson, C. (1991), *Educational Leadership: The Moral Art* (Albany: University of New York Press).

Holmes, M. (1994), *Education Policy for the Pluralist Democracy: The Common School, Choice and Diversity* (London: Falmer).

McCarthy, R. M., Oppewal, D., Peterson, W., and Spykman, G. (1981), *Society, State and Schools: A Case for Structural and Confessional Pluralism* (Grand Rapids: Eerdmans).

Marshall, P. (1994), 'Shaping God's World: The Christian Calling to Culture', lecture given at the 1994 Conference of the European Educators' Christian Association (EurECA) in Basle, Switzerland.

Moltmann, J. (1967), *Theology of Hope: On the Grounds of the Implications of a Christian Eschatology* (London: SCM).

—— (1972), 'The Crucified God: A Trinitarian Theology of the Cross', *Interpretation* 26: 278–299.

—— (1974), *The Crucified God* (London: SCM).

Nelson, R. (1987), 'Faith Discipline Integration: Compatabilist, Reconstructionalist and Transformationalist Strategies', in H. Heie and D. Wolfe (eds.), *The Reality of Christian Learning* (Grand Rapids: Eerdmans).

Outhwaite, W. (1994), *Habermas: A Critical Introduction* (Oxford: Blackwell).

Pratte, R. (1977), *Ideology and Education* (New York: McKay).

Skillen, J. (1992), 'Living by Principle in a Complex Social Order', in S. Hauerwas and J. Westerhoff (eds.), *Schooling Christians* (Grand Rapids: Eerdmans).

Walford, G. (1994), *Choice and Equity in Education* (London: Cassell).

Young, R. (1995), 'Liberalism, Postmodernism, Critical Theory and Politics', in R. Smith and P. Wexler (eds.), *After Post-Modernism* (London: Falmer).

PART 3

BEYOND THE
DOMESTICATED
PERSON

COMMENTARY

The purpose of this section is to provide a Christian view of the educated person. This includes an account of a Christian view of the person and of some of the alternative views which are influential in thinking about education, an exploration of ways of promoting Christian concepts of mature personhood through education for adolescents and a study of how the value and success of the process are and should be measured.

Stanton Jones maintains that both psychologists and educationists work in the context of 'presumptive understandings of what human beings are ... anthropological models ... background ideologies' which ground and shape their practice. Contemporary competing (and overlapping) views of the person that he considers are those of Cartesian rationalism, behaviourism, sociobiologicism (*e.g.* Richard Dawkins), and postmodernism. His main objections to such accounts are on the philosophical grounds of reductionism and 'dissonance with our fundamental sense of higher meaning in life'.

Dr Jones sketches out the broad parameters of a (not *the*) Christian view of the person. These include value (because we are made in God's image and are worth the death of his Son), purpose (in this life and in the one to come), individual relationality (because God is relational and love is at the heart of it all), damaged and limited moral agency (because we are free to choose and, having chosen to rebel, not free to be perfectly good), rational *and* passionate (like God), and soulishly embodied (not body and soul).

Education is always conducted in the context of what Stanton Jones terms 'a vision of ultimacy'. If this were the Christian vision, a number of consequences would follow, including seeing education as 'the cultivation of the responsible agency of the developing person to decide rightly', and certain practices would be challenged, such as the values-clarification approach to moral education.

Luke Bretherton lists a number of features of the experience of many young people at the end of the twentieth century. These include fragmentation through fractured relationships, 'living in Paradox Lane' where competing worldviews can be held without finding contradictions, and struggling to discover identity when freedom and responsibility seem illusory. Mr Bretherton says that personhood is centrally about 'other-awareness and undistorted sets of human and divine relationships', and maturity is a journey rather than an end-point.

Adopting a vision of mature personhood as the goal of education requires listening, an incarnational approach to communication, cross-generational and informal learning methods, curricular integration, learning together as a lifelong enterprise of discovery, teaching people to listen and think, and a balance between deductive and inductive approaches. Luke Bretherton roots all of these in a vision which is centrally relational, so that communicating with young people is about seeking, with them, 'to re-imagine the future from the resources of our shared history and building, with them, in the present'.

Why and how should we measure the value and success of the educational process? Brian Hill (in the first of his two contributions to this volume) says that Christian educators should ask fundamental questions about the whole ideology of current practice, which is too easily taken for granted in educational measurement. Sadly, he says, many Christians 'fail to question the system because in each case they themselves are members of the most privileged groups'. He lists a whole range of purposes that could be served by assessment and calls upon Christians to oppose any which deny large numbers of children 'the right to equality of educational opportunity and maximization of their personal abilities'. Christians should be concerned for individual worth and difference. They are called to be. 'stewards of the rights of the unenfranchised in a manipulative world'. Christian concern for the individual dignity of bearers of the divine image should lead them to favour assessment which is criterion-referenced, wherever possible, over that which is norm-referenced. There should be regard for the diversity of individual gifting and forms of creativity.

The capacity for making considered personal choices is valued by God and should not be undervalued by Christians in an overreaction to rationalism. Neither should the human capacity for forming responsible relationships.

Our key themes of the role of worldviews, the importance of a vision of human nature and society, and the centrality of the relational all come together in the subject of this part of the book. The three writers all bring them together in a way that makes strong appeal to the notion of being made in the image of a relational God. In working this out, Stanton Jones and Brian Hill also emphasize rationality and moral responsibility. Luke Bretherton's emphasis is strongly on an incarnational model, according to which teacher-learner and learner-teacher walk together on the risky pilgrim pathway to discovery.

6

Recovering the person

Stanton L. Jones

Christian doctrine includes more than distinctive ideas about the nature of God and how humans might relate to him; it includes beliefs about human persons as well. The relevance of these types of metaphysical beliefs to education and social science is discussed. Some prominent alternative visions of the person, including rationalistic, behaviouristic, sociobiological and postmodern views, are described briefly and difficulties noted. Prominent features of a Christian vision of persons are then outlined, including issues of value, purpose, bounded rationality, moral agency and freedom, relationality, and soulish embodiment. Some possible educational implications of such an understanding of persons are discussed.

I shall strive to outline a Christian vision of the person and to explore its possible implications for contemporary education. But what possible justification can be mounted for the relevance of a religiously grounded understanding of the person for education? Examination of an equally difficult case, the relevance of such a vision for the academic discipline of psychology, may provide the support needed.

I have previously argued (Jones 1994) for a respectful and dialogical relationship between psychology and religion, in contrast to the tendency of psychologists to see religion only as an object for study, service delivery or reform. One facet of such a cordial relationship would be the opportunity for religious visions of the person to sharpen and transform the questions psychology seeks to pursue about human experience and character. The major obstacle to such a relationship is the perceived fundamental incompatibility of science and religion. Science and religion are judged unsuitable for mutual dialogue and influence because it is believed that, first, science rests on facts and religion on faith; secondly, scientific claims are verifiable or falsifiable while religious claims are utterly subjective or existential; and thirdly, the criteria for choosing between scientific theories are clear and objective, while the criteria for choosing between religions are ambiguous and subjective (Barbour 1974).

Incompatibilists err in their understanding of both science and religion. The portrait of religion as merely subjective is a caricature which ignores the way that religions usually manifest a declarative dimension which asserts or presupposes views of the nature of our experienced world and of the ultimate reality beyond that world, of human nature, and the nature of morality.

Regarding the former, our understanding of science has been evolving rapidly in this century. In contrast to the premise that science rests on facts, contemporary philosophy of science asserts that data are theory-laden. We see data through a lens of assumptions about the nature of what we are viewing. Theories, the observations that support those theories, and the metaphysical visions of the world out of which theories are born, are more intimately, even organically, interrelated than previously recognized. In contrast to the claim that scientific claims are verifiable or falsifiable, philosophy of science teaches that scientific theories are evaluated by theory-laden observations, but that these observations can unequivocally neither verify nor falsify any particular theory, and that the data alone never unambiguously point to only one theoretical explanation. Finally, philosophy of science instructs us that the criteria for choosing between scientific theories are not utterly clear and objective. Instead, theory appraisal is a highly complex and sophisticated form of value-judgment involving empirical and extra-empirical factors; thus, science is a cultural and human, as well as empirical, undertaking.

When a contemporary understanding of science is combined with a more balanced understanding of religious faith and belief, the barriers preventing dialogue, mutual support and critique between psychology and religion collapse. Contemporary philosophy of science does not support a categorical separation of science from other forms of human knowing, including religious knowing or belief. While the relative differences between, and unique identities of, psychology and religion deserve to be carefully observed and maintained, we can encourage a dialogue about how religious beliefs shape the assumptions we bring to psychology. As Browning has argued,

> ... the clinical psychologies, especially, cannot avoid a metaphysical and ethical horizon and, for this reason, they should critically ground these features of their systems rather than unwittingly lapse into them (1987: xi).

This conclusion holds for education as well as psychology. Education, like psychology, is always done in the context of presumptive understandings of what human beings are, of what we might call anthropological models. These models, however rigorously or casually they might be articulated, shape what we regard as data, what we view as legitimate methodologies of study, what we value as outcomes, and so forth. Sadly, in education as in psychology, these background ideologies are often ignored, and thus educational practice is frequently grounded uncritically in implicit and unexamined contemporary anthropological models.

Contemporary and competing views of persons

We live in a time of transition and pluralism in western culture today, and no one anthropological model appears to dominate. Multiple religiously grounded models vie for attention, from those rooted in the major institutionalized religions (traditional and liberal Christian, Judaic, Hindu and others) to the modern revivals of other ancient traditions such as pagan nature worship (seen in contemporary Wicca, white witchcraft, or Gaia worship) or the ancient mystery religions. Anthropological models, however, do not derive only from explicitly religious traditions. The technical and scientific culture of the West has spawned several models of the person which have influenced education, a few of which I will soon discuss. I have dubbed these 'competing' models, and will implicitly emphasize their points of incompatibility with Christian views of persons. Nevertheless, there are inevitable commonalities in the understandings of persons across these models, rooted in the common realities of human existence, and constructive dialogue can progress between traditions around these commonalities. But each of these traditions, explicitly religious or not, produces its own unique family of views of the person owing to its unique emphases and concerns, and thus each, despite laudable strengths, must be distinguished from the others (here from a Christian understanding).

Cartesian rationalism, grounded in the separation of the mind from the body and material world, and of the individual, autonomous intellect from its community and tradition, has had a profound impact upon western culture, leading many to identify Descartes as the father of the Enlightenment and of modernity. Many have thus seen education only in terms of the individual's acquisition of analytic skills and objective knowledge; this tradition has been especially strong in Britain (see MacIntyre's [1990] discussion of the Scottish rationalist or 'encyclopaedia' tradition). This model errs in presuming that humans are only rational, in denigrating our non-rational qualities (such as emotion and our aesthetic capacities), and in seeing knowledge as decontextualized, objective, impersonal and merely technical.

Enlightenment culture has produced psychological views of the person which are quite at odds with rationalism. Behaviourism, for example, broke down the Cartesian wall between mind and body, subsuming mind as a part of the general capacity of the physical organism for adaptive learning by associationistic laws. B. F. Skinner reduced humanity to mere conditioned responders who do what environmental experience programmes them to do, eliminating both human freedom and dignity. Education, for the behaviourist, becomes a distilled experience of the more general shaping and learning process that describes all of life. The goal of education for the behaviourist must ultimately be to aid adaptation of the behaving organism (the child) to the environment in order to enhance survival of individual and species. Behaviourism, with its reduction of humans to response patterns and materiality, and with its supposition that humans ultimately do only what they are conditioned to do, is deficient as a view of persons. (For more on behaviourism and other psychological models of the person such as psychoanalysis, see

Browning 1987; Jones and Butman 1991.)

Another recent model rooted in modern science, particularly in Darwinian thought, is the sociobiological model (see the writings of Richard Dawkins). This view suggests that projection of one's genetic material into the next generation is the highest good and point of all existence for every life form (as sociobiologists say, 'A hen is just an egg's way of making another egg'). Rationality, emotion, religion and culture, including education, must all be understood in the light of this comprehensive fundamental motivation, and each can ultimately be reduced to the pursuit of reproduction. Explicit implications of this model for education are as yet unarticulated, though sociobiology would teach that the ultimate value of education can only be to allow one to climb higher on the social-status ladder, which gives one increased access to more genetically desirable mating partners and more skills with which to advance one's progeny. This bleak vision of human nature must be evaluated in terms of the philosophical merit of its reductionistic agenda and on its scientific merit, but also in light of its dissonance with our fundamental sense of higher meaning in life.

Though many other models deserve comment, I will close by mentioning the powerful influence which postmodernism is having today. Postmodernism began as a critical response to the Enlightenment's disregard for all non-rational aspects of human experience and to its impossible ideal of objectified, impersonal knowledge, and has deep connections with Romantic, Marxist, neo-Marxist and post-Nietzschean thought forms (MacIntyre, 1990). More extreme forms of postmodernism have challenged the idea that truth *per se* really exists, arguing rather that there is only (at most), truth-from-a-certain-point-of-view. All human knowing is seen as peculiar to a certain symbol system and culture. Truth then becomes peculiar to each symbol system or subculture, and thus becomes fragmented; my truth may not be your truth. Given the incommensurability of truth with truth, some postmodernists go on to argue that the real agenda in the 'pursuit of truth', including education and science, is the exercise of power and dominance. The implication for education would seem to be that education must become non-imperialist, non-prescriptive, relativistic, deconstructionist and responsive to all subgroups in a culture.

A Christian view of persons

Several preliminary concerns should be mentioned before sketching a Christian view of persons. First, there is no monolithic Christian view of persons. In the spirit of this book, I here offer *a* (not *the*) Christian understanding with which many evangelicals might agree. Secondly, I offer this account knowing that 'Christian' views or justifications have been argued, for example, for a heliocentric cosmology because of biblical references to the immobility of the Earth, for the callous rape of the environment in the name of exercising dominion over the earth, for the domination and subordination of women in the name of godly family structure, and even for the extermination of the Jews under Hitler. Religious traditions, however, should be judged on their own terms and not on the basis of their most distorted manifestations. Christian understandings should no more be judged by Hitler's extermination of Jews or Galileo's trial than Islam should be judged by the violent acts of its most fanatical adherents, sociobiologists by the eugenics movement, or atheists and Marxists by the genocidal purges of Stalinist Russia.

Thirdly, the broad parameters sketched below do not constitute a Christian theory of human development or personality in a form which psychologists or educators would recognize as scientifically proper. Rather, these are metaphysical starting-points from which more formal theories of personality, human development or education might be constructed. Again, many of these conceptions are quite broad, and share points of contact and agreement with the models described above as 'incompatible' (*e.g.* with sociobiology that sexuality is important, or with postmodernism a concern for abusive uses of power). Finally, I would argue that a satisfying vision of the person must be sufficiently complex to explain the heights and depths of human character and experience; it must not be one-dimensional or simplistic. The sketch I give here is an incomplete outline of a very complex and non-unitary tradition. (For more depth, see Berkouwer 1962; Brunner 1939; Evans 1990; McDonald 1981.)

A Christian vision of the person would include at least the following elements.

Value

We all sense that we are meant to have value, and yet there is a modern crisis of valuelessness. As our place in the physical universe has receded from being at its centre to being an insignificant speck in an immense cosmos, and as our vision of humanity has shrunk from being the crown of creation to 'this eon's accidental species occupying the top of the food chain', the puzzle of how to attain value has become increasingly vexing. Where does value come from if there is no external referent of valuing? Some, such as the brave existentialists, urge us simply to face an empty universe and embrace meaninglessness and valuelessness.

Two basic Christian doctrines serve as our foundation for asserting that human beings are valuable. A Christian view of persons starts with humans as created in God's image. Female and male, we are made in his image and likeness (Genesis 1 - 2). Christians disagree on the mode of that creation, but many argue that the deeper issue is whether God actually created us, regardless of the means used. If we were created intentionally and in God's own image, then we must have value. Secondly, the Christian understanding of how God has acted to give his own life for all his children testifies to our value in his eyes; God so loved his children 'that he gave his only Son' (John 3:16) to die for us. God's objective sacrifice is the measure of our value.

Temporal and eternal purpose

Our search for value is answered not only by an internal sense of being valued by God, but also by a deep sense that our lives have meaning. The God of the Bible is a creating and sustaining God, and we are created in his image. Genesis 1 - 2 tells us that one of God's first declarations to his children was that they, like God, had work to do - to exercise dominion over the created order, to act as stewards who would care for the rest of creation as his agents. We are meant to work, and our work has value. All work, from digging ditches to neurosurgery, from cleaning toilets or changing nappies to international diplomacy, is potentially meaningful because it can contribute to the working out of God's purposes among his people.

And yet the value of work, and the value we feel in performing it, are complicated and compromised in several ways. Our human rebellion against God has driven a wedge between us and our work, with the result that work is always in danger of becoming mere toil, or driven by greed, or otherwise distorted. Evil can become imbedded in work cultures, with the result that people are demeaned or damaged by their work or blocked from meaningful work at all. Also, we long not just to fill the purposes of our work in this life, but for a greater life purpose rooted in a personal relationship with our creator God. Our lives have more than temporal purpose, but more foundationally are a preparation for some greater reality of which we now see only a foreshadowing. We need both kinds of meaning, and so there is a sense in which earthly work can never quite satisfy us.

Individual relationality

The God in whose image we were made is a relational God. This is one profound implication of God's existence as triune personal being. We are relational as God is relational. The Christian understanding of persons is a curious blend of the individualistic and the communitarian. The value of the individual is implied in the emphasis upon the individual's approaching God to receive forgiveness and everlasting life. Yet we are not plunged into radical individualism, because the Bible also instructs us that we are a part of a body that transcends individualism (1 Corinthians 12). Our individuality is secure and can never be swallowed up in the collective, and yet we do not and must not stand alone. The ideal of the one family of humanity, which must be seen as mere naïve sentimentalism in most other anthropological models (such as the sociobiological view, which paints a picture of cruel competition for scarce resources as the background of our natures), assumes real meaning in the light of God's intentional creation. The Christian imperative to love God and love our neighbours as ourselves adds further weight to this idea of our deeply relational nature.

As part of our relational nature, we are sexual beings. Our sexual nature, both as gender and as a drive to mate and propagate, are acknowledged quite explicitly in the creation narrative. But Christians would argue that we are relational not because we are sexual (as a Freudian might), but that we are sexual because we are relational. The sexual is the concrete embodiment of the grander truth of our relational natures. Our sexuality serves as concrete daily proof of our inextricable ties with the 'other'; this is one concrete reason to celebrate and respect gender. And our erotic desires are not a narrow urge to

112

propagate as the sociobiologists argue; rather, the teaching that sexual union results in and facilitates an experience of being 'one flesh' in marriage (Genesis 2:24; 1 Corinthians 6:12-20) suggests that sexual urges are meant to be tied to loving, monogamous, lifelong union with another. This union, in turn, serves as a concrete symbol on earth of the faithful union we are meant to have with God.

Damaged, limited moral agency

It is common for psychological models, such as behaviourism or psychoanalysis, to assert that all human actions are the necessary result of the causal influences which impinged on us prior to acting. Christians disagree. Human beings are endowed with a precious gift of freedom by virtue of our creation in the image of God who, as the sovereign of the universe, is perfectly free. We see freedom reflected in the moral choice offered to the first persons in the Garden of Eden, a choice which carried enormous consequences. Christianity views humans as moral agents who can be held culpable for their choices. It is only in this light that the most central Christian teaching – that we all sin and all need God's forgiveness and mercy – makes sense. Further, Christianity teaches that our moral choices contribute to the formation of our moral character, so that our choices have not just immediate but long-term consequences as well. In our sinfulness, we can steadily erode our capacity for making free choices by making wrong choices, with the result that we become ever more slaves to evil, as in the case of the alcoholic or drug addict.

Yet Christianity does not ascribe unbounded freedom to human beings. Our freedom is limited in at least three ways. First, we are finite beings, in contrast to God's unbounded power and wisdom which result in unbounded freedom. We have the capacity for real choices, but we cannot choose without restrictions. Secondly, the Christian faith would seem to assert that we make free choices, but there is no reason to think that this implies that all our choices are free or that any are utterly free. Some of our reactions may well be the conditioned results of past experience, and indeed past experience or biological variables may make some choices more likely than others. Finally, our capacity for choosing is damaged by the reality of sin and evil. The doctrine of total depravity teaches that every part of the human person is contaminated to some extent (though not necessarily to the maximum extent) by our sinful rebellion against God. We are free to choose, but one option which is not open to us is to choose to be perfectly good.

Bounded rationality

God, in whose image we are made, is a rational being. He knows all things and hence all things are potentially knowable. Thus the church has historically and correctly taught that we are rational beings, capable of knowing truth (Romans 1) and invited us to come and reason together with God (Isaiah 1:18). Christianity is not anti-intellectual; in exercising our rationality we 'look for the fingerprint of the Creator in creation'. Christian faith has not had the uniformly negative impact upon science or scholarship which its critics would like to claim (Lindberg and Numbers 1986).

But in contrast to Enlightenment understandings of rationality as objective, impersonal and mathematical, the Bible presents God as a passionate being whose rationality is not alienated from his love. Similarly, our rationality can never be separated from the deepest recesses of our personhood, or what the Bible calls our 'heart'. Wisdom in the Old Testament can not be equated with intelligence, as wisdom has the additional element of valuing the right ends and those values guiding all choice. Interestingly, recent work in the brain sciences supports an intimate connection between human rational capacities and our values and emotions; individuals with intact intellect but impaired capacities to feel and to value are debilitated in their capacities to decide rightly in life (Damasio 1994). Another distortion of our rationality is our capacity for self-deception; Romans 1 teaches that we are capable of knowing truth, but that we can suppress or distort the truth as well. Our rationality is not absolute.

Soulish embodiment

Christianity is sometimes characterized as a religion of the disembodied soul; indeed, church teaching has erred in that direction at several points in history. Three Christian doctrines reinforce the goodness of our embodiment: creation (God intentionally made us embodied beings and called his creation 'very good'), incarnation (God, in the second person of the Trinity, became an embodied human being and dwelt among us), and resurrection of the dead (1 Corinthians 15; we will not be disembodied spirits in the afterlife, but will be restored to perfect bodily existence). Embodiment is not a second-class state, and our souls are not incongruous attachments to bodily existence. The most literal reading of Genesis 2:7 is that God breathed life into the man's body and he 'became a living soul'. Adam was not *given* a soul, but rather in his embodied totality he *became* a soul. Bodily existence is part of being a human soul!

Though other aspects of our personhood could be elaborated, these give us a good start in understanding people from a Christian perspective. The reader should remember that the utility of this Christian vision is not that it allows us literalistically to deduce a complete educational or personality theory; for instance, there is no 'Christian theory of cognitive development and dyslexia'. It cannot serve to generate highly specific guidelines for educational practices; for instance, it does not prescribe how or when praise or punishment should be meted out in schools. Rather, it sets broad parameters for understanding people and suggests to us when our vision of persons is deficient. It describes the horizon toward which we want to lead pupils, envisions some of the goals of education, and grounds values which might embedded in our educational processes and allows us to debate them critically.

Implications for education

We face a pressing dilemma. Value-free education, like value-free counselling or science, is a mirage. Education is a task which is always conducted in the context of a vision of ultimacy – which includes an understanding of who and what our students are, a vision of their optimal character and personal development, a vision of the good society to which we want our students to contribute, and a vision of the valued information, skills and perspectives that merit attention in contrast to those which do not. Yet the days when state schools can be sites of religious indoctrination are gone. Schools are not churches, synagogues, mosques or temples. The dilemma is: how is education to be conducted when our human diversity seems to demand neutrality, and yet neutrality is impossible? Perhaps the only workable solution is self-consciously and critically to ground what we do in some explicit vision of ultimacy; the Christian vision is a candidate (though not the only one) for such a role. A further dilemma then is: where and when should that grounding occur? At the broad level of institutional policy, at the level of individual schools, or only of individual teachers, or in response to the commitments of the families that entrust their children to the educational process? In all content areas across the curriculum, only in specific content areas (such religious education, sex education, and others), or only in non-academic areas such as the model of morality and citizenship toward which students are being shaped?

Were the Christian vision to undergird the entire educational enterprise, a number of consequences would follow. A firm grounding would be secured for the value of students, of the skills and abilities they can acquire, and of the work toward which they are being prepared. A holistic vision of the person that values the body and the non-physical aspects of the person would lead to a balanced curricular focus that strives to develop the whole person. The study of all subjects would be infused with an explicit examination of value. The process of education would not be conceived as the mechanistic conditioning of a responding organism, but as the cultivation of the responsible agency of the developing person to decide rightly. The teacher, rather than being the 'master behavioural technologist', would be the role-model and midwife who strives to guide the learning process to encourage (but not to force) the child to make right choices. As an outcome, educators would aim to produce a person with enhanced faculties – a person with more knowledge and skills to utilize in the exercise of his or her rationality and more clearly articulated values with which to guide decision-making.

A Christian model of the person does question or challenge some educational practices. Humanistic models, for example, would suggest that human beings are intrinsically good. Based on this premise, pedagogical methods like 'values clarification' have been developed for instruction in such areas as sex education. This approach presumes that children will make right choices if options are clarified and the native values of the child are brought to the fore of his or her consciousness. But this presumes that children naturally have the right values, and that values are something that are distilled rather than taught and developed. Alternatively, a Christian vision presumes that while we bear the stamp of divinity as the residue of being made in God's image, we are also disordered beings who want the wrong as well. Clarification of a person's true values reveals evil as well as good. Christian-based education would then serve as a mirror in which each of us could examine our true (and profoundly mixed) motives, and as a scale which would weigh our various motives, providing instruction in a vision of virtue toward which we might aspire.

BIBLIOGRAPHY

Barbour, I. (1974), *Myths, Models, and Paradigms* (New York: Harper and Row).

—— (1990), *Religion in an Age of Science* (New York: HarperCollins).

Berkouwer, G. C. (1962), *Man: The Image of God* (Grand Rapids: Eerdmans).

Browning, D. (1987), *Religious Thought and the Modern Psychologies* (Philadelphia: Fortress).

Brunner, E. (1939), *Man in Revolt*, trans. O. Wyon (Philadelphia: Westminster).

Damasio, A. (1994), *Descartes' Error: Emotion, Reason and the Human Brain* (New York: Grosset/Putnam).

Evans, C. S. (1990), *Søren Kierkegaard's Christian Psychology* (Grand Rapids: Zondervan).

Jones, S. (1994), 'A Constructive Relationship for Religion with the Science and Profession of Psychology', *American Psychologist* 49/3: 184–199.

—— and Butman, R. (1991), *Modern Psychotherapies: A Comprehensive Christian Appraisal* (Downers Grove: IVP).

Lindberg, D. C., and Numbers, R. L. (1986), *God and Nature: Historical Essays on the Encounter between Christianity and Science* (London: University of California Press).

McDonald, H. D. (1981), *The Christian View of Man* (London: Marshall, Morgan and Scott).

MacIntyre, A. (1990), *Three Rival Versions of Moral Enquiry: Encyclopaedia, Genealogy, and Tradition* (Notre Dame, IN: University of Notre Dame Press).

7

Communicating with youth culture[1]

Luke Bretherton

This chapter outlines some of the ways in which the current problems in our society are experienced by young people. It details reactions and the ways young people express this experience. This ranges from eco-warriors actively seeking to change society through to fatalistic resignation and passive consumption. Based on a relational view of personhood and maturity, I then develop some possible responses whereby we as teachers might walk alongside young people in seeking ever-widening horizons of hope and possibility. The final section gives some practical ways of doing this. Communicating with the young is not about accommodating them to the present situation but about taking risks and imagining a different way of being in the world.

Setting the context

Fragmented experience

Fragmentation is becoming the core experience of young people at the end of the twentieth century. Any claim to a coherent view of life is met with a multitude of other, variant and apparently equally valid claims of interpretation. There is an element of despair here. The fragmentation is experienced not as a liberation, but as the pain of broken families, paranoia about violent crime and lack of face-to-face local community. Divorce rates are but one indicator of this.

Living on the surface

As Marshall McLuhan proclaimed in the 1960s, the image or medium has become the message. It is memory, however, not technology or image, which opens up the possibility of a future. The story of God's faithfulness to Israel in the exodus is constantly reiterated by the prophets. It is this memory which directs the people to hope in God's continued faithfulness. In our culture the forgetting in instant gratification, for instance, through drugs, pornography, virtual reality, television and violence, is a tragedy. It cuts short the possibility for hope, leaving passivity and numbness in its wake.

Many young people seek depth in mystical or spiritual experiences of their own making. The high one gets from dancing all night on Ecstasy can be seen as a spiritual experience, although for most it is just a 'buzz'. Being lost in a computer-generated world of sensation-stimulating technology can be likened to the ecstatic feeling of connection with the Brahman. Is this depthless pleasure-seeking or a genuine quest for meaning?

Life in Paradox Lane

Sometimes militant, sometimes apathetic, young people live in the middle of society's contradictions. Politics and activism are changing into a series of single-issue, localized movements that see themselves as bypassing the compromise of party politics and established political structures. Many young people are involved in such activity. They are to be found among protestors camping out at engineering projects which threaten fragile ecosystems, 'Reclaim the Streets' parties,[2] and protests at live animal exports. We must remember the 'eco-warriors'. They fight to save the planet and the rights of marginal groups, finding enough conviction in their own faith, often home-made, to risk persecution, suffering and imprisonment.

Others, however, see this as ineffective. They have resigned themselves to a fatalistic and eventually nihilistic relinquishing of all motivation to anyone or anything outside of themselves. Instead they buy into the consumer dream of gratifying their every material desire. Others are so numbed by the barrage of voices and consumer choices that the possibility of change has not even occurred to them. The inherent paradox here is that the 'materialism as faith' and 'screw the system, I'm dropping out' mentalities share the same origin. The questions raised by later modernity often lead to many different wordings of the same answer. As Benjamin Barber (1995) puts it:

> Belonging by default to McWorld, everyone is a
> consumer; seeking a repository for identity, everyone
> belongs to some tribe. But no-one is a citizen.

It is now possible to hold two or more competing worldviews without finding any contradictions. Living in paradox could be interpreted as necessary for new possibility, energy coming from integrating the contradictions. For most people, however, the experience is like watching a parade of many and varied floats pass by. They are free *not* to make any choice or preference. In fact, to make a choice ties them down, and where is the freedom in that? So the conclusion is to not choose, but to live for ever watching the parade with the pleasure of knowing that choice is available.

This suspicion of the definite and particular forms part of the wider cultural and philosophical shift towards rejecting purely rational and empirical ways of perceiving the world around us. This opens up the possibility for new modes of learning which incorporate experience and allow for the playfulness of ambiguity and contradiction. But a note of warning is needed. It is a small step from playfulness to deconstructing binary oppositions such as good *versus* evil.

The cult of youth

We live in a culture that narcissistically worships its youth. The new and the young are the ideal. The singers Cher and Madonna are cyphers for this phenomenon. Madonna has made an art of constantly reinventing herself with a new image. Cher is virtually a piece of sculpture, remoulding her body in plastic surgery to resemble a thirty-year-old when she is in fact over fifty. As Christ says in Luke 12:34, 'Where your treasure is, there your heart will be also.' Where we invest our energy, money and worry, that is where we worship with our heart.

Cher and Madonna are indicative of this characteristic of an autonomous self-construction. A sense of call, and of life as a gift containing the possibilities for awe, discovery and wonder, has largely been lost. This capacity is something to be treasured. As Douglas Coupland warns in his novel *Life After God*:

> Sometimes I think the people to feel saddest for are people who once knew what profoundness was, but who lost or became numb to the sensation of wonder (1994: 51).

The problem of identity

Young people are growing up in a world where for many identity is seen as a game and a choice. Which role shall I choose today? Am I a woman or a man? Which one do I want to play? For others there is no choice at all; identity involves being at the butt end of forces (economic, environmental or genetic) beyond their control. For them, free will, and hence responsibility, are pure illusion. Developing a clear sense of identity with a mature, self-giving and responsible character is clearly very difficult in the present cultural context.

Adult/child tension

All of the above are added to the normal adult/child tensions that already exist during adolescence. During the time of transition from child to adult, our whole sense of identity is questioned. Today, this constitutes a transition from uncertainty (Am I a child or an adult?), to even greater uncertainty (Will I get a job? Do the planet and the environment have a future?). This contrasts with the 1950s and 1960s where adulthood was seen as a 'place' of security and stability.

Many in this present generation of western young people are increasingly aware that technological and economic progress will not meet every need. Young people cannot expect (although many will still want) the same security in life as their parents, be it in terms of finances, relationships or employment. Adults are seen as responsible for feeding the children a lie about progress and security for all. It is adults (or more correctly 'adultism', the abuse by a previous generation on the next) that are seen as responsible for environmental collapse, global poverty, unemployment and the fact that I can't afford a new pair of Nike trainers.

What is our goal?

Assumptions about personhood and maturity

In relation to this context, what kind of person do we want our education processes to help nurture? I believe that human being is human communion. To quote John MacMurray:

> It is only in relation to others that we exist as persons; we are invested with significance by others who have need of us ... We live and move and have our being not in ourselves but in one another; and what rights or powers or freedom we possess are ours by the grace and favour of our fellows (1961: 211).

It is through relationships with others, and most notably with God, that 'I' come into being. The nature and character of these relationships will affect an individual's capacity to fulfil his or her personhood. This view of ontology (and its commensurate view of epistemology as not exclusively rational or cognitive) is most clearly expressed in the work of John MacMurray (1961), John Zizioulas (1985) and Alistair McFadyen (1990). The prevalent view of personhood states that an individual has no dependence on other persons but depends on the realization of a pre-social, unencumbered self. This contrasts with seeing the self as situated in different social and cultural relationships.

If personhood is about other-awareness and undistorted sets of human and divine relationships, a key element in maturity is developing and sustaining relationships. This involves the ability to communicate. A vital part of communication is the intention behind the communication. The intention to understand another person and seek his or her good, rather than manipulate or seek to impose a pre-determined good on the other person, is a mark of maturity. With this comes the need for responsibility and discernment (neither of which is dependent on intelligence or ability). Truly seeking to understand the 'other' involves being open to change and being able to deal with change as it affects one's identity and ways of understanding the world. Maturity involves a constant struggle with personal integrity. It is a journey, a pilgrimage, rather than a static point of being. This struggle is a creative enterprise. Ceasing to struggle leads to disintegration, when creativity and ultimately hope are lost.

So where now?

We are very far from a situation in which this view of personhood is the reality experienced by young people or the goal of the education they receive. Inevitably a certain degree of accommodation to, and involvement with, the existent culture is necessary. Even while we work towards renewing the present situation, we are part of the problem. There is no spectators' gallery. We are part of this culture as much as the young are. The issue is: are we prepared to see young people as peers, and not as subjects or objects? Can we walk alongside them, seeking ever-widening horizons of hope and possibility, rather than directing them into ever-narrowing conclusions about life and God?

Boundary-markers

Boundaries are important. To a certain extent teachers are at an advantage when they are naïve about 'youth culture'. Their naïvety gives space for children to 'educate' the teacher, telling him or her about their music, computer games, and the like. This is the children's gift to the teacher. At another level teachers must also be chameleons. One friend dresses in her trendiest clothes when working with her church youth group and wears executive-type suits when teaching. The same applies to behaviour: a teacher cannot always be matey, but must also be an agent of discipline and order. Ultimately young people do not want a trendy teacher submerged in their culture. They want good learning. Good learning, however, is premised not just on good content but on good relationships, and this involves a listening attitude.

The art of listening

To listen we must take young people seriously. Three tentative biblical perspectives on communication liberate us to have a different attitude to young people from that of contemporary society. The first is that of the prophetic voice which calls into question the established structures. Jeremiah, Daniel, Samuel, Mary and David were all very young when God called them into positions of leadership and prophecy. They were not conditioned by the established ways of thinking. They could reappropriate God's promises to Israel and imagine and so seek to build a different world where God was sovereign and the people of God were free. This is not to say that all young people are prophetic; those cited above had consciously responded to God's call. In general, however, young people do have the courage to ask the questions 'adults' have forgotten to ask or find too difficult to face.

The second biblical perspective on communication comes from the doctrine of the incarnation. There has been a great deal of work on incarnational approaches to mission and communication in recent years. In summary, Christ came to first-century Palestine under Roman occupation. This was a specific cultural and geographic locality. He was involved in every aspect of life in that locality, and it was as Christ became incarnated into the most intimate details of a specific situation that the radical difference between God and humans, between God's kingdom and the world, was drawn. We too must be intimately involved in the culture and lives of those with whom we are trying to communicate.

Lastly, in the kingdom of God, it is what the 'world' sees as foolish that shames the wise. It is the weak who are strong. In the context of old/young communication, it is the old who stand in a position of strength – economic, educational and experiential. Old and young, however, must learn together. Neither pupil nor teacher has 'arrived'; both are on a pilgrimage to greater understanding. To quote Brother Roger (1995) who founded the Taizé community which thousands of young people visit each summer:

At Taizé, we strive to be, above all, men who listen. We know well that trust in God is not communicated by forceful arguments that, wanting to persuade at any price, will only awaken disquietude and fear ... Christ does not turn us into people who have 'made it'.

To work in partnership takes humility. We need to regain a vision of strength in weakness, of Christ as Lamb, of sacrifice, not coercion. People cannot be commanded into freedom. No-one can instruct another human how to be a mature, responsible, committed person. Anyone, however, can model the struggles, pain and times of joy that mature personhood involves.

If we seek biblical approaches to communication, this will fundamentally reorientate our relationships with young people. It will free us to listen with respect, engaging in genuine dialogue.

Relating for partnership

We cannot expect the young to enter our world until, by our actions and attitudes, we demonstrate interest in theirs. Only then can we lead them to other worlds and different perspectives. Is this not what the Father, through the Son, by the Spirit did for us?

We can enter their world by listening to their music, watching the films they watch, reading their magazines, and the like. The easiest way to find out what they are into is a questionnaire.

The information we glean as we enter their world is invaluable for communication - illustrations, stories, conversation, humour. Some of the best communicators in our culture are comedians; they can have an audience listen to them for hours. One thing they do is establish common ground. Ben Elton, Mr Bean and Victoria Wood all tell stories about everyday life - shopping, going to the doctor's, getting on with parents - things that we identify with and that we have done. They have entered our world.

The basic question here is whether our educational practice brings greater relationship between people and creates space for relational interaction. Alternatively, does what and how we teach reinforce the atomistic, relationally fractured experience of most young people?

Don't generalize

The term 'youth culture' can be misleading. It implies that there is a culture specifically for young people, independent of the rest of culture. We need to see beyond this. Young people are part of a matrix of intersecting circles of identity which include their relational allegiances (family, peer group), their geographic localities (village, city, country), entertainment interests (TV, magazines, music, sport) and consumer patterns. Young people are embedded in the wider culture to which they belong.

The term 'youth culture' also misleads because it implies homogeneity of experience. These divisions of experience can be very subtle.

Within each school there will be cultural dividing lines drawn up by elements such as music, clothes and peer group. In the press, for example, there has been much discussion of the link between drugs and the so-called 'rave scene'. The 'rave scene' itself is fragmented into a host of different sub-cultures, many of which would not associate themselves with being rave at all. To name a few there are ragga, drum and bass, bangra, techno, ambient, house, jazz-funk and garage. Each has its own nuances when it comes to dress, drug use and lifestyle. Each will have a wide variety of socio-economic, racial and religious groupings among its adherents.

Once we have listened, what should we do?

The one and the many

The twin tendencies of homogenization (*e.g.* national schooling) and fragmentation (*e.g.* segmented curriculum) are symptomatic of modernity's inability to deal with the particular or engage with the whole.[3] The remedy must involve asking some basic questions.

First, *why?* The present impetus of education is utilitarian and functionalist. Ours is not to reason why, but to focus on the right technique and grade. The French philosopher Jacques Ellul details how the link between technique and human purpose has been severed, such that technique justifies itself. The boom in self-help literature, with techniques for everything from joyful sex to bluffing at being a postmodernist, is but one indicator of this phenomenon. Technique and utility have replaced faith, ethics and tradition as our source of authority. We must constantly challenge our assumptions and ask: why are we educating?

Secondly, *who?* The segregation of learning to the formal location (classroom), time (school) and age (under eighteen) are also symptoms of modernity. Informal learning environments with all ages present (such as the Passover meal) are not viewed as 'proper' education, that is, education for qualifications. But in virtually all societies – except our TV-dinner, 'snax' culture – meal-times are central to the shared life and learning of a community.

In a so-called 'fatherless' society, the need to develop cross-generational, informal learning methods is even greater. The circulating schools established by Griffith Jones in eighteenth-century Wales provide an excellent example. It is estimated his schools raised literacy from 20% to 80% in a population of half a million in thirty years. A key factor was that adults and children learnt together in a flexible, seasonal structure.

Thirdly, *how?* By three means in particular. (1) *Project learning or cross-curricular relationships.* Integrating all areas of a curriculum through focusing on a particular project to which all lessons relate is one way of doing this. During National Poetry Week, one friend arranged for each subject to be taught in relation to poetry. History taught the Industrial Revolution using Blake. Physics discussed the elements, comparing poetic ideas of truth with scientific ones. Religious education looked at the link between faith and creativity using poets like R. S. Thomas. And so on.

(2) *Learning for life.* The emphasis needs to be on learning as a lifelong enterprise of discovery. It is the patterning of relationships and approaches to learning which is to be communicated, not a fixed body of knowledge. This mirrors the call of Christ to follow him in all of our life, for the whole of our life. We are to be disciples in the peripatetic school of Jesus. And as we go along the path of life, we are to invite others to be disciples (Matthew 28:19–20).

(3) *Teaching people to listen and think.* We have to be constantly looking for creative ways to encourage pupils to take responsibility for thinking and learning. Jesus was brilliant at getting people to think – leaving stories unexplained, answering questions, being enigmatic about who he was. When his followers asked why he was like this, he replied, 'I tell stories to create readiness, to nudge people towards receptivity' (Peterson 1993).

Much educational practice attempts to direct people to a fixed conclusion. Perhaps a more fruitful approach would be to plant seeds and then provide the kind of space and environment in which these seeds can grow. Some will take root, some will not (as Christ relates in the parable of the sower), but, as in the parable of the mustard seed, the seemingly small and insignificant is often what grows to be of great influence.

Some ways of seed-planting and enabling pupils to think for themselves are the following. (1) *Evoke grief.* We live in an age when the horror of war (for example in Bosnia) or the genocide in Rwanda is presented to us as a media event, entertainment to be watched on TV. We are numb to the pain around us, cocooned by material

127

comfort or by the white noise of all-consuming entertainment. Evoking grief is an effective way of waking people up to ask questions about the world around them. An example of this is to start correspondence with refugees or prisoners of conscience via Amnesty International or the Jubilee Campaign.

(2) *Fuel imagination.* Much education has lost any place for wonder and awe. An example which could be used in education comes from a friend who counsels pregnant teenagers. She shows them a film of the foetus in the womb as it develops. She says the effect is often profound, leading the girls to ask questions about when life begins, an issue they had never considered before. Another approach is to raise the horizon of what is expected or possible.

(3) *Subvertising.* The subverting of the media and advertising by pointing out its hypocrisy and inconsistencies enables pupils to begin questioning. For example, a large billboard campaign by Volvo depicted a scene of beautiful countryside and bore the words 'Buy a Volvo'. In the same typeface and colouring a group of media terrorists had pasted 'Buy a Bicycle' over the top of it. Another example is to record an alternative voice-over to an existing television advert, subverting the original message. When watching television the pupils will remember the alternative message instead of the intended one. This approach is popular in British media studies courses and should be used more widely. The magazine *Adbusters*[4] specializes in promoting ways of subvertising. Its manifesto proclaims:

> We will take control of the role that the tobacco, alcohol, fashion, cosmetics and fast-food corporations play in our lives. We will hold their marketing strategies up to public scrutiny and set new agendas in their industries ... On the rubble of the old media culture we will build a new one with a non-commercial heart and soul.

Fourthly, there is enormous scope for developing rituals for expressing anger or joy in a class using everyday objects as symbols. Perhaps developing a common symbolic and ritualistic language with pupils is a way of levelling the playing-field for children because ritualistic expression does not depend on intellectual or physical ability. An example of ritual in the classroom comes from a friend who asks his pupils to write poetry. Before asking them to read it out, he closes all the windows and lights a candle in the middle of the room to indicate that they are now in a special space and that something different is taking place.

Fifthly, we are now in a period when visual literacy and associative ways of learning influence all education. Most schools still teach in a rational, didactic way, contrary to the surrounding environment. A caricature of a typical lesson plan is that it begins with an explanation of what we are going to do in the lesson, some teaching is given on that, pupils then write down notes or read a section of a text book about it, do some exercises and then the teacher recaps at the end.

A balance must be struck between this deductive approach and a more inductive one. This includes use of storytelling, surprise and being cryptic. It means avoiding statements like 'That's not logical', 'Be practical', and 'That's not my area.'

Finally, we must practise what we preach. Who we are will model as much as what we teach or the way we communicate. All of us matured by having role models on whom we 'grew ourselves'. A good teacher often becomes this for pupils. As Francis of Assisi said in relation to telling people about the gospel: 'Preach God at all times and when necessary use words.' Our integrity and authenticity are ultimately the test of whether to take seriously what we say. The teacher must be prepared to incarnate what he or she teaches. If we want a child to learn, we must ourselves be seeking to learn. If we want a pupil not to abuse his or her power or strength, we must model humility and vulnerability.

This is all very well but ...

Some may feel that none of the above engages with the reality of the classroom. It lacks the taste of chalkdust in the mouth, or in this day and age, the hum of CD-ROM in the ear. But are we about accommodating ourselves to the realities of the classroom? To quote Emil Brunner, 'the Church went wrong when it adopted the language of the classroom instead of the community'; perhaps education went wrong at the same time. Should we really be accommodating people to a situation that is disintegrating before our eyes? One management pundit, Jeremy Rifkin (1995), sees patterns of work degenerating into a tiny knowledge-élite, with a cadre of professional task-organizers managing just-in-time contract labour, people with 'McJobs'. Is this what we want to prepare people for? Rifkin recommends that education emphasize relationship and belief. I agree.

Conclusion

Communicating with youth culture is not about finding the right technique by which we can transfer a set of cognitive data so that most of it is remembered. It is about seeking, with young people, to re-imagine the future from the resources of our shared history, and building, with them, in the present. Remember: 'Adventure without risk is Disneyland.'[5]

NOTES

1 I am deeply indebted to Jonny Baker and Gary Collins for all their ideas and input into this chapter. God go with you.
2 'Reclaim the Streets' is an underground movement committed to direct-action environmental protest. The parties suddenly occur (always unannounced) in streets where they strategically cause the greatest disruption to the domination of traffic. The road is unilaterally closed off and all members of the community are invited to participate in this celebration of life. Parties are usually allowed to continue for a few hours by the police, before being closed down.
3 For a full discussion of this, see Colin Gunton, *The One, the Three and the Many: God, Creation and the Culture of Modernity* (Cambridge: Cambridge University Press, 1993): 11-71.
4 *Adbusters* is produced by the Media Foundation, 1243 West 7th Avenue, Vancouver BC, Canada, V6H 1B7.
5 Douglas Coupland, *Generation X* (New York: St. Martins Press, 1991): 153.

BIBLIOGRAPHY

Barber, Benjamin (1995), *Jihad vs. McWorld* (New York: Times Books).
Coupland, Douglas (1994), *Life after God* (London: Simon and Schuster).
McFadyen, Alistair (1990), *The Call to Personhood: A Christian Theory of the Individual in Social Relationships* (Cambridge: Cambridge University Press).
MacMurray, John (1961), *Persons in Relation* (London: Faber and Faber).
Peterson, Eugene (1993), 'Matthew 13', in *The Message* (Colorado: Navpress).
Rifkin, J. (1995), *The End of Work* (New York: Putnam's).

Roger, Brother (1995), quoted by Nicholas Gonzales in *Regeneration Quarterly* 1/2 (Spring): 30.
Zizioulas, John D. (1985), *Being as Communion: Studies in Personhood and the Church* (London: Darton, Longman and Todd).

8

Evaluation and assessment: the tail that wags the dog?

Brian V. Hill

Educational assessment can never be a purely technical, value-free activity. Schooling favours standardized procedures of assessment, grading and reporting which, unless we ensure that they serve our educational objectives, may well subvert them. External examination systems in particular tend not only to 'commodify' knowledge and endorse ruling-class values, but increasingly to put national economic priorities before those of personal development. Many Christians, because they themselves are members of the privileged groups who benefit most from schooling, fail to question these things. Lulled into complacency by their social advantage, they cannot hear the cries of the oppressed.

Educational assessment is such an accepted feature of the schooling monolith today that we tend to take for granted much current practice that should be critically interrogated. Formal assessment often de-motivates the act of learning, creates institutional hiatus at the end of each term, scarifies the self-esteem of low achievers, and leads to invalid and unedifying inter-school comparisons in the popular press. Such effects attract too little critical comment from academics, though students and some teachers are sharply aware of them.

Latterly, the clay-footed divinities that shape our ends at national level have urged a return to the good old days when assessment was confined to a one-shot unseen written exam at the end of each term or year. It is high time that we asked fundamental questions about the whole ideology of educational measurement. The tail is wagging the dog.

Christians in particular should be alarmed at the evolution of an industry under the patronage of Procrustes which applies the calipers of 'the national interest' to all students and rides rough-shod over attempts to do greater justice to the infinite variety of human gifts, learning styles and domains of experience. The rhetoric of national interest is even fuelling a distrust of school-based continuous assessment, thanks to a conservative backlash which has brought together in militant alliance both economic rationalists and religious fundamentalists.

The questions that need to be asked do not lie exclusively within the province of psychologists and matriculation boards, but also call for continuing scrutiny by moral and social philosophers, theologians and Christian educators.

The rise of industrious measurement

Teaching has always involved assessment. From informal impressions gathered in contexts of voluntary learning, to formalized appraisals in the classroom context, assessment provides feedback for both the teacher and the student, usually with respect to how much the student has learnt (and, less often, how well the teacher has taught).

Special impetus was given to the development of the field of educational measurement, however, by the rise of mass education in the nineteenth-century western world and a concomitant interest in empirical psychology. The quantitative precision of Thorndike's studies (Wynne 1963, chapter 5) of animal learning and the psychometric research paradigm which developed from them appealed because they seemed to overcome the vagaries of subjective judgment and inherited privilege. Mass teaching must, it was thought, necessarily rely upon standardized mass measurement.

The result was that norm-referenced[1] sorting procedures – not a new thing, for they were being used centuries earlier in China in entrance examinations for the civil service – became increasingly sophisticated. Unfortunately, they were and are more suited to meeting the selection requirements of industry and academia than the priorities of personal development.

Christians condoned such ideas. And why not? The motives which led the sixteenth-century Reformation leaders to advocate universal education had included a concern to equip ordinary people for the duties of citizenship (*e.g.* Luther 1931). John Knox wanted 'those that be apt to learnyng', whatever their social status, to go as far as they were able (Boyd and King 1972: 201).

In the nineteenth century, mindful of the servitude into which the labouring classes were slipping as a result of exploitation in the mines and factories, reformers found additional reasons to bring education to the masses. And external examinations were hailed as a way of levelling the playing-field and enabling the able poor to advance on merit.

Initially, such examinations were coarse-grained affairs relying mainly on the ability to write urbane essays. It was soon recognized that this criterion was insufficient to test all that needed to be measured, and it was also biased towards the classes most in tune with high culture. The testing movement in America worked hard to develop procedures that were more culture-fair – at least for Anglo-Americans! – and the 'objective test' was born, with its bank of items requiring specific short responses whose statistical significance could be precisely calibrated. But the responses required were still mainly literary and numerical.

Such procedures were not, and cannot be, value-free. The more precise the response required from the learner, the stronger are the underlying assumptions that human beings are plastic and programmable, and that convergent responses are truer to the nature of human understanding than divergent ones. The same goes for assessment, to the extent that it is routinized, standardized, and taken out of the hands of participant observers such as teachers.

In a century where the mass of human beings was being deployed in mechanical tasks on assembly lines, and where creative thought was a perceived liability in all but the few, this approach might have seemed plausible. It is no longer so in the present day, as automated machines replace human ones, and there is an increasing demand for such skills as information processing and social negotiating. Add to this the need for creative and lateral thinking to address the moral and ecological problems which confront us, and mainstream views of assessment are looking increasingly deficient.

Assessment and educational values

One of the difficulties in developing a Christian view of the matter is that the term 'educational assessment' embraces a number of different purposes and processes. Taken at its broadest, it signifies an attempt to estimate the value of something. This makes it cognate with the term 'evaluation'. The questions most often begged, however, are about who and what are being assessed, and for the benefit of whom.

The diagram on the next page shows in simplified form those who are the interested parties in assessment at classroom level. It also shows that assessment can serve a number of purposes, most of which are cited in standard textbooks on the subject (*e.g.* Macintosh 1976; Satterly 1989). Unfortunately, such texts generally seem to imply that only technical questions are involved, whereas, as we have said, assessment cannot be value-free.

Society or the individual?

It is evident from the diagram, for example, that some assessment is intended to be of direct benefit to the student, some serves institutional purposes which may even be to the student's detriment, and the remainder can go either way. In regard to assessment to predict the areas in which the student will be likely to have future educational success, for instance, the information *could* be very helpful to the student, but it could also be used by an educational institution to deny admission to that student.

So which comes first, society or the individual? The question is a basic philosophical one which one Christian writer has addressed in terms of a fundamental ideological conflict between the classical, Renaissance and Enlightenment assumption that the primary responsibility for educating citizens lies with the government, and the Judeo-Christian affirmation that the primary responsibility and

Purposes served by assessment

Of whom or what? — For the benefit of whom?

Of whom or what?	student	teacher	parent	accrediting educational institutions	school administration	future student employment
of student						
for reinforcement	■					
for correction	■					
for goal setting	■					
for educational prediction	■		■	■	■	
for vocational prediction	■		■			■
for certification (of achievement)	■			■		■
for curriculum evaluation		■			■	
of teacher						
for student placement	■	■	■			
for teacher evaluation		■			■	
of curriculum						
for teacher evaluation		■			■	
for curriculum evaluation		■		■	■	

authority for educating children rests with parents (Skillen 1987: 86).

As we shall see in chapter 12, Christian parents must take seriously the claims of many social analysts (*e.g.* Apple 1982; Giroux, Penna and Pinar 1981) that schools function to preserve the privileges of the dominant power blocs in society. Government and government-subsidized schools are constrained by an examination system which 'commodifies' knowledge, and endorses ruling-class values and high culture, moderated by an emphasis on national industrial priorities. Non-government schools, in their turn, serve sectional interests – religious or class – which again subordinate the child to the system.

Sadly, many Christians fail to question the system because in each case they themselves are members of the most privileged groups. The examination system appears to work reasonably well for them. Lulled into complacency by their social advantage, they cannot hear the cries of the oppressed. Am I saying that Christians should oppose such devices as national testing, or vocational training coupled with 'competency-based assessment'? The answer is: 'Yes, if the methods used deny large numbers of children the right to equality of educational opportunity and maximization of their personal abilities.'

Individual differences in learning styles

Schools tend to privilege those whose primary modality of learning is literary-academic. It is well known, however, there are many high achievers in business, politics and the arts who did poorly at school. Their true intelligence did not emerge until they had escaped the schooling paradigm.

The point has been underscored in recent years by the work of Howard Gardner on 'multiple intelligences' (Gardner 1982). In each individual, he claims, different kinds of intelligence appear in different strengths. The seven kinds he postulates are musical, bodily-kinaesthetic, logical-mathematical, linguistic, spatial, interpersonal and intrapersonal. He is not just talking about personality differences or special talents separate from some general factor called intelligence, but about different modalities of intelligence itself, which in turn imply different routes by which individuals learn similar things – and, it may be added, by which they should be assessed on what they have learnt.

To put it at the lowest level, where persons are regarded merely as entries under 'human resources' in the national accounts, there is great waste when these various modalities are not taken into account. How much more should the Christian show concern for individual worth and difference? Even in the parable most attuned to economics, the parable of the talents (Matthew 25:14–30), Jesus represents God tailoring his expectations to our individual differences. And of course the parable's deeper meaning goes well beyond economics.

Intended outcomes

In the best circumstances, assessment is derivative from the explicit objectives of the curriculum. To put this another way, it all depends on what teachers and others hope will result from the teaching act. In another context (Hill 1994b: 7), I challenged teachers in the area of the social studies to ask themselves whether their intention was (1) to pass on to their students a body of information as such; (2) to persuade their students to conform to the *status quo*; (3) to train their students in the skills of social enquiry; (4) to develop in their students the capacity to engage in reformist critique of the *status quo*; or even (5) to encourage their students to work for the radical disruption of the *status quo*. None of these represents a value-neutral option. A similar range of possibilities exists in each of the other curriculum areas. But the most common methods of assessment tend not to get much beyond the level of testing information-transfer, within an ethos which presumes that the examiner, or the discipline, knows all the answers, and convergence is the most prized response.

Methods of assessment

The further the assessment process is removed from the immediate context of learning, the more difficult it is to do equal justice to the more personalistic aims of education and the various modalities of intelligence. Similarly, communicating via the two-dimensional medium of pen and paper severely limits the range of responses by which we might judge what has been learnt.

Again, reporting on the learner's achievement in terms of five or six letter-grades, or through one aggregated percentage, provides only the crudest idea of where a person's range of abilities lies, or what his or her suitability might be for the task in hand. Marks of this kind are usually related to a distribution curve which bunches the greatest number of students at the very part of the curve where it is hardest to make fair cut-offs.

Such procedures also tell us nothing about the abilities of learners to exercise initiative or shoulder responsibility, and convey no idea of their moral and interpersonal capacities. The argument that assessment would lose its objectivity if it included such factors founders on the poverty of what there is left to report on when they are excluded.

Uses of assessment evaluated

With the above reservations in mind, it is useful to evaluate the various uses to which assessment is put in the schooling model, as indicated in the diagram.

Diagnosis of learning

Three uses relate entirely to the diagnosis of learning on the learner's behalf. They concern the reinforcement of correct learning, the correction of errors in previous learning, and the setting of personal goals for future learning. Psychological theory advises us to ensure that this kind of feedback occurs promptly and in relation to specific learning tasks.

Educational and vocational selection

It is also in the interests of students to compare their general rate and level of progress with the average of their cohort, provided this is done in the spirit of helping them to gain a true estimate of their chances in the wider world. As the diagram shows, however, the data collected for these purposes are also often made available to interested outside bodies such as universities and prospective employers, which can easily lead to disregard for the particular individual's life-chances.

A potential conflict of purpose therefore exists. If, for instance, teachers record marks every time they assess, then learners will be inhibited from confiding in the teacher, admitting difficulty, and seeking help. 'Continuous assessment' conducted in this spirit causes students to become jaded and distrustful. Unfortunately, this is something the current demand for 'quality assurance' tends to encourage, as a means of quantifying the teacher's supposed 'efficiency'.

Yet continuous assessment *does* give better clues to both achievement and future potential than one-shot final assessments. The solution is to draw a clear distinction between frequent feedback for immediate diagnostic and guidance purposes, and less frequent assessments recorded over the period of cumulative learning to gauge overall achievement and future potential.

School reports

The question of making reports on the results of formal assessment to persons other than the student needs to be taken further. Schools are a very invasive form of social intervention. They have been too easily granted an unchallengeable right to report on the progress and behaviour of their students to anyone whom they deem to have a proper interest in the information.

It is reasonable to ask how much of this 'proper interest' has to do with social control rather than *bona fide* educational and vocational guidance. Christians are called to be stewards of the rights of the unenfranchised in a manipulative world. In any case, all students have a right to know how they are faring, and their parents do too, since it is usually they who choose the school.

Teachers themselves also have a right to the information, for all the reasons already given, plus the help such information can give them in deciding what placement in the school best suits the child, and what effects their teaching is having on the child's learning. At one remove, the school administration also needs the information, at least in a general form, to monitor staff and overall school performance. All these possibilities are represented in our diagram.

More contentious is the release of information to other educational institutions, future employers, and the public media. The usual minimal safeguard is to give students discretion as to who sees their report. But even within the reporting process, as I have argued elsewhere (Hill 1994a), the assessment of *educational* achievement is one thing; a *character* assessment is another. The latter should be a personal and moral testimonial compiled only at the request, and disclosed only at the discretion, of the student.

I speak as both a Christian and a moral philosopher. Such points of order may appear trivial to people habituated to accept the paternalism of schools, but they are all the more necessary in a day when extensive dossiers on citizens are being compiled and accessed on the information highway, for commercial and political purposes as well as educational.

One of the more recent innovations in the reporting of school learning has been the idea of the student profile.[2] More's the pity that this more humane, though not less rigorous, approach to reporting has been overshadowed by the priorities of recent national testing initiatives.

Teacher, school and curriculum evaluation

Another class of uses for assessment in schools focuses on teachers, schools and curricula, rather than on the students *per se*, though testing of the students often provides much of the data for such evaluations. The problem, however, with using the same set of data for both student assessment and professional evaluations is that it is not always easy to judge whether the good marks should go to the teacher or to the student. After all, much good learning has resulted from students being thrown on their own resources by bad teaching. Any university student can attest to that.

Teachers should be encouraged to evaluate regularly their own teaching behaviour and the curriculum processes for which they are responsible. School administrators also need to monitor these things, in the interests of the children and their parents. And at a further remove, general statistics of overall school performance are relevant to the confidential moderation which local education authorities and other educational authorities should exercise over school-based assessment.

If less money were spent on expensive external examinations, and more on comparative statistical analysis of school cohorts, so that schools could be provided with benchmarks against which to measure their own estimates of student performance, then post-school selection procedures in education and the workforce would be both more just and more reliable.

The evidence for that has been around at least since 1940, when the results were released of the famous 'Eight-Year Study' in the USA.[3] Its findings, which have often since been confirmed by other studies, were that school recommendations are at least as reliable as external entrance examinations in predicting future educational success. The study was mostly concerned with correlations between school estimations and continuing success at college level, but the same logic applies to estimating success in the workforce.

Christians should be the last people to express surprise at such findings. The attributes one would expect to be most relevant to future educational and vocational success include many characteristics which only interpersonal appraisal can detect. Subject to suitable internal checks on teacher performance and student placement, class sizes and frequency of same-teacher contact, and effective statistical moderation between schools, the ones most likely to know best are the teachers-in-consultation.

What will not provide this kind of justice is misuse of moderation data by the media and politicians to compile public rankings of schools. In the name of competition, they promote social division and an élitism which owes more to class than to either learning or character. Such crude rankings disregard the number of variables which must be taken into account, and unjustly denigrate both the needs and the achievements of schools in disadvantaged areas.

We do need, of course, to identify schools which are grossly failing their clients, but such scrutiny must be exercised case by case, taking all the relevant factors into account. Moreover, the remedies will usually involve improving staffing ratios and better leadership, rather than allowing such schools to run down and become, as some social reformers have predicted, 'sink schools'. Christians must not desert the most vulnerable in the rush to take care of their own.

The Christian bottom line

We said earlier that the 'value-free' posture adopted in many textbooks on assessment is a fraud. No researcher or assessor is without underlying normative assumptions about human nature and society. Nor can any technique for assessing human performance be value-neutral. If we elect to test information recall, we assume at the least that humans have the ability to remember, and to link ideas together. If we set cognitive problems to be solved, we assume in addition the capacity for rational thought.

Again, if we look for ways to assess how students respond to aesthetic stimuli, or how well they are able to empathize with people from different cultural backgrounds, it is because we value those aspects of human experience. On the whole, the external written tests which determine so many students' futures do not. Nor do they reveal much about the individual's capacity to stay on task over an extended period, or to take the initiative in exploring the wider environment and solving real-life dilemmas. But they do imply utilitarian value priorities which students may well take on board in lieu of higher life-purposes.

Ironically, when people talk about the aims of education, they profess to be interested in many of these wider values. In reply, some admit that formal assessment can pick up only short-term gains (mainly of a cognitive and physical-skill kind), but say that we should still teach with higher ends in view.[4] Such naïveté underestimates the pressure on teachers, especially when confronted with syllabuses which are overloaded with required knowledge content, to 'teach to the test'. Thus does the tail wag the dog.

Christians must reject the thesis that a value-neutral theory of assessment is possible. Previous chapters in the present book have explored some of the personal values which we should defend, but in the context of the present discussion a few deserve special mention.

The worth of the individual

One is the Christian respect for the dignity of each individual, understood as a being made in the image of God and treasured by him. Systems of assessment which automatically brand many students as failures or educational rejects must be opposed. Every person in society can and should be given a meaningful role and the educational opportunities to improve his or her ability to perform it.

This is why Christians might be expected, for example, to favour the use of criterion-referenced assessment, wherever possible, in preference to norm-referenced assessment. The former assesses learning in relation to whether the conditions for *mastery* of a particular learning task have been met. It lends itself to individual diagnosis and paced learning. The latter compares the performances of many students with each other, to obtain a 'normal curve' of distribution of scores. Except at the extremes of the curve, these decisions tell us very little about the actual level of mastery attained in particular aspects of the course, or the steps that the learner would be well advised to take next.[5]

Enhancement of gifts

These comments lead in to the second value-cluster in Christian thinking: namely, the diversity of human talents and forms of creativity which was earlier referred to in the discussion on modalities of intelligence. This diversity applies, of course, to much more than just intelligence.

The New Testament church brought into being a new form of human community based on recognition not only of the equal worth but also the unique gifts-profile of each person. This was seen not merely as an accident of birth, but as an endowment of the Spirit of God. Moreover, most of the 'spiritual gifts' listed in the New Testament are familiar human attributes literally raised to a higher power by God's Spirit.

Such gifts range widely, from teaching and pastoring to offering hospitality, administering organizations, giving generously, and being of practical help. Their scope implicitly rebukes the caste system in many traditional churches which accord more status to verbal skills than to relational, and which are in bondage to attitudes in the secular culture that Christians should have forsworn long since.

Critical rationality

What I have elsewhere claimed (Hill 1990 *passim*) to be a further Christian value important to educators is critical rationality. To summarize the argument: we see evidence, throughout the Bible, that God sets great store by the capacity he has planted in us to make considered personal choices.

Critical rationality has also been strongly advocated by some recent secular philosophers of education, and in reaction to this, some Christians have equated it with human rebelliousness. In its place they counsel submission to authority. But the two are not antithetical. Critical rationality is a capacity, to be used for good or evil purposes. As a weapon of faith, it has had an illustrious history.

Hence it is quite appropriate to develop methods of assessment which test the extent to which this capacity has been developed. That secular philosophers have often overstated its priority, in comparison to the other values we are here commending, is no reason for Christian educators to undervalue it.

Responsibility in relationships

Critical rationality calls for objectivity. Complementary to this is the warm commitment to responsible relationships which the gospel also urges upon us. There is more to this than the formal school curriculum can be expected to handle. To assess personal commitments of this kind for the purpose of assigning grades, for instance, would be a violation of personal space.

Nevertheless, there are many capacities of knowledge, understanding, values clarification and justification, empathy, social negotiation, and the taking of responsibility for one's decisions, which contribute to successful learning in this area. Such capacities *can* be assessed, in ways which are both morally legitimate and technically accurate. Paper-and-pencil tests are of some use, but need to be complemented by teacher–participant observation in a variety of settings. Some of the appropriate methods will be drama, role-plays, simulations, debates, group projects and other ways of representing relational learning.

To argue for the relevance of relational learning in the workplace and community would be a stating of the obvious. Higher educational institutions need more convincing, for they are generally over-confident that higher learning is to be equated with cognitive knowledge and skills, and tend to leave the affective and relational aspects of learning to informal agencies.

It is not surprising that they are now being called to account for their neglect of ethical issues. The idea of a professional person includes notions of interpersonal confidentiality and social responsibility. Expertise is to be moderated by professional ethic. From school to university, the gospel emphasis on responsibility in human relationships has relevance, and the capacities touched on above can and should be subject to assessment.

Assessment in other learning contexts

The principle of assessing what is learnt is not confined to the school context, for learner, teacher and curriculum come together in many other ways. To mention only a few: we also learn from parents, friends, preachers, leaders of voluntary groups, employers, sports coaches, and advertisers in the media. Perhaps it is only those in the commercial world who take as much interest in 'curriculum evaluation' (they call it 'market research') as schools. And their intentions are rarely as benevolent.

Yet the logic is just as applicable. Teachers need feedback on the effectiveness of their teaching. Learners need feedback on the effectiveness of their learning. We are all constantly engaged in reality-testing, to stabilize our identity in a changing world. Parents need to know how they are being perceived by their children, and so on.

For the most part, however, such contexts leave us at liberty to utilize the feedback for our own benefit, without fear that the evidence will be used to box us in to someone else's grand design. Indeed, learners are much freer to assess whether the ideas and experiences being presented to them will contribute to their own life-plans. And moral responsibility for one's own choices is more easily invoked in a voluntary milieu.

In these contexts, the notion of evaluating one's teaching has some special nuances. How many preachers, for example, actually seek reliable feedback on the efficacy of their preaching? How many leaders of study groups and youth clubs see the need to evaluate their programmes, independent of whether they are sustaining good attendances or not?

Conclusion

Assessment is a natural part of learning, but it can easily be subverted to uses which hinder the learner. I have suggested that Christian people are, in general, too complacent about the assessment procedures which are used in formal schooling, overlooking the extent to which they erode self-esteem and the joy of learning.

We should nevertheless embrace its good uses, in schools, and in other learning contexts including the church, in the spirit of Paul's advice (1 Thessalonians 5:21-22) to 'Test everything. Hold on to the good. Avoid every kind of evil.'

NOTES

1 See later, p. 143.
2 One of England's leading exponents of this approach is Roger Murphy at Nottingham (Murphy, 1988). It is no accident that Murphy holds to Christian assumptions about the nature and dignity under God of human persons.
3 A crisp account appeared in Best 1959: 300-305.
4 Exemplifying this attitude, the secondary education authority in the State

of Western Australia decrees that syllabuses submitted for approval should specify – in the dated style of Bloom's *Taxonomy* – cognitive, affective and psychomotor objectives. It goes on to say, however, that recommended forms of assessment should not include measurement of affective gains, presumably because the authority has been misled by Bloom's inclusion in the affective domain of objectives related to valuing and personal commitment. As might be expected, the examinations set by the authority are therefore dominated by information transmission and analysis.

5 Obviously, at the end of the day, some norm-referencing is unavoidable, in the interests of estimating one's life-chances in a competitive and often callous society, but there is no good reason for every act of assessment in the classroom to fit into this paradigm.

BIBLIOGRAPHY

Apple, M. E. (1982), *Cultural and Economic Reproduction in Education: Essays on Class, Ideology and the State* (London: Routledge and Kegan Paul).

Best, J. W. (1959), *Research in Education* (Englewood Cliffs, NJ: Prentice-Hall).

Boyd, W., and King, E. (1972), *The History of Western Education* (London: Adam and Charles Black, 10th edn).

Gardner, H. (1982), *Frames of Mind: The Theory of Multiple Intelligences* (New York: Basic Books).

Giroux, A. H., Penna, A. N., and Pinar, W. F. (eds.) (1981), *Curriculum and Instruction* (Berkeley, CA: McCutchan Publishing Corporation).

Hill, B. V. (1990), *That They May Learn* (Exeter: Paternoster).

—— (1994a), 'May We Assess Religious Development at School?' *Spectrum*, 26/2: 125–140.

—— (1994b), *Teaching Secondary Social Studies in a Multicultural Society* (Melbourne: Longman Cheshire).

Luther, M. (1931), 'To the Councilmen of all Cities in Germany that they Establish and Maintain Christian Schools', in *Works of Martin Luther* 4 (Philadelphia: Mahlenberg Press): 103–130.

Macintosh, H. G. (1976), *Assessment and the Secondary School Teacher* (London: Routledge and Kegan Paul).

Murphy, R. (1988), *The Changing Face of Educational Assessment* (Milton Keynes: Open University Press).

Satterly, D. (1989), *Assessment in Schools* (Oxford: Basil Blackwell, 2nd edn).

Skillen, J. (1987), 'Changing Assumptions in the Public Governance of Education: What has Changed and What Ought to Change', in Richard John Neuhaus (ed.), *Democracy and the Renewal of Public Education* (Grand Rapids: Eerdmans): 86–115.

Wynne, J. P. (1963), *Theories of Education* (New York: Harper and Row).

PART 4

BEYOND A
REDUCTIONIST
CURRICULUM

COMMENTARY

As we move into Part 4, the focus shifts from the person to the curriculum and, in particular, to the exploration of a curriculum that will best promote the development of whole persons as discussed in Part 3.

Richard Wilkins sketches out a proposal for the 'basics' of the formal curriculum for a general population. Although, as he says, our basics follow from our presuppositions and his are no exception, his concern is that he should avoid defining them in a way that can be applied only in a Christian school. Mr Wilkins looks at three understandings of the overall purpose of education – socialization, development of rationality, and natural development – and finds that, while 'each cries out for complementation from the others', they are incompatible. As he puts it, they constitute 'three inadequate accounts in fissionable contiguity'.

A list of basics could be arrived at on the basis of consensus and, in a culture deeply influenced by religion, these, Richard Wilkins says, are likely to be language, number, science and moral religion. Consensus, however, is fragile, so a better way of arriving at basics is needed. This he finds in Christianity as 'a durable view of life, the universe and everything'. Drawing on the doctrines of God, creation, fall and redemption, Mr Wilkins finds a basis for the basics of, again, science, language, number and morality. To base them in Christian beliefs (such as, 'morality derives from the revealed character of God and his declared will for his creatures') is admittedly controversial, but that does not mean that this basis has to be dismissed. In addition, Christian doctrines 'support powerfully the hopes about education that others deny' (and here Richard Wilkins refers particularly to postmodernism).

Postmodernism, with its Babel of multiple narratives and multiple forms of rationality, can nevertheless 'lend credence' to the idea of a uniquely Christian curriculum. That it can do so, and how it can, are the subjects tackled by Elmer Thiessen in the next chapter. The influence of presuppositions and worldviews on what we take to be knowledge is now widely recognized in the postmodern world. Dr Thiessen says, however, that this may tip us over into a relativistic abyss unless we hold on to some elements of modernism and adopt the 'middle position' of a form of critical realism. This he finds consonant with a Christian view that there is a reality to be known by finite and fallen human beings.

The 'foundations' for a Christian curriculum are found in the combination of, and 'dynamic interplay' between, God's general and special revelations (in nature and in Scripture). But in both cases we have to reckon with the hermeneutical problems of our faulty and partial understandings. In relation to the place of the Bible, Elmer Thiessen goes on to describe a range of models for the way biblical presuppositions operate in curriculum construction. He dismisses simple deduction as being inadequate to the task, and untrue to the nature of the Bible. The analogies of a filter (removing the impure), a motor (injecting some elements), and a lens (through which we view the world) are all mentioned as having something to offer. But, following David Smith's application of it to the curriculum, it is Tom Wright's analogy of actors acting out the unwritten final act of an unfinished play that Dr Thiessen finds the most helpful. Faithfulness to the Creator of the first four acts is the goal, and this provides plenty of space for both variety of outcome and incomplete success.

Elmer Thiessen balances an emphasis on the uniqueness of the Christian curriculum with one on the common (but non-neutral) ground between different worldviews. This leads him to adopt transformationalism as a strategy, and dialogue, with criticism, as a method, in constructing a curriculum along with those of other perspectives.

Ron Elsdon takes us right back to the beginning, to the book of Genesis, in his proposals for education for an ecologically sustainable society. Here, and not in Babylonian creation myths, he finds creation to be an act of love and humanity to be endowed with real responsibility and power. In Genesis, the land of Canaan is a gift from God rather than a commodity to be marketed for economic growth *per se*; and the people are called by God to faith-inspired ways of caring for creation rather than technique-driven ones. Dr Elsdon finds reasons here for the evident inadequacy of simple solutions to environmental problems that rely on either science and technology or economics, and, as he puts it, 'in human hands, they have become part of the problem, therefore they cannot be the complete answer'. He also finds New Age solutions inadequate because they fail to take human sinfulness seriously.

For a better approach to environmental care and for education to that end, Ron Elsdon recommends the Christian worldview as a basis. It can integrate the disciplines and motivate the carers. It also presents an understanding of human sin along with the 'ongoing goodness of creation', which gives grounds for purposeful activity with a careful eye to the possibility of the consequences of greed, complacency and the like.

The second of our key themes is seen in the dynamic interplay between biblical principles and contemporary situations, which is a common thread through this part of the book. Simple logical deduction from doctrines to curricular applications is by no means all there is to it. Creativity is called for in playing out the final act. The other key themes are also present. Worldview considerations are of central importance and the vision extends beyond the sort of people and society we wish to bring about through education to the environment itself. The doctrines of the creation of humanity and of the world are appealed to in different ways by the three writers. Human sinfulness and its effects upon our knowing and doing, and our relationships, are also there, especially in Ron Elsdon's chapter.

9

What are the basics?

Richard Wilkins

The basic subjects of the curriculum are generally agreed to be the three Rs; science, moral and religious education are other strong candidates. Disagreement about the purpose of the basics is due to differences about the overall purpose of education. Three recurring statements of purpose are found wanting separately and together. Democratic demand for basics is accepted with reservations. Divine revelation as a presupposition of knowledge is stated, and accommodation strategies in teaching the basics are outlined.

What matters most?

At one level the identification of 'the basics' is easy. The basics are those elements of educational provision to which schools are periodically urged to 'get back'. The implication of the common slogan is that education's providers have been seduced by inessential frills, to the neglect of the fundamentals of education. Inadequate provision of any of these fundamentals is, to a person's education, the equivalent of a diet lacking essential nutrients.

It is easy to conceive of an irreducible minimum curriculum

without which a 'basic education' cannot be described. Needless to say, beyond the point of slogan and general conception, the identification of the basics becomes problematic. Here, if anywhere, the general thesis of this symposium is confirmed: what each of us defines as 'a basic' depends heavily on what education is designed to do; our basics follow from our presuppositions.

The most everyday of conversations will demonstrate this truth. An assertion in the public bar that schools should stick to 'readin', 'ritin' and 'rithmetic' will almost always provoke the comment 'Yeah, but I think the kids need a bit of ... as well.' And so it will go on, until the basics make up a very long list indeed. More erudite discussions follow the same course. After the three Rs, other knowledge, skills and disciplines are lobbed in as each conversationalist feels inwardly deprived of something important. Our senses of what is important arise from our presuppositions.

This unavoidable experience is not, however, a reason for avoiding the task of defining the basics. Limited time, resources and educational opportunities mean that some prioritization is desirable.

What are deemed to be 'the basics' will, of course, depend on perceived shapes and purposes for the curriculum as a whole. The basics are to the whole curriculum like a ship lightened of all cargo not essential for survival during a short trip or a violent storm. To vary the metaphor, any curriculum delivery must start somewhere, and to progress through stages of learning requires foundational skills at the beginning. Layers of measurable sophistication may be added with abundant time, but abundant time is not available for the education of many children. If Jane leaves school tomorrow, will she take with her 'the basics' for future living and, perhaps, for resumed formal education later in life?

Pious hopes

In handling the topic I hope to maintain three resolutions. The first might seem a truism. I shall confine discussion of the basics to deliberate adult interventions in children's development in the form of a planned curriculum. Not all children's learning, of course, results from such interventions. There is a primary teachers' dictum that children come to school for the first time knowing 50% of all that they will ever learn. This suggests that children's learning experiences are not confined to the formal curriculum. In the context of the formal curriculum, however, defining the basics is largely a task for adult educators. It is, therefore, in the setting of adult-driven education that the basics will be discussed.

Secondly, I shall try to build up a picture of the basics for a general population so that, if possible, evangelical Christian insights might contribute to common schooling. I hope to avoid *defining* them in such a way that they could live only in a Christian school serving a devout community; although it may be only in such communities that we could expect the basics to be fully understood and exploited in the ways I shall describe. The least helpful approach, it seems to me, would be one which identified different lists of basics springing from all the presuppositions in the world.

Thirdly, however, I shall address such evangelical views as I deploy chiefly to the common educational task of stating the purpose of the basics. This projects what I have just said into the realm of distinctive contribution, even challenge and apologetic. A purely intra-Christian debate would merely invite the reader to spectate a wrestling-match over peculiar problems in education with which evangelicals have lumbered themselves by voluntarily choosing to obey the teaching of the Bible. I prefer not to do that here.

You could say that ...

Much narrative could be woven from the yarns of various definitions of the basics. That might not get us very far. Some preliminary distinctions might usefully be drawn, however; not with a view to knocking down the inadequate, but rather to collect a 'basic' toolkit to use in tightening up parts of any structure of basics that we can put up. These distinctions often arose from contending schools of thought. Each is inadequate as a complete way of prescribing the basics, but each might have something to contribute to an adequate understanding of basic education.

There is, for example, one distinction which is easy enough to put into words. This is on the question of whether the basics are those essential skills which schools are good at delivering; or whether, like more elaborate curriculum models, they are what adults regard as the most important things that every child ought to know. These are not identical. The first view can include a recognition that there are basic areas of learning which every child ought to acquire, but which are not the business of schools (just as a vegetable store is not required to supply a complete diet).

In practice, these emphases oscillate. Even if there were agreement on the basic needs of a child which a school is not required to meet (such as a nose-blowing technique or a philosophical reason for staying alive), there is not always uniform provision for those needs from other quarters. Schools cannot easily leave all such needs unmet, even if they stoutly believe that they should. The Samaritan traveller in Jesus' story ignored any theory he might have had about the duty of Jews to look after their own; similarly, schools demonstrate 'Christian love' in their attempts to provide basic education according to the known needs of all their students.

This somewhat rustic example illustrates the life-chances in practice of more sophisticated models.

What's it all for?

The starting-points, basics or core content of a curriculum will derive from an understanding of what it is hoped the curriculum will achieve. Three such understandings may be briefly identified; their advocates believe respectively that each is the governing purpose of education, to which all other considerations should be subordinated.

Socialization

Any community which educates its children hopes that such education will help them to survive and, if possible, prosper, when they grow up. Educational socializers draw out the basics from the needs of members of particular societies at particular times. Thus, in some societies, education will enable every boy to read tracks so as to travel towards the deer rather than away from it; and every girl will learn the signs showing that meat is not yet cooked. In other societies, every boy and girl will learn how to work with a computer modem. Anything common to education in different societies is accidental; each society sovereignly determines education's purpose.

Development of rationality

By contrast, educational rationalists see the purpose of education as the eventual transcending of the familiar, the instinctive and the utilitarian. The learner should seek and appreciate 'truth', which is perceived as having universal and somewhat abstract properties. Rationalists, following Plato, believe that, despite appearances, the universe is essentially orderly and harmonious. So they believe that reason, which pursues order and harmony, is the proper mode for learning about the universe. The effect of this belief on education is profound. Platonic rationalists believe that mathematics, a supremely rational (and, incidentally, a most abstract) discipline, models both the highest mental activity *and* the truth about the universe. 'Platonists maintain that the objects and structures of mathematics have a real existence independent of humanity' (Ernest 1991: 29). Education on this model sets up mental reasoning almost in defiance of human feeling and social utility. Accordingly, if young children find their basic education distasteful and pointless, that is unfortunate, but irrelevant.

Natural development

Natural developers, following Rousseau, believe that children's instincts and interests have value in themselves. They believe that nurturing what is already in the child from birth will allow the systemic growth of appropriate adult qualities, making for personal happiness and social cohesion. They view the imposition of units of adult-approved learning in bolted-on components or grafts imposed on children by adults as forms of child abuse. Education should, rather, aim to develop most fully each child's potential, by extending, enriching and elaborating the experiences to which the child seems spontaneously inclined.

Each of these starkly outlined theories has a view on the way in which education should go, and a corresponding view on where it should start and what is central to it. As distinct sources of policy their outworkings do not coincide, although it is possible for their advocates to form coalitions. That is just as well, because in practice none of them is ever completely excluded. Each theory, when in the saddle, can be damagingly criticized for palpable failures of service. While each could, in itself, provide a coherent curriculum direction and content, each also cries out for complementation from the others. In the curricula of nearly all schools, all three objectives are routinely honoured. The necessary compromises are invariably incoherent and unstable. Indeed, Kieran Egan maintains that the fulfilment of the aims of any one of these curriculum theories so detracts from the others that no curriculum seeking to combine them can hope to succeed (Egan 1990: 11). Yet such a composite curriculum seems almost inevitable, given public and parental expectations.

Three ways out – together

Practical education is, then, in a triple bind of incompatible theories, all of which supply priorities which the public demands of its schools. This would be enough in itself to explain why schools find success difficult, and why the most successful schools are those which exclude children who most need educating. Can Christians point to a way out of this trilemma? If so, there will be distinctively Christian features of their identification and understanding of the curriculum and its basics, as well as some particularly Christian reasons for teaching the basics. At the same time, Christians will not be embarrassed to find some consonances with those of other participants in education.

Where there is agreement, embrace it

Thus, a first way of proceeding is to note *consensus*. It seems sensible at the present time to say that literacy and numeracy are foundational basic skills. Parents, employers, politicians, higher-educators and journalists are clamouring for young people to be competent in these disciplines. Christians, in so far as they have a special view, place a high value on reading the Bible, and see in mathematical experience something of the Creator's orderly mind.

Positive results flow from acquisition of these skills. They enable the child to progress with the accumulation of knowledge and they offer the possibility of relatively independent learning; for example, a literate child with a set of encyclopedias is not limited by the knowledge and understanding of an individual teacher. Anyone with a grounding in mental arithmetic is not at the mercy of a shopkeeper's whim or a calculator's battery. Following Lev Vygotsky at a safe distance, we may say that the child's mental structure has been altered by acquiring these skills, so as to open up possibilities of learning not confined to logical progression from the information on which they were first exercised.

The early and continuous teaching of science helps to relieve a nest of adult anxieties about the future, such as concern for children's socialization and employability. Empirically based science is the facilitator of technology which is, in turn, the inescapable environment of modern society. Furthermore, the scientific paradigm reigns over nearly all modern discourse. Underlying practically all social practice are the theoretical procedures which characterize positivistic western science: neglect of first causes, prioritizing questions on which there might be publicly agreed answers, and generalizing into formulae the results of a few experiments. These procedures are profoundly inadequate, but their very ubiquity makes it necessary to understand them, and their inadequacy. Science is, therefore, a 'basic'.

Education is inevitably practised amid certain moral assumptions. It requires civilized behaviour by participants, but such behaviour is seldom adequately derived from education's need for it. It normally rests on a set of principles imported into or assumed by the school. In other words, we may educate within socially agreed moral limits, but the needs of education alone are not always enough to secure that moral agreement. This is more obvious when we recognize that education invites our judgment, during our studies, on behaviours in contexts other than education; the Holocaust cannot be adequately appraised by English public-school tradition or in the progressive-school moot. Where morality cannot be assumed it must be taught. Morality is, therefore, a basic dimension of education.

Finally, education assumes (not always correctly) a common understanding of its purpose. The three theories described above derive in their purest form from different understandings of the meaning of life. As we have seen, each contributes something essential to the curriculum; but Christians among others will reject them as adequate accounts of ultimate reality. Such accounts are, in the broadest sense, 'religious'. There are, of course, religious views of life that encompass meaning and morality, so in the case of a culture deeply influenced by, for example, Christianity, some such term as 'moral religion' might come into the public consensus.

We have, then, four basics: language, number, science and moral religion. These happen to be the 'core' and 'basic' subjects in the English National Curriculum. It cannot be stated too often that such politically accountable documents seldom issue from a line of pure educational reasoning; such reasoning may be sound in itself, and it may justify the presence of basics in a curriculum, but it seldom explains adequately how they got there.

This, perhaps unsatisfactory, state of affairs highlights the fragile provisionality of a consensus/coalition case for particular 'basics'. None of the accounts of education and life given above is adequate. With three inadequate accounts in fissionable contiguity, plus democratic political pressure, plus a society in disorderly transition, some better account is needed. The second way out is to explore a durable view of life, the universe and everything, from which education's meaning might be derived.

Meaning, morality, children and knowledge – where do they come from?

Christians believe that the personal, infinite God described in the Judeo-Christian Scriptures is the existing being of ultimate worth. He is characterized in the Bible as 'holy', meaning uniquely and perfectly possessed of good qualities which we perceive dimly reflected in human nature at its rare best. The biblical description is not merely of a being in whom good qualities reside, so much as one who actively and personally *is* those qualities: God not only has love, he is love and he loves. He is, moreover, a social being, in the divine order of Trinity, so that he is complete also in relational qualities.

All that exists apart from him was created by him. According to Jonathan Edwards (Edwards 1966: 236ff.), God created the universe in which we live for his own glory, and that will be the universe's end result. His creatures depend, not upon their rights, but on his free grace which enables them to share his glory. It is by the grace of God that everything came into being, continues to exist, and will come to final fruition.

Human beings are particularly designed to reflect in miniature the personal nature of the holy and eternal God; his holding them responsible for not doing this is also for his glory. His redemptive

160

involvement in human history as Jesus Christ of Nazareth acts out both his intention in creating human beings and his sacrificial love for them in their guilt and failure.

This at least is a prelude to stating the special nature of persons in education. Only when some account has been taken of God himself does any significance attach to saying that those to be educated are 'made in the image of God'. Such a statement means much more than the projection on to the clouds of positive feelings for human nature. Instead, the biblical revelation and its historic extrapolations describe human beings as in a twofold 'special relationship' with their divine Creator. Their purpose is to represent God's care for his creation, including themselves. Failing that (as they have) they relate again to God as persons in the consciously redeemed community of the church.

Even apart from its awareness of redemption, humanity retains qualities imbued by its divine creation. Intellectual, social and moral attributes still reflect the divine character, although now flawed as well as finite. With particular reference to the basics of education, this means that the minds that learn about the world have some likeness to the mind of the one who created it. Therefore, Christians understand the connection between our perceptions and what is really there as stronger than is possible for those who see no connection between origins and perceptions.

Christian understandings of nature have been effective in human knowledge far outside the Christian community. For example, modern science springs directly from a Christian view of creation as good, orderly, contingent (therefore to be explored as it is), and open to discussion (Allen 1989). Language is affirmed by the realization that God uses it to communicate with his world. Numbers and their logical relationships describe many of the relationships built into God's creation, making them more predictable than if the Creator God had no use for logic-in-time. Morality derives from the revealed character of the personal God and his declared will for his creatures.

These understandings are not to be dismissed because they are controversial. All understandings of knowledge and education are controversial. Christians hold Christian doctrines because they believe them to be God's truth; but in addition these doctrines support powerfully the hopes about education that other views deny.

Compare, for example, Richard Rorty's postmodern description of objectivity – 'the agreement of everyone in the room' (cited in Tomlinson 1995: 89) – with that of Calvinist philosopher Cornelius Van Til: 'For the Christian, facts are what they are, in the last analysis, by virtue of the place they take in the plan of God' (quoted in Warfield 1959: 18).

The instability of postmodern factuality may be exciting to the intellectually sophisticated, but a belief in ultimately unknowable truth undermines all basic education, or at best subsumes it under child psychology, of which, of course, we have no objective knowledge.

The other basics are equally circumscribed in non-Christian theories. Language, following one common interpretation of Jacques Derrida, can teach us only about itself, not what it claims to signify; language is a self-contained, non-referential environment beyond which there is no reality (Tomlinson 1995: 90–91). If this is so, it is not possible to teach young children without lying. The relation of mathematics to anything outside the workings of the chance-originated human brain is highly problematic (Ernest 1991). Morality, lacking public agreement, is virtually unteachable. Yet the cry goes up from social commentators that in deregulated global economies societies need a culture of trust and responsibility, and that *governments* should create this culture (Perri 6 1995: 2–8). Such cultural transmission will, no doubt, be a basic task for the curriculum.

Non-Christians might envy the epistemological assurance that Christians seem to enjoy. The signs are that such assurance is increasingly needed to fund the educational enterprise. Christians themselves will doubt whether sheer necessity can mother the invention of reality on the scale required to make education a meaningful activity. In particular, they will insist that while they believe that reality about God's creation supports meaningful education, access to that reality originates in a top-down encounter with God himself. Such access is not a need-driven divinization of knowledge and learning processes. In one of his letters, D. H. Lawrence argued that if 'the Word was God' (as John 1:1 states), words about the anatomy below the human waist are as much God as words for physical parts above. That dramatizes the mentality which we are rejecting. Truth, and the ability to learn it, are gifts of God, not human attributes invested with religious dignity; any more than divine revelation is the effulgence of the human self, or Christian worship our own good qualities flung upwards.

Through learners' eyes

This does not mean, however, that we can learn only if we have a prior grasp of Christian theology. God accommodates his teaching to our state of mind; teachers must do the same. This may even mean that they will sometimes downplay the priority of the basic skills. Hans-Ruedi Weber, giving basic Christian instruction to a preliterate community in Indonesia, resisted his initial western response, 'we must teach them to read', and developed Bible knowledge with storytelling, drama and clay modelling (Tomlinson 1995: 121–122).

Teaching the basics in western societies also requires appropriate accommodation to learners' outlooks. Howard Gardner's understanding of multiple intelligences suggests that teachers should play to individual children's strengths, via their personal linguistic, logical, spatial, musical, bodily-kinaesthetic or problem-solving aptitudes (Gardner 1993).

More fundamental is the analysis of children's developmental stages by Kieran Egan. Egan identifies these as outlooks on life which give special means of access to knowledge. 'Mythic' thinking is preliterate and interprets knowledge by sharp polarities according to whether the learner finds it good or bad, nice or nasty, hot or cold or whatever. Literacy engenders a feeling of distance from perceived objects, giving rise to 'romantic' desires to overcome the 'otherness' of an indifferent or hostile world. From the mid-teens, a learner may move from a feeling of distance from observed nature to a feeling of being controlled by it; this creates a need for some 'philosophy' to explain causal chains of events. In each mode, according to Egan, students acquire knowledge and develop skills to meet their own emotional need to feel secure in the world as they see it at the time. Teaching material, selected by adults, should be *presented* in terms of the students' emotional needs. Progress should be assisted by maximizing learning in each stage. The student may then pass to later stages while retaining fully developed emotional learning tools from earlier stages. The role of education is to nourish all types of understanding or 'good ways of knowing'.

Whether or not Egan's scheme is generally acceptable, the possibility that children learn best if knowledge nourishes their spirits should be taken very seriously. In our culture, an anxious public demands early introduction of the four basics and their continued development.

A Christian understanding of knowledge endorses independently their importance and validity. There may be a third requirement for efficient teaching, which is that learning the basics should seem to children to be worth while. If so, and if the task of making that happen dovetails all learning into education for spiritual development, Christians need not complain.

BIBLIOGRAPHY

6, Perri (1995), *Demos Quarterly* 7 (London: Demos).

Allen, Diogenes (1989), *Christian Belief in a Postmodern World* (Kentucky: Westminster/John Knox).

Baker, Mike (1994), *Who Rules Our Schools?* (London: Hodder and Stoughton).

Boden, Margaret (1992), *The Creative Mind* (London: Sphere).

Bullivant, Brian (1981), *The Pluralist Dilemma in Education* (Sydney: George Allen and Unwin).

Cooling, Trevor (1994), *A Christian Vision for State Education: Reflections on the Theology of Education* (London, SPCK).

Dearing, Sir Ron (1993), *The National Curriculum and its Assessment: Interim Report* (London: School Curriculum and Assessment Authority).

—— (1994), *The National Curriculum and its Assessment: Final Report* (London: School Curriculum and Assessment Authority).

Edwards, Jonathan (1966), *Basic Writings* (New York: New American Library).

Egan, Kieran (1979), *Educational Development* (New York: Oxford University Press).

—— (1986), *Teaching as Story Telling* (Ontario: Althouse).

—— (1988), *Primary Understanding* (London: Routledge).

—— (1990), *Romantic Understanding* (London: Routledge).

—— (1992), *Imagination in Teaching and Learning* (London: Routledge).

Ernest, Paul (1991), *The Philosophy of Mathematics Education* (Basingstoke: Falmer).

Gardner, Howard (1993), *Demos Quarterly* 1 (London: Demos).

Goleman, Daniel (1995), *Emotional Intelligence* (New York: Bantam Doubleday Dell).

Gordon, Peter, and Lawton, Dennis (1978), *Curriculum Change in the Nineteenth and Twentieth Centuries* (London: Hodder and Stoughton).

Tomlinson, Dave (1995), *The Post-Evangelical* (London: SPCK).

Warfield, B. B. (1959), *The Inspiration and Authority of the Bible* (London: Marshall Morgan and Scott).

Wells, David (1993), *No Place for Truth* (Leicester: IVP).

10

Curriculum after Babel[1]

Elmer J. Thiessen

Accepting elements of the postmodernist critique of universal rationality, this chapter will argue for the possibility of a Christian curriculum which rejects relativism and yet is rooted in a particular story. It will clarify the relation between faith and learning, and address the question whether a Christian curriculum can be unique and yet share elements with other curricula rooted in other worldviews. Finally, it will briefly work out the implications of this for both Christian and state-maintained schools.

There would seem to be two Babels, an ancient and a postmodern one. In Genesis 11:1 we read that 'the whole world had one language and a common speech'. But after Babel, the LORD confused the language of the whole world and scattered the people over the face of the whole earth. Hence the 'problem' of linguistic diversity and all that that entails. Attempts have been made to return to pre-Babel times. Postmodernists like to describe modernism in terms of another attempt to devise a universal language and a universal rationality. But we are experiencing another confusion of tongues, and various philosophers have invoked the image of Babel to describe postmodernism with its emphasis on multiple narratives and multiple forms of rationality (Stout 1988: 1–2).

In the first section of this chapter, I want to argue that the postmodern Babel lends credence to the idea of a uniquely Christian curriculum. But how does one describe the way in which a Christian worldview shapes the curriculum? And can one affirm the uniqueness of a Christian curriculum and yet allow for commonness with curricula based on other worldviews? After addressing these issues, some implications will be drawn for education in both Christian and state-maintained common schools.

Defence of the possibility of a Christian curriculum

There are some who have objected to the very possibility of a uniquely Christian curriculum (Hirst 1974: 77).[2] Such opposition to the very possibility of a Christian curriculum, however, seems strangely antiquated in the light of more recent developments in philosophy. Since the ground-breaking work of Thomas Kuhn (1962/1970), it is generally recognized that observation is theory-laden. The doctrine of 'immaculate perception' which was at the heart of the traditional conception of science is now regarded as fundamentally flawed (Leahy 1990: 140).

This, and other more recent epistemological developments, would suggest that rationality, knowledge, the justification of our beliefs and, by implication, the curriculum, are, to some degree, shaped by presuppositions and worldviews, by historical, social and even psychological conditions.[3] The idea of a universal and neutral rationality is now recognized to be itself an expression of a particular narrative, an Enlightenment narrative. All this is at the core of postmodernism, and all of this would suggest that the idea of a uniquely Christian curriculum is not at all far-fetched.

The problem of relativism

There is, however, a danger inherent in the above justification of the possibility of a Christian curriculum. An appeal to postmodernism raises the spectre of epistemological relativism. While all postmodernists stress that our access to 'objective' reality is always mediated by our own particular perspectives, worldviews, or conceptual constructions, some go much further, suggesting that reality is a purely human construct. Thus, any 'truth' we claim for our cherished positions becomes problematic and is often radically relativized.[4]

But postmodernists who carry their views to such an extreme invariably contradict themselves. They are forced to concede that we can communicate, despite our conceptual differences. They also seem unable to avoid talking about their postmodern viewpoint as better than that of old-fashioned modernism. But better in terms of what? Better presupposes a best!

The private worlds of extreme postmodernists also tend not to remain entirely private. Human constructions of reality seem to be subject to certain constraints, suggesting the inescapability of the notion of an objectively 'given' reality. And we also seem to find it difficult not to talk about objective and universal truth in some sense.[5]

It would thus seem that we need to retain some elements of modernism. We therefore need to find some way to reconcile the epistemological insights of modernism and postmodernism, avoiding the extremes in either position (Toulmin 1990: 175).[6] Clearly our beliefs are to some extent human constructions, but this is not to say that they are *just* that (Clark and Gaede 1987: 82). Hence many writers have adopted a form of 'critical realism' as a middle position. Our knowledge is always partial and particular, but it is not just that. There is a non-relative goal to our search for truth, and there are criteria by which to assess the adequacy of our human constructions in relation to this goal, although this is admittedly a complex process.[7]

William James, the American pragmatist, prophetically captures this reconciliation between modernist and postmodernist themes when he describes the absolutely true as 'that ideal vanishing point towards which we imagine that all our temporary truths will someday converge' ([1948]1968: 170). For the orthodox Christian the aim of temporary truths is to produce human constructions of knowledge that conform to the ideal of God's truth (Clark and Gaede 1987: 84).

The 'foundations' of a Christian curriculum

It is time to move on more specifically to a consideration of a Christian curriculum. In what follows, my indebtedness to what has come to be known as Reformed epistemology will be apparent.[8] I want to deal with some of the key issues that have arisen in contemporary discussions of a Christian curriculum, responding in particular to a lively recent exchange on this topic in *Spectrum* (Allen 1993; Velten 1994; Smith 1995).

It would seem self-evident that for the Christian, the sacred writings of the Old and New Testaments should play a foundational role in the development of a uniquely Christian curriculum. Here it should be noted that there are some Christians who seem to deny this, claiming that the Scriptures are concerned only with salvation and spiritual matters.[9]

Clearly, the Bible is first and foremost a book of religion and not a textbook in history or science. But as David Smith observes, although the Bible does provide the answer on how to be saved, it also contains a great deal of information on how Christians are to interact with the world once they are saved (1995: 11). Further, the scope of redemption is not limited to persons, but includes the whole of the cosmos (Romans 8:18-25; Colossians 1:19-20). The above objection to Scripture as a 'foundation' to a Christian curriculum rests on a sharp divide between spiritual and earthly or cultural matters, an unfortunate legacy from American fundamentalism which most evangelicals today reject (Buss 1994).

It is important, though, to recognize that the Bible is not the only 'foundation' for a Christian curriculum.[10] In addition to God's special revelation, there is what theologians refer to as 'general revelation' – God's revelation in nature (Romans 1:20; Psalm 19:1-4). Indeed, general revelation is the more immediate and normal source of much of our knowledge, even for Christians – a point stressed by Catholic theologians, but one to which evangelical and Reformed theologians have not always paid sufficient attention (Curtis 1994: 94). It needs to be stressed, though, that for the Christian this general revelation is still God's revelation.

Here it might be well to draw attention to a problem that arises in taking special and general revelation to be the 'foundations' of a Christian curriculum. Reformed epistemologists, very much in keeping with some emphases in postmodernism, stress that we must not forget the human interpretative dimension in understanding both God's special and general revelation. It must not be assumed that Christians can read the Bible in a neutral or positivistic manner which bypasses all problems of interpretation. Hermeneutical problems also arise in the reading of God's general revelation. Christians come to the Scriptures and also to the world around them with presuppositions and biases, and these can lead to distortions and even errors in interpretation. Hence there is a constant need for critical discernment and re-evaluation of one's reading of the Scriptures and nature.

It is not possible here to explore the complex relation between special and general revelation, except to note that these need to be kept in balance in developing a Christian curriculum (Curtis 1994: 100; cf. Wolterstorff 1984, chapter 13). And it needs to be stressed that because God is the source, guide and goal of all that is (Romans 11:36), there must be a unity to all knowledge and truth. All truth is God's truth (Holmes 1977). Hence there must ultimately be coherence between the conclusions drawn from special and general revelation.

Deducing curricular implications from the Scriptures

The Bible occupies a central position for the evangelical Christian. Given what is often seen as the Christian scholar's mandate – taking captive every thought to make it obedient to Christ (2 Corinthians 10:5) – it would seem that it should be possible to deduce a uniquely Christian curriculum from biblical presuppositions. It is this implication that has prompted perhaps the strongest objections to the Reformed perspective on curriculum. Christian scholars often find it difficult to provide concrete examples of conclusions that follow from biblical presuppositions for their discipline. Indeed, to cite just one example, neither Planck's quantum theory nor its denial could be derived from the Scriptures.[11]

Indeed, many of the claims of the sciences cannot be directly deduced from the Bible. And therefore there is some justification for giving the label 'pious rationalism' to the suggestion that it is possible in every case to get a direct derivation of curricular content from the Bible (Velten 1994: 63–64).

But if we are to make anything of the idea of a Christian curriculum, biblical perspectives and presuppositions must have some sort of influence on the curriculum. But how is this influence to be described? I want to review various models that have been proposed to help us understand how the Bible serves to delimit and inspire a Christian curriculum.

169

Allen introduces a commonly used analogy: 'Our Christian beliefs should act, not so much as a pump pushing fuel into an engine, but more as a filter, letting through what is clean and keeping out what is impure' (Allen 1993: 19). The filter analogy highlights an important scholastic emphasis that our beliefs in geology or psychology must not *contradict* any revealed doctrine of truth (Clouser 1991: 95). But the negative function of filtering out what is impure can ultimately be restated positively. Every exclusion entails an inclusion. Thus Allen too makes certain deductions. For example, a Christian anthropology entails the inclusion of physical education in the curriculum, and the doctrine of creation entails respect for diversity (Allen 1993: 21, 23). The Bible therefore works not only as a filter, but also as a motor and impulse (Velten 1994: 66).

Some writers prefer to talk about a Christian 'worldview' which changes our ways of looking at the world and hence shapes a curriculum. David Smith, for example, suggests that 'worldviews are primarily lenses with which we look at the world' (1995: 21). For example, the Bible serves to open our eyes to creation and its normative structure, thus encouraging us to look for norms governing the political, economic, aesthetic and other spheres of life (Wolterstorff 1980, chapter 2).

Various writers introduce the notion of presuppositions - basic theoretical assumptions at the core of our belief system, that are often held unconsciously and that shape the rest of our thinking (Clouser 1991: 101–107). Wolterstorff describes these presuppositions in terms of 'control beliefs', which lead us both to reject certain sorts of theories which are inconsistent with these control beliefs, and to devise theories which are consistent with them (1984: 67-68). Sometimes these presuppositions merely act as a general guide to developing curriculum. But sometimes they entail specific truths for curricular content.

Here it is important to see that the influence of Christian presuppositions will be mediated at various levels. The following diagram of a belief system serves to illustrate how presuppositions lead to philosophical theories, which in turn lead to scientific theories, which in turn finally lead to specific claims (see figure 1).[12] All beliefs, however far removed from the centre of one's belief system, are influenced by one's presuppositions, though clearly those beliefs closer to the centre of one's belief system (for instance, those related to one's view of human nature) will be more significantly shaped by one's

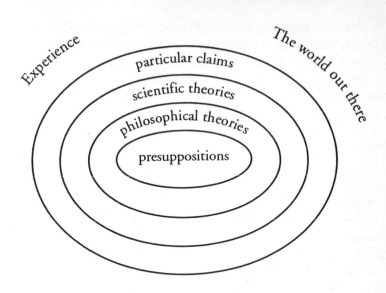

Figure 1: Belief systems

presuppositions. This explains why the influence of Christian presuppositions is more apparent in some subject areas than in others.

It should also be noted that influence does not only move from the centre outward. Sometimes our experiences cause us to revise our theories and even our presuppositions. As pointed out earlier, there needs to be a dynamic interplay between the conclusions Christians draw from general revelation and those drawn from God's special revelation. Not only do Christian presuppositions influence science, but science sometimes causes Christians to correct their fallible interpretations of Scripture (Wolterstorff 1984: 94).

Lessons from a Shakespearian analogy

Tom Wright, in a discussion of the nature of biblical authority, has provided us with a very helpful analogy (1992: 140). He posits a Shakespeare play, most of whose fifth act has been lost:

The first four acts provide, let us suppose, such a wealth of characterization, such a crescendo of excitement with the plot, that it is generally agreed that the play ought to be staged. Nevertheless, it is felt inappropriate actually to write a fifth act once and for all: it would freeze the play into one form, and commit Shakespeare as it were to being prospectively responsible for work not in fact his own.

Instead, it is felt to be better

... to give the key parts to highly trained, sensitive and experienced Shakespearian actors, who would immerse themselves in the first four acts, and in the language and culture of Shakespeare and his time, and who would then be told to work out a fifth act for themselves.

David Smith, in an illuminating commentary on this analogy, applies it specifically to the area of Christian curriculum construction (1995: 22–24). This analogy wonderfully highlights the need for creativity on the part of Christians in working out the implications of the biblical story in all spheres of life, including the academic sphere and the development of curriculum.

Tom Wright's analogy further underlines the importance of the actors immersing themselves in the first four acts and in the language and culture of Shakespeare. The development of a Christian curriculum similarly requires a careful reading of God's special revelation, which plays a foundational role in such development.

While each of the actors will no doubt have to study the first four acts on their own, they will finally have to get together in order to discuss the best way in which to work out the fifth act as a group. Christian scholarship too should be conducted within the context of a community, allowing others to critique proposed suggestions on what a Christian curriculum should look like (Walsh and Middleton 1984: 159–161).

Tom Wright's analogy warns about the dangers of freezing the play into one form. David Smith highlights this point, arguing that it is impossible to arrive at a final, correct version of a Christian curriculum. The first four acts should not be seen as a code, or a blueprint, 'entailing one and only one set of practices', or leading to 'a static picture of reality'. The analogy 'allows for different (yet perhaps equally faithful) performances for different audiences and in different theatres, thus making room for the fact that the same principles will have different practical outworkings in different educational contexts' (Smith 1995: 22-23).

In seeking to be faithful performers in the area of education, Christians will not always get it right. Though God is the author of the first four acts of the play, the Christian's understanding of it is always incomplete. The fact of human sin further leads Christians to resist and distort the truth. There is the further danger of the actors being steeped more in contemporary ways of thinking and seeing than in the original characteristics of the play and its author (Smith 1995: 23).

But there are public criteria by which to assess the appropriateness of the fifth act in relation to the first four acts. Some things are simply required by the earlier acts and are not open to variation, as David Smith points out (1995: 24). Even in the creative applications of the first four acts, 'there will be a rightness, a fittingness, about certain actions and speeches, about certain final moves in the drama' (Wright 1992: 141). Then of course with regard to curriculum there is also the fittingness with God's revelation in nature. And a final more general criterion of faithfulness to the Christian narrative is a life of faithfulness, a life of responsible action (Wolterstorff 1980).

The analogy finally serves to remind Christians that every attempt to develop a Christian curriculum is in the end a human construction, at least in part. David Smith therefore reminds Christians not to credit human ideas to God or to claim his authority for the fruit of human invention (1995: 22). And therefore also, any attempts to work out the implications of special revelation for curriculum must be offered tentatively and must be open to correction. This calls for critical thinking and constant re-evaluation of suggested offerings of Christian thinking in various disciplines. Humility and open-mindedness on the part of Christian scholars are essential. But there is a goal – faithfulness to the original creator of the play!

Transformationalism, uniqueness and commonness

Much of my argument thus far has been stressing the uniqueness of a Christian curriculum. Such thinking can easily lead to an extreme position in which communication with others starting with a different worldview or with different presuppositions is deemed to be impossible.[13]

This extreme position flies in the face of ordinary experience. Christians do communicate with others despite their differing presuppositions. Further, Christians maintain that all human beings are created in the image of God and have access to the same general revelation. This point is often expressed theologically in terms of the notions of 'natural law' or 'common grace'. Obviously, those who reject a Christian view of human nature and reality will interpret this commonness differently, but, as was argued earlier, some kind of an appeal to a common reality, leading to some degree of commonness in beliefs, seems to be inescapable for all human knowers.

I would suggest that here again we need to try to maintain a balance between an emphasis on the uniqueness of Christian thinking with the rather obvious fact that Christians do, to some extent, agree with those holding other worldviews. I suggest that it is possible to affirm, at one and the same time, that one's belief system is unique, and that it shares truths with other belief systems (Smith 1995: 21, n. 47; cf. Wolterstorff 1984: 83).

Here a picture might be useful (see figure 2).[14] Imagine a series of ellipses, each representing a different worldview or belief system, but all overlapping to some degree. Each ellipse is unique, and yet there is some common ground. The common ground represented by the area of overlap of these ellipses will be interpreted and justified in very

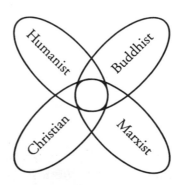

Figure 2: Overlapping ellipses

different ways in each particular belief system. But what this common ground allows is for a pragmatic consensus to develop in a pluralistic world after Babel.

Here it is important to recognize that this common ground should not be seen as a neutral autonomous sphere - an error inherent in liberalism and sometimes made by Christians in discussions on the integration of faith and learning. Further, we must be careful not to see convergence as a criterion of truth or as a sign of intellectual respectability (1 Corinthians 2:15-16; Plantinga 1984). Interpretation of experience is inescapable and the interpretative dimension of knowledge does not have an epistemological status different from that of so-called 'facts' with which all agree.

An approach which tries to do justice to the need for a balance between an emphasis on the uniqueness of a Christian curriculum and an emphasis on the common ground which Christians share with those starting with different presuppositions is sometimes referred to as 'transformationalism.' The transformationalist works from within disciplines as presently constituted, seeking to transform them, where necessary, so as to come closer to a biblically inspired understanding of that discipline (Nelson 1987; Shortt 1991, chapter 5). Cooling labels this a 'work-with' strategy, emphasizing the importance of Christians working with other scholars with differing worldviews, while trying to achieve a creative interplay between theological reflection and scientific and cultural analysis (Cooling 1994: chapter 10; 1995: 156).

There is of course always the danger that in seeking to work co-operatively with those who do not share their own presuppositions, Christians will dilute or even betray their own distinctively Christian perspective to the discipline in question. Transformation of disciplines is possible only if Christians have something new to contribute (cf. 2 Corinthians 5:17). Hence it is imperative that Christian scholars do two things at the same time, keeping these two activities in balance: working within their respective disciplines together with other scholars, whatever their worldviews, and immersing themselves in God's special revelation which will help them to gain a uniquely Christian perspective to the discipline in question.

One other danger of a stress on the uniqueness of Christian truth is that it can lead to isolationism and even to a proud distancing from those who 'haven't got the full truth'. This is wrong, and betrays the incarnational emphasis of the gospel, as Velten correctly stresses (1994: 66–67). Just as the Word became flesh and dwelt among us, so Christian academics too are called to identify with the academic world. God calls Christians to be servants, both in the citadels and in the grimy houses of our civilization.

And how do Christians relate to others adhering to different worldviews and belief systems? There needs to be dialogue in which each side remains true to its own presuppositions, and seeks to understand the presuppositions of the other. The Christian can approach the other with a genuine attitude of wanting to learn from the other. Truth in other belief systems needs to be affirmed (cf. 2 Thessalonians 5:21). Such affirmation can further serve to invigorate the Christian's own understanding of truth.

Genuine dialogue, however, does not preclude criticism. Unfortunately, this point is very often not acknowledged in today's postmodern climate. Given that most disciplines today are governed by presuppositions which are at variance with Christian ones, Christians will need to expose and critique these. But this must be done humbly and lovingly. A defensive posture and confrontational critique might in fact be a betrayal of the spirit of Christ, who taught us to love even our enemies. Clearly I am here introducing ethical considerations. But epistemology must not be divorced from ethics, a point stressed by the anabaptists and their peace emphasis. The ethical and the personal might in fact have a priority over the epistemological (cf. Yoder 1992).

Conclusion and some practical implications

I have tried to show that a Christian curriculum is possible. Indeed, developing a Christian curriculum is both a necessary and urgent task if Christians are to do justice to recent developments in the theory of knowledge. This does not entail subjectivism or relativism as there is an objectively 'given' reality against which all interpretations rub. Differing human interpretations of truth also do not preclude the overlapping of these particular interpretations. I have also argued that the Bible has a key role to play in shaping curriculum for Christians. But this is not meant to imply a simplistic model of how that happens.

Christian schools are therefore justified in developing a uniquely

Christian curriculum. A religiously neutral curriculum is impossible. Thus, within a Christian school, the entire curriculum will be coloured by Christian presuppositions, and Christian education will be seen as taking place in all subjects. This will further serve to combat the unfortunate fragmentation inherent in today's widespread disciplinary approach to curriculum. There is still, however, a place for courses which focus particularly on gaining an understanding of Christian presuppositions and a Christian worldview.[15]

By extrapolation, other religious traditions are justified in designing curricula in keeping with their own religious presuppositions. The argument of this chapter would therefore seem to point in the direction of a plurality of schools. Of course, many other factors come into play before one can draw such a conclusion. State-maintained common schools would seem to be in a unique position to facilitate dialogue with various religious traditions, something that can and should take place within religious schools as well. How common schools can do justice to the inescapable religious particularity of curricula is of course another issue. I would suggest this as a main agenda item for future discussion about common schools and religion.[16]

NOTES

1 I am very grateful for the helpful comments made when I first presented a draft of this chapter at the 'With Heart and Mind' Conference at Regina, Saskatchewan, 14–17 May 1995. My thanks also to the independent reader and to the editors of this volume for their many helpful suggestions and careful editing of earlier drafts.

2 For a response to Hirst, see Thiessen (1985). It should be noted that Hirst now expresses some dissatisfaction with the idea of a universal, secular rationality, thereby acknowledging at least the second Babel (Hirst 1993).

3 See, for example, Clark and Gaede 1987; Young 1971; MacIntyre 1988; Clouser 1991; and Middleton and Walsh 1995.

4 Hence the title of a recent book on postmodernism by Middleton and Walsh, *Truth is Stranger Than It Used to Be* (1995).

5 For a defence of objective knowledge from a Christian point of view, see Helm 1987.

6 Jeffrey Stout also attempts such a reconciliation with regards to ethics in *Ethics after Babel* (1988).

7 Various writers, including postmodernists, have identified such criteria

as the ability to interpret and encompass all empirical data, consistency, breadth, simplicity, fruitfulness and pragmatic considerations (Kuhn 1977; Walsh and Middleton 1984: 36–39; and Cooling 1994: 79–85).

8 Reformed epistemology can be traced back to John Calvin and other leaders of the sixteenth-century Reformation. Key figures in its development are Abraham Kuyper in the nineteenth century and some contemporary American philosophers such as Alvin Plantinga and Nicholas Wolterstorff. See Shortt (1991) for a recent account of this aproach to epistemology and its educational implications.

9 Velten, for instance, characterizes the Bible as primarily theological in nature, and this leads him to draw the rather extreme conclusion that 'there are no biblically-deduced subject-area contents' (1994: 60–64, 69–70).

10 This is a rather unfortunate error that is at times made by those adhering to a Reformed epistemology, for example Van Til, who holds that education should be 'based exclusively on the Bible' (quoted in Shortt 1991: 70).

11 See, for example, Wolterstorff 1984: 59; Heie and Wolfe 1987: vii; Nelson 1987: 328, n. 6).

12 This diagram is inspired by Quine's important essay, 'Two Dogmas of Empiricism' (1953: 20–46, esp. Section 6). Shortt addresses the issue of varying degrees of influence of Christian presuppositions by introducing the notion of a 'hierarchy of perspectives' (1991: 70).

13 For example, Perks argues that Christians and humanists 'can never agree fundamentally on the interpretation of the facts of reality at *any* point if they are consistent with their presuppositions [so that] for the Christian and the humanist, therefore, there can be no common ground' (1992: 28, my emphasis).

14 I have borrowed this from a presentation made by Trevor Cooling, who also argues for overlapping belief systems (1994: 115).

15 For two excellent resources on this, see Wolters 1985, and Walsh and Middleton 1984.

16 For a defence of state education based on an epistemological framework similar to the one outlined in this chapter, see Cooling 1994. See Thiessen 1995 for a criticism of this defence and Cooling 1995 for a response. See also chapter 4 of this present volume.

BIBLIOGRAPHY

Allen, R. T. (1993), 'Christian Thinking about Education', *Spectrum* 25/1: 17–24.

Buss, Dietrich G. (1994), 'Educating Toward a Christian Worldview: Some

Historical Perspectives', *Faculty Dialogue* 21 (Spring-Summer): 63–89.

Clarke, Robert A., and Gaede, S. D. (1987), 'Knowing Together: Reflections on a Holistic Sociology of Knowledge', in Heie and Wolfe (1987): 55–86.

Clouser, Roy A. (1991), *The Myth of Religious Neutrality: An Essay on the Hidden Role of Religious Belief in Theories* (Notre Dame, IN: University of Notre Dame Press).

Cooling, Trevor (1994), *A Christian Vision for State Education: Reflections on the Theology of Education* (London: SPCK).

—— (1995), 'A Reply to Elmer Thiessen and Arthur Jones', *Spectrum* 27/2: 153–164.

Curtis, Edward M. (1994), 'Some Biblical Contributions to a Philosophy of Education', *Faculty Dialogue* 21: 91–110.

Heie, Harold, and Wolfe, David L., (eds.) (1987), *The Reality of Christian Learning: Strategies for Faith-Discipline Integration* (Grand Rapids: Eerdmans).

Helm, Paul (ed.) (1987), *Objective Knowledge: A Christian Perspective* (Leicester: IVP).

Hirst, Paul (1974), *Moral Education in a Secular Society* (London: University of London Press).

—— (1993), 'Education, Knowledge and Practices', in *Beyond Liberal Education*, ed. R. Barrow and P. White (London: Routledge): 184–199.

Holmes, Arthur (1979), *All Truth is God's Truth* (Leicester: IVP).

James, William ([1948] 1969), *Essays in Pragmatism* (New York: Hafner).

Kuhn, Thomas (1962/1970), *The Structure of Scientific Revolutions* (Chicago: University of Chicago Press).

—— (1977), 'Objectivity, Value Judgment and Theory Choice', in *The Essential Tension*, ed. Thomas Kuhn (Chicago: University of Chicago Press): 320–339.

Leahy, Michael (1990), 'Indoctrination, Evangelization, Catechesis and Religious Education', in *British Journal of Religious Education* 12/3: 137–144.

MacIntyre, Alasdair (1988), *Whose Justice? Which Rationality?* (Notre Dame, IN: University of Notre Dame Press).

Middleton, J. Richard, and Walsh, Brian J. (1995), *Truth is Stranger Than It Used to Be: Biblical Faith in a Postmodern Age* (London: SPCK).

Nelson, Ronald R. (1987), 'Faith-Discipline Integration: Compatibilist, Reconstructionalist, and Transformationalist Strategies', in Heie and Wolfe (1987): 317–339.

Perks, Stephen C. (1992), *The Christian Philosophy of Education Explained* (Whitby: Avant Books).

Plantinga, Alvin (1984), 'Advice to Christian Philosophers', in *Faith and Philosophy* 1/3: 253–271.

Quine, W. V. (1953), *From a Logical Point of View* (Cambridge: Harvard University Press).

Shortt, John (1991), *Towards a Reformed Epistemology and its Educational Significance* (PhD thesis, University of London Institute of Education).

Smith, David (1995), 'Christian Thinking in Education Reconsidered', *Spectrum* 27/1: 9–24.

Stout, Jeffrey (1988), *Ethics After Babel: The Languages of Morals and their Discourses* (Boston: Beacon).

Thiessen, Elmer John (1985), 'A Defense of a Distinctively Christian Curriculum', *Religious Education* 80/1: 37–50.

—— (1995), 'Review Article on *A Christian Vision for State Education*', *Spectrum* 27/2: 145–152.

Toulmin, Stephen (1990), *Cosmopolis: The Hidden Agenda of Modernity* (New York: Free Press).

Velten, Dieter (1994), 'Christian Thinking in Education', *Spectrum* 26/1: 59–70.

Walsh, Brian J., and Middleton, J. Richard (1984), *The Transforming Vision: Shaping a Christian World View* (Downers Grove: IVP).

Wolters, Albert M. (1985), *Creation Regained: Biblical Basics for a Reformational Worldview* (Grand Rapids: Eerdmans).

Wolterstorff, Nicholas (1980), *Educating for Responsible Action* (Grand Rapids: Eerdmans).

—— (1984), *Reason Within the Bounds of Religion* (Grand Rapids: Eerdmans, 2nd edn).

Wright, N. T. (1992), *The New Testament and the People of God* (London: SPCK).

Yoder, John Howard (1992), On Not Being Ashamed of the Gospel: Particularity, Pluralism and Validation', *Faith and Philosophy* 9/3: 285–300.

Young, Michael F. D. (ed.) (1971), *Knowledge and Control: New Directions for the Sociology of Education* (London: Collier-Macmillan).

11

Towards the ecologically sustainable society

Ron Elsdon

The need for an ecologically sustainable society demands a proper understanding of the nature of creation. The Old Testament describes three sets of relationships, involving God the Creator, humanity and the physical world. The relevant texts are grounded in Israel's occupation of, and care for, the promised land. Having a polemic character, they continue to challenge the adequacy of worldviews that do not take into account the range of the relationships involved. A Christian contribution to the ecological debate is therefore to offer a worldview that can integrate all the other disciplines which will be needed to move realistically towards a society which is ecologically sustainable.

In 1995 the Church of Scotland published a survey of the ethical thinking of a group of young people. Among its findings was the widespread view that the church should stop majoring on issues such as personal sexuality, and say more about global issues like poverty and pollution. However surprising this may be to older people, it ought not to surprise those who work with young people, whether in the classroom or the church youth club.

The youngest of children learn something about environmental problems in their classrooms. Whereas there is still a powerful lobby which believes that science and technology alone can solve even the most stubborn and global of environmental problems, given enough time and resources, many young people are learning about the care of creation in a much more multi-faceted manner, involving religious education among other disciplines.

Religious education can be seen as simply one piece of the jigsaw; preferably, it should be approached as a means of constructing a worldview within which problems and solutions alike can be analysed. It is essential that a correct worldview be found within which to work. This is partly because of the scale, complexity, cost and severity of some environmental problems, which are beyond any kind of easy solution.

Appropriate and long-term solutions will be costly. Thus it is dangerous for a Christian speaker to answer the question 'What shall we do?' simply in terms of popular 'tips'; these are popular because they cost nothing except for occasional minor inconvenience. They are also attractive because, as Tony Walter points out, they help middle-class people, aware of being increasingly powerless in a world governed by market forces, to feel (wrongly) that they are doing something innovative and influential (Walter 1978, 1982).

The need for a correct worldview within which to work also reflects the nature of today's young people. Some, with awareness, energy and idealism, are not only outraged by the mistreatment of the Earth meted out by their forebears; they believe they can save the planet. Rightly, some of them are well aware that science and technology alone are inadequate guides on the way, and the rise of modern alternative religious movements reflects in part this disillusionment with a materialistic or mechanistic worldview. If, however, they are persuaded to operate within a worldview that later proves inadequate, and their work is then seen to have achieved nothing, the end result may be cynicism and despair, and everyone will be the poorer.

Different worldviews compete for the attention (and the loyalty) of young and old alike, including those of New Age philosophy, liberal brands of Christianity, and technocentrism. With fundamentally different views of humanity and the world, and of the divine, they offer confusingly different futures. One of the issues this chapter addresses is some of their shortcomings. More important, however, is the worldview offered by evangelical Christianity, with its emphasis on the trustworthiness and authority of the Scriptures, which are God's inspired word to humanity. This has too often been ignored in debates about environmental issues. For evangelical Christians this is a dangerous omission, and the main task of this chapter is to demonstrate the relevance of the Old and New Testaments alike, in the particular context of educating young people for the responsible care of creation.

The way the Scriptures address this issue, from the opening verses of Genesis onwards, is one which immediately sets itself against other worldviews. To take a biblical approach to environmental care seriously is, therefore, to commit oneself to a radical reappraisal of the way Christians have often swallowed secular and sub-Christian ways of thinking. This is one of the accusations which can be levelled against at least some expositions of a more 'liberal' Christianity which, in praiseworthy attempts to make the gospel relevant to the modern world, yet cuts it off from its scriptural foundations (McGrath 1993).

The polemical character of the Genesis creation narrative

The assertions in Genesis 1 relating to the care of creation have now been worked over repeatedly by modern Christian writers (see Berry 1991 for a review). They are twofold: first, there is the repeated statement of the goodness of creation. Secondly, humanity's creation in the image of God is inextricably linked in the text with the charge to responsible dominion over the rest of creation (1:26ff.).

What is repeatedly missed, however, is the polemical character of the Genesis text. In the history of Israel, this polemical dimension surfaces at two separate stages.

1. With respect to ancient near-eastern creation myths

The composition of 1:1 - 2:4 is to be seen as confronting the Babylonian creation myths whose superficial similarities with the Genesis text are significant. The sun, moon and stars appear only on Day 4, after the mysterious reference to darkness and light. The Babylonians believed that these heavenly bodies decide the world's destiny. But in Genesis these are merely created entities. This polemic surfaces elsewhere in the Old Testament, including the Psalms (*e.g.* 121:6):

> ... the sun will not harm you by day
> nor the moon by night.

John Goldingay shows how the account of the creation of humanity in Genesis 1 also confronts the Babylonian myths (Goldingay and Innes 1994). In these myths the gods, tired of fighting each other, created a race of people to serve them and make life easier. These myths reflected upon how human life was full of violence, frustration and disenchantment, and saw this as a reflection of what the gods were like. In this sense, they, too, believed that humanity was made in the divine image!

Genesis 1, then, uses similar categories (deliberately) to present a radically different worldview. Creation was an act not of selfishness (as was the motivation of the Babylonian gods) but of love; humanity was created not as a drudge for the gods, but with real responsibility and power, generously given by the God in whom all power resides.

2. With respect to Israel's encounter with Canaanite religion

The Genesis 'primeval history', which goes through to chapter 11, is a sort of historical prologue to the calling of a man (Abraham) and a people (Israel), called to live as a light to the nations in the land God gave them. This land was one 'flowing with milk and honey' (Exodus 3:8, *etc.*), not just in promise, but in reality, as the panic-stricken spies reported from their fact-finding mission (Numbers 13:27).

Biblical references to Canaanite geography reveal a landscape with many steep slopes watered by sparing rainfall that sometimes failed. Such a combination of land and climate meant that irresponsible techniques such as unregulated clearing and burning of forests could set off massive conflagrations and soil erosion. When Israel entered Canaan, responsible care of the land became a major issue, as the Pentateuch makes clear (*e.g.* Leviticus 25:1–7). But how did this relate to their religious life?

The Old Testament taught them that the right way was by humble dependence upon the God who, in creation and in the exodus, had showed them his love and power; he could be relied upon to bless their national life if they would only be obedient (Deuteronomy 28:1-14; cf. 28:15ff.).

The Israelites were warned about the people already living in Canaan. It is not simply that they believed in different gods, and practised abominable rituals such as sacred prostitution and child sacrifice. As various Old Testament scholars have shown, the Canaanite view of the land was totally different. Instead of being a gift from God, it became merely a marketable commodity, and economic growth became a prime goal (Brueggeman 1977; Samuel and Sugden 1982; Wittenberg 1979).

Why did not Israel take the warnings seriously? The answer is that basing prosperity on faith and obedience was more than they were willing to cope with. It was at this point that Canaanite religion, in spite of its corrupt practices, became fatally attractive. The role of Canaanite religion was inextricably tied up with nature, and with how to ensure good harvests. The idea was simple: the role of the religious rituals was to persuade the gods to ensure a good harvest. Religious techniques, under the control of their adherents, were found to be less demanding than the way of faith in Yahweh (Wright 1983).

Once in Canaan, the people of Israel encountered technologies superior to their own. On the one hand they inherited cities as they forsook their agrarian, nomadic way of life; on the other they were hard pressed to withstand the onslaught of the Philistine armies, with their range of weapons unlike anything seen before. So there was also the temptation to rely on these for their stability and prosperity, expressed, for example, in seeking alliances with nations such as Egypt in their attempt to stave off the unwelcome attentions of the Assyrians.

It was not, then, simply a matter of two different kinds of 'religion'. It was a clash between two worldviews, one based on faith and obedience to a God whose redeeming acts were supposedly already built into the memory of his people, and the other based on whatever techniques, including religious ones, could be relied on to 'produce the goods'. This dichotomy between faith-inspired and technique-driven views of religion has a modern ring to it: we must dwell on this theme at some length.

The continuing relevance of the polemical character of Genesis

The use of science and technology

The impact of science and technology upon modern society has persuaded many that, given the right techniques, any problem can be solved. Supremely these techniques are supplied by science and technology. Even Christians are tempted to think, speak and act this way.

This persuasion is embedded in the way we are educating the next generation. Science and technology, vital as they are, are often taught in a vacuum, increasingly so as subject specialization increases as young people progress through the educational system. These disciplines seem to have no connecting points with the world of faith. It is easy for a Christian to criticize, of course. But how does one persuade others who have a different worldview? There are various hints that this can be done.

First, however much society would like to continue to believe that all ecological problems can be solved with the right techniques, increasing numbers of young people are turning their backs on careers in science and industry. Some are disillusioned with the impact of science and technology on the world around us. These young people and their concerns need to be listened to carefully by others who up to now have always assumed that 'we know best'.

Secondly, there is an enormous question of motivation. We have seen that it is foolish to assume that world environmental problems will simply go away when the right techniques are found. Some of them are too severe in nature, too global in extent, and too inextricably tied up with the greed and insecurity of the nations for such a simplistic approach.

It is therefore vital that people find a motivation strong enough to persist with long-term solutions that may well involve profound changes to western lifestyles. The 'compassion fatigue', now well documented after countless heart-rending appeals of the 1980s, is an instructive parallel. Without the correct motivation for environmental care, something similar could set in if enough 'yet-another-environmental-crisis' presentations go out on television news bulletins.

Thirdly, technique-oriented ways of looking at the care of creation also overlook the fact that many environmental problems – whether those which have come upon us gradually or sudden disasters – have human negligence as one of the most important factors. In the former category we may mention the greenhouse effect, first predicted as long ago as 1849; in the latter the list is seemingly endless, but includes various oil-tanker disasters (of which the *Torrey Canyon*, wrecked off the English coast in 1968, was the first of many) and nuclear incidents (not 'accidents') such as Three Mile Island and Chernobyl.

Yet a wholesale loss of confidence in science and technology could be equally disastrous. The scale and severity of environmental problems demand the very best that these disciplines can offer in the years ahead. It is therefore urgent that young people in their education are persuaded that even better science and technology (and their practitioners) will be needed in the years to come. It is also vital that ways be found to integrate these with other equally important disciplines. Many Christians are convinced that the Bible is God's self-revelation and thus affords the basis for a comprehensive worldview. They would wish to seek an integration of these disciplines within a biblical framework.

The use of religious techniques

An important feature of the modern cultural climate in the western world is the appearance of a religious mood that wishes to reintroduce a spiritual dimension to the impoverished existences of modern people. Because awareness of the need to care for creation is high on the agenda of many thoughtful people, the spiritualities which arise seek to incorporate some kind of spiritual awareness of what creation is.

Matthew Fox's 'creation spirituality' has been attractive to many, especially since Fox is a member of a Christian religious order. As some commentators have shown, however, his understanding of creation owes far more to influences other than to biblical Christianity (*e.g.* Osborn 1993, Berry 1994).

More influential, because it appears to incorporate the valuable biological work of James Lovelock, is the so-called 'Gaia hypothesis'. Lovelock argues that the global ecosystem is a complex entity in its own right. It involves negative feedback systems to maintain stability of climate, atmospheric composition, and the chemical composition of sea water.

The systems involve two-way interactions between organisms and their abiotic environment. Lovelock's work has therefore been picked up by advocates of green spirituality as an expression of the fundamental interconnectedness of everything. This is true, for example, of the New Age movement with its concept of 'planetary consciousness'. Osborn shows how, in its moderate form, this is expressed as a spiritualization of the international world order, as formerly dreamt of by socialists; in its more extreme form it is seen as the emergence of a single planetary brain of which human beings are the brain cells. An analogy is drawn between the mammalian central nervous system and that of Gaia. Osborn comments:

> Freed from rational criticism and empirical testing, interconnectedness can function once more as a fundamental philosophical concept and (in its Gaian form) as a religious myth (1993: 55).

Although the biblical view of creation strongly supports such a picture of interconnectedness (Elsdon 1992), Osborn goes on to show how it is often used to lead towards a pantheistic influence, where the natural world is a profound expression of the divine. Whereas eastern pantheism so emphasizes oneness that diversity becomes an illusion, modern western ecological pantheism takes diversity seriously as well. But in this form it has had a long historical association with gnosticism and antipathy towards material reality, so that its potential to lead to responsible care for creation remains doubtful. It also leaves little room for personhood. Human beings exist only 'as islands of subjectivity in an impersonal cosmos', and evil exists only as a form of ignorance (1993: 59).

The primacy of economics

Economic growth is not only a preoccupation of governments and individuals. It is also widely seen as a necessary prerequisite to the elimination of environmental problems. This is most clearly seen in the influential Brundtland Report (shorthand for *Our Common Future*, the 1987 report of the United Nations World Commission on Environment and Development. The commission was chaired by the Prime Minister of Norway, Gro Harlem Brundtland). The thesis can be stated simply as follows: most environmental problems are due to poverty, therefore economic growth in poor countries will, in raising people's living standards, result in the elimination of the resulting environmental problems.

It is not surprising that the report has been widely criticized on this (and other) counts (*e.g.* de la Court 1990). Of particular importance here is the fact that it ignores the role that western economic and technological influences have had in promoting poverty in the rest of the world, and the impact of western technology on world ecosystems. Thus Capra's statement seems nearer to the truth:

> Excessive technological growth has created an environment in which life has become physically and mentally unhealthy. Polluted air, irritating noise, traffic congestion, chemical contaminants, radiation hazards, and many other sources of physical and psychological stress have become parts of everyday life for most of us. These manifold health hazards are not just incidental byproducts of technological progress; they are integral features of an economic system obsessed with growth and expansion, continuing to intensify in high technology in an attempt to increase productivity
>
> (Capra 1982: 249).

This is not to condemn the idea of economic growth. Rather, it is to dispute the idea that economic growth *per se* is the answer to pressing problems where it is in fact the cause.

Towards the ecologically sustainable society

What is 'the ecologically sustainable society'? It is certainly not what others have labelled 'eco-utopia', because so long as sin remains in the world, giving rise to greed, fear, complacency and idolatry, it will be impossible entirely to eradicate the causes of environmental damage.

Rather, 'the ecologically sustainable society' is one which so values the created order that it seeks, as a matter of priority, to minimize the deleterious effects upon the environment of the kinds of human activity that the Bible describes as 'sinful', whether these be the long-term effects of global processes such as the greenhouse effect, or once-off disasters such as Chernobyl and Bhopal.

The question then arises as to how this is to be achieved, and what particular contributions Christians can make. The foregoing sections have attempted to show that 'solutions' to the problem of how to care for creation using science and technology on the one hand, and economics on the other, are dangerously inadequate. In human hands they have become part of the problem, therefore they cannot be the complete answer. Similarly, popular spiritual frameworks such as New Age thinking are inadequate because they fail to take seriously the reality of human sin, which so often manifests itself in concrete situations such as environmental problems.

The role of Christians is, then, one of persuasion. This will mean on the one hand that there is a place in evangelism for emphasizing the goodness of creation, which reflects something of the character of God (Psalm 19; Romans 1:20). On the other, Christians involved in science, technology and other related disciplines should work together to integrate the worlds of their faith and their professional work, and to join together in a cross-fertilization of ideas which draws together the best insights of all in a concerted attempt to show how these can lead to proposals for 'the ecologically sustainable society'.

What biblical Christianity offers here is a worldview which can incorporate all the other disciplines that will be needed in order to care responsibly for creation. Its potential for teaching environmental care as part of an educational curriculum is enormous. In the Old Testament, the goodness of creation is stated not only as a theological principle; as we have seen, it is set in the context of a people called to care for a particular land. So the Pentateuchal laws are as much to do with the practicalities of this task as with any other aspect of Israel's life before God. What is then needed is a consideration of how the principles behind these Pentateuchal laws can be re-applied in a crowded, high-consumption, high-technology world.

It has been argued that biblical Christianity presents an other-worldly picture of the future; the return of Christ at the end of history consigns creation to oblivion. In fact, the opposite is the case; creation is renewed and transformed, to prepare it for its place in the 'new heaven and the new earth' (Revelation 21:1; *cf.* Romans 8:18–25). As is the case with the Old Testament emphasis on the goodness of creation, this is not abstract theology. Such visions of the future are closely linked to exhortations to live in a faithful and committed way here and now. Thus at the end of his exposition of the 'resurrection body' in 1 Corinthians 15, Paul urges his readers to 'stand firm. Let nothing move you. Always give yourselves fully to the work of the Lord, because you know that your labour in the Lord is not in vain' (verse 58).

Biblical Christianity also presents an understanding of human sin which, while doing nothing to underplay its seriousness, still emphasizes the ongoing goodness of creation, seen supremely in the incarnation. It thus presents the possibility of purposeful human activity continuing to sustain the goodness of creation, while continuing also to warn about the consequences for creation of greed, fear, complacency and idolatry. This avoids both the unrealism of utopian approaches, and the prospect of despair over finding that there is nothing we can do.

With its emphasis on the goodness of creation, and particularly through the theme of the Sabbath, where God's rest on the seventh day is more to do with celebration than fatigue (Atkinson 1990), Scripture challenges the view that science and technology alone can solve environmental problems. Alongside the technological aspects of the care of creation, there is a need for that thankfulness which is essential for motivating environmental care. This must form part of the ongoing educational agenda wherever care for creation is taught.

Scientists should be offered opportunities (voluntary or through new course structures) to learn economics – and *vice versa*. Scientists and economists should be required to learn ethics; the use of their disciplines should not merely be left to 'someone else'.

It must also lead to an endeavour to demonstrate clearly to the secular western world that attempts to 'solve' the world's environmental problems while ignoring the Creator and a biblical worldview will have very limited success. It is doubtful whether any concerted attempt to do this has ever been tried.

In one sense this kind of proposal may seem absurdly inadequate. People want *solutions*. But, as was suggested early in this chapter, personal actions such as electing to use lead-free petrol and bottle banks, however admirable, are themselves hopelessly inadequate. The response must be not only personal but corporate; not only easy but sacrificial; not only short-term but sustained.

This means that such disciplines, as taught at every level of education, must not be compartmentalized, but integrated. These proposals sound simple enough (and are easily written!). What lies behind them is an enormous challenge that the Christian community often seems singularly ill equipped to take on. Where are those with the ability and conviction to engage with the assumptions of a secular worldview and demonstrate that they are lacking in the field of the care of creation - *and do it on secular ground* (rather than within the comfort of a conference in the church hall)? Where are those who can produce the material that can be used in the cross-fertilization of disciplines (biblical, scientific, technological, economic - and others) that can lead towards 'the ecologically sustainable society'?

If those people cannot be found, we will have little cause to complain if environmental problems in the third millennium go from bad to worse before our eyes.

BIBLIOGRAPHY

Atkinson, D. J. (1990), *The Message of Genesis 1 - 11: The Dawn of Creation* (Leicester: IVP), especially pp. 48–50.

Berry, R. J. (1991), 'A Bibliography on Environmental Issues', *Science and Christian Belief* 3: 15–18.

────── (1994), 'Creation and the Environment', *Science and Christian Belief* 7: 21–43.

Brueggemann, Walter (1977), *The Land* (Philadelphia: Fortress).

Capra, Fritjof (1982), *The Turning Point* (London: Fontana).

de la Court, Thijs (1990), *Beyond Brundtland: Green Development in the 1990s* (London: Zed Books).

Elsdon, Ron (1992), *Greenhouse Theology* (Eastbourne: Monarch), especially chapter 9.

Goldingay, John, and Innes, Robert (1994), *God at Work*, Grove Ethical Studies 94 (Nottingham: Grove Books).

McGrath, Alister (1993), *The Renewal of Anglicanism* (London: SPCK).

Osborn, Lawrence (1993), *Guardians of Creation* (Leicester: Apollos).

Samuel, Vinay, and Sugden, Chris (1982), 'A Just and Responsible Lifestyle - An Old Testament Perspective', in Ronald J. Sider, *Lifestyle in the Eighties: An Evangelical Commitment to Simple Lifestyle* (Exeter: Paternoster).

Walter, Tony (1978), 'Home or Castle? A Christian Sociological Approach to the Family and Ecology', *Third Way* 2: 3-6.

────── (1982), *The Human Home* (Tring: Lion).

Wittenberg, Gunther (1979), *Good News to the Poor: The Challenge of the Poor in the History of the Church* (Maryknoll: Orbis).

Wright, Christopher (1983), *Living as the People of God* (Leicester: IVP).

PART 5

BEYOND THE
SCHOOLING PARADIGM

COMMENTARY

Schooling and education are not synonymous terms. Schooling is neither necessary nor sufficient for education but, nevertheless, the schooling paradigm dominates and restricts our thinking about education. The two chapters in this part of the book are concerned to focus on the contexts in which education takes place and to examine the relationship between schooling and alternative educational paradigms.

Although, as he points out, the Bible has nothing to say about schooling, Brian Hill examines the assumptions behind the schooling paradigm in the light of his Christian beliefs. A paradigm is a conceptual framework, a mindset and way of doing things and, as such, it is something into which we can become locked. Christians, Christian churches and Christian mission agencies have been locked into it for a long time – with their church schools, training colleges, Sunday *schools* and, more so nowadays, their home *schooling*. Schooling also consorts with two other influential paradigms: 'scientific' assessment and economic rationalism.

Although he allows that schooling has its undoubted and very significant achievements, Prof. Hill feels that it can be justly criticized for its instrumentalism in promoting social inequalities and for its poor record and ethically questionable methodology in values education, the heart of education. The teaching methods of Jesus point us to a need to humanize the schooling paradigm and to take alternative teaching–learning paradigms seriously. Brian Hill goes on to look at some of these: 'school without walls' (which reduces isolationism and segregationism), home schooling (which can never be afforded by the poor), workplace experience (which affirms the dignity of work), education in voluntary contexts (which has much to offer because it is free from the problems of compulsion) and learning exchange through the internet (which offers superb resources and greater engagement, but makes 'computeracy' a prerequisite), and so back to school. Prof. Hill's conclusion is that our education theory 'should accommodate a range of complementary educational sites' including voluntary contexts.

Mention of the internet takes us to Ian Barns's chapter on the new media technologies. He points out that these are 'not just tools which expand our instrumental powers for good or for ill ... they are also forms of life ... and ... cultural products'. And, he argues, they express a particular cultural frame – that of 'liberal capitalist modernity' – and, therefore, their worldview is that of the Enlightenment. This means that, in the long term, they undermine the 'deeper communal and relational sources of human selfhood'.

Ian Barns, using Colin Gunton's writings on the Trinity, says that we need to return to the relational, communicative God and to embody his life in the practices of Christian community. Christians should participate in public policy-making, not to Christianize it by force of law, but as a leavening influence which maintains 'a genuine, dialogically open public sphere'. As regards policy debates about the media, Christians should challenge the policy framework of economic liberalism and advocate a renewed social democratic framework instead. As far as education is concerned, Ian Barns sees exciting possibilities of a greater array of learning resources, a move to more flexible interdisciplinary practices, teachers becoming facilitators rather than instructors, and schools becoming open-learning centres. But all of these developments need to be framed by a richer vision of person-in-community, a vision which Ian Barns says that Christianity provides and in which purpose is found in 'the trinitarian love of God'.

Both these chapters challenge dominant and often unquestioned paradigms. Both Brian Hill (more implicitly) and Ian Barns (very explicitly) find that the Christian worldview provides an alternative framework. Ian Barns, in ways that chime in particularly with Luke Bretherton's earlier chapter on communicating with young people, finds the Christian doctrine of the Trinity a powerful focus and motivation to transforming, leavening activity. Worldviews, Christian constants in a changing world, vision, relationships and love? Yes, they are all there. Perhaps the changing world and the possibilities of change for good or evil are the themes that come across most strongly as we look into tomorrow's world.

12

Evaluating the school paradigm: curriculum for life?

Brian V. Hill

Schooling is a particular way of handling the task of education, with both strengths and limitations. Despite the fact that the Bible has nothing to say about schools, the Christian church has invested vast resources in them and has extended the paradigm to 'Sunday schools' and 'home schooling'. Such strategies underestimate the deterrent effect of compulsion on attempts to inculcate beliefs and values. Christians must reinstate other educative contexts as well, especially such biblical models as discipleship, peer sharing and intergenerational learning. Schools will continue to be potentially helpful in developing basic skills, cultural understanding and critical thinking.

There is nothing given, or value-neutral, about schooling. For all but two centuries of the human story, it was a resource available only to the privileged few. It cannot therefore be considered inevitable that we should handle learning in this way. Schooling is, in fact, a highly structured social institution of a particularly invasive kind.

By the end of the nineteenth century, most countries in Western Europe and North America had made schooling compulsory for all children aged roughly six to fourteen. In many places the age limits have since been extended in both directions. It was then, and continues to be, a massive interventionist strategy. All this places a heavy burden of proof on those who insist that it is necessary. We had better be very sure we have got it right.

Christians in particular, as people concerned to seed the values of the kingdom of God in society, need to be alert to the implications of the schooling paradigm, not least because much research suggests that it is at the level of values education that the paradigm is weakest. Yet great energy and vast resources have been invested in church schools and, in the last two centuries, Sunday schools.

All this is despite the fact that there is nothing in the Bible about schooling (see Hill 1982: 75-76). It does, of course, say a great deal about teaching and learning. But these are not synonymous with schooling. There are other ways in which both can and do occur. It is therefore urgent that Christians re-evaluate their attachment to the schooling paradigm.

The schooling paradigm

It is important, for the sake of what follows, to clarify how the phrase 'the schooling paradigm' is being used. Two points need to be made.

First, the phrase needs to be defended from the criticism that it is simply a piece of pretentious jargon, easily replaced by the single word 'schooling'. On the contrary, the word 'paradigm' implies a particular mindset and way of doing things.

We owe to Thomas Kuhn (1970) the realization that conceptual frameworks, in any domain, are never direct reports of the aspects of reality they purport to describe, but mental simplifications based on beliefs about the underlying nature of those aspects. These accounts can be so general and persuasive, as in the case of the Newtonian paradigm in physics, that we think they are obvious 'fact'. The illusion is dispelled when our unexamined assumptions are successfully challenged. This is what must happen in regard to the schooling idea.

Schools have been with us from earliest recorded times, but only recently have they come to be regarded as the prime agency of education, and made mandatory for all children. One effect of this has been to denigrate other agencies which formerly provided important learning experiences, such as the family, the master–apprentice relationship, discipling, private tutoring, voluntary interest and service groups, and travel.

Those who are locked in to the schooling paradigm see such avenues of learning as untidy, amateurish and miseducative. And they often are. For such people, education at best *is* schooling, because schools are best able to control the process. 'Control' is a key word here. We think of schools primarily as educational sites. But schools are also instruments of social control, as typified in the first instance by the requirement that all children shall attend them. Any analysis of what schools are doing must therefore include attention to the social functions and power relations associated with them. These elements are as intrinsic to the schooling paradigm as the educational purposes. They can even have an inhibiting effect on the realization of the latter.

It is important to be aware of these potential conflicts when we consider the criteria most commonly associated with the schooling paradigm. The paradigm is characterized by the presentation and assessment of a compulsory curriculum by professionally trained teachers, working with graded class groupings on sites designated 'educational'.

Sites of schooling

Secondly, the schooling paradigm embraces not only places specifically called 'schools' but, given the defining characteristics we have just identified, other institutions of formal education, such as colleges and universities. To the extent that they fulfil these conditions, they too are operating within the paradigm.

Christians and schooling

As was noted earlier, the Christian churches have long had a stake in the schooling paradigm. They entered the field from the fourth century of the Christian era (Judge 1966), though primarily using schools and universities for the education of a leadership élite. It was in the Reformation that the ideal of universal schooling came fully into focus, and thereafter philanthropic agencies in both the Protestant and Catholic sectors laboured to enfranchize the masses.

Governments, in general, were reluctant to take on this responsibility until the Industrial Revolution destroyed the stability of the domestic system of home-based manufacture, and the opportunities for family life and vocational learning which were built into it. The churches alone could not meet the new needs of the dispossessed masses, and governments now conceded that universal schooling was in the state's interest.

Today, in every country, state systems outstrip private provision. What Connell (1980) admiringly describes as the 'western schooling model' has been fervently embraced not only in the West but also in Asian and Third World countries. This has not led to a reduction of the energy and resources invested in the schooling paradigm by the churches. Not only do church schools dominate the sizeable non-government sectors that one finds in most western countries, but theological training and Sunday schools also draw strength from the general paradigm, and schooling is still one of the services which go hand in hand with cross-cultural missionary effort.

Consorting paradigms

Meanwhile, two other paradigms are currently affecting the way we perceive the task of schooling. One is the paradigm of 'scientific' educational assessment, discussed in chapter 8. It has had a lot to do with keeping the emphasis on social priorities rather than personal development. The pity of it is that we live in competitive societies in which the distribution of rewards is markedly unequal, and educational grades are widely used to deny many people a fair quality of life.

This prostitution of educational purposes has been reinforced by that other recently ascendant paradigm, economic rationalism. In many countries, a managerialist discourse has been imposed on educational systems. In this discourse, the student becomes the raw material, the curriculum a manufacturing process, and vocational competencies the product.[1] Similarly, examinations are viewed as quality assurance mechanisms for ensuring that the product will contribute to the national interest (see Hill 1993; Hukins 1993).

Nothing could be better suited to the realization of the objectives of both 'scientific' assessment and economic rationalism than the social instrument of schooling. It is tailor-made for the exercise of social control. Christians who perceive other, more person-centred possibilities in this instrument must strive to counter the inimical effects of the school culture. This requires that we have a more realistic appreciation of what it is, and is not, possible to achieve through schooling.

Scope and limits of schooling

Achievements

First let it be said that universal schooling has contributed significantly to the general uplift of the masses. It has helped them to understand the modern world in which they must survive and brought useful knowledge and skills within the reach of most children. It has also somewhat reduced their fears of ethnic difference in increasingly multicultural communities. It has given them access to a workforce requiring minimal levels of competence which most could not have obtained in any other way. It has widened their options for leisure. And it has empowered them to exercise more discerningly whatever political freedoms are available to them.

Ironically, though many of the power-brokers who supported the introduction of compulsory education did so in the interests of economic productivity and social control, the net effect was to raise the general level of consciousness and change the power structures of society. As Wardle (1974: 151) puts it, while authorities often perceived schools to be 'defenders of the status quo, one of the principal results of their efforts was to raise their pupils' levels of aspiration, while they conspicuously failed to prevent them from questioning the social and political establishment'. Similarly, the Swedish educator Torsten Husen (1979) has deduced from comparative international statistics that the more societies have become schooled, the more their citizens have become involved in the processes of democratic decision-making, social critique and community action.

Criticisms

Such testimonies notwithstanding, telling criticisms have been lodged against the schooling paradigm. One of the best-known critiques is Illich's *Deschooling Society* (1970). As a Christian, Illich was reacting with the passion of a prophet to exploitative practices in Third World countries, and sometimes he overstates his case – a trait that may perhaps be forgiven in the prophet, but not in the scholar.

201

Illich exposed important limitations in the schooling paradigm. He saw it as an essentially middle-class and upper-class instrument, confirming social inequalities and further disempowering the lower classes by eroding their self-reliance and turning them into dependants and consumers of more education and material goods.

Neo-Marxist critics like Marcuse (1964) have gone further in arguing that the paradigm has been a deliberate ploy of political-industrial élites to domesticate the rising generation; in effect, to nurture a false consciousness which gives them a sense of freedom while preventing them from seeing how they are being exploited and 'kept in their place'. But far from wanting to abolish the paradigm, neo-Marxists seek to subvert it to their own purposes in order to upset the capitalist *status quo* (Sarup 1979).

Another irony is to be noted. The way neo-Marxists talk about schooling is not dissimilar from the attitude of some of the defenders of Christian schools. The basic assumption in each case is that the self is socially constructed, therefore schooling is the best way to guarantee the desired outcome. In some Christian schools, this sets at a discount the individual's right and responsibility to make an informed choice about allegiance to Christ.

Empirical considerations

The schooling paradigm must be reassessed at both the empirical and the ethical levels, as I have attempted to do in several other places (*e.g.* Hill 1990: 22–28). Space will allow here only a brief synopsis.

First, the empirical evidence[2] suggests that the compulsory classroom environment as such is poorly adapted to bringing about attitude change. It can facilitate the learning of facts, processes and concepts, and it can encourage the development of skills of critical thinking, empathy, problem-solving, communication and negotiation. But in the matter of securing commitment to specific values, it is continually outflanked by the home, the peer group, the media, and other outside influences.

Why should this be so? After all, many hours of a child's day are invested in schooling. And some schools do in fact appear to achieve a great deal in this area. In these cases, however, it generally turns out that they are schools where the values of the school mirror closely the primary nurturing influences in the life of the child, and the main credit for the values embraced should go to them, not to the school.[3]

But even where the match between home and school is closest – indeed, sometimes because of it – there can be a perplexing level of nonconformity in graduating students, depending on the degree of pressure to conform which has been applied within the school. This pressure may occur through school rules, teacher coercion, presumptive teacher language (Mavor 1985), group pressure, compulsory acts of commitment, formal assessment of values, and so on.

When human beings, however young, sense that they are being manipulated – even, supposedly, for their own good – they can and do frequently resist. They are far from being totally plastic. If this violation of private space is continual, then they can become seriously alienated from the process (see *e.g.* Fensham *et al.* 1986 and Blishen 1969).

There is increasing evidence that a serious degree of alienation is affecting not just the low achievers and children from ethnic minority groups, who might have been expected to resent the put-downs they so often experience in school, but even those who have coped well with the system and shown a capacity to achieve at a high level (Collins and Hughes 1982).

Ethical considerations

But even if more sophisticated educational theory could equip us with ways of overcoming the empirical hurdles we have just been considering, there would remain the ethical question of whether we should even try. The hinge of the problem is the propriety of applying pressure for value change in the context of compulsory instruction. It is one thing to seize this opportunity to improve the *capacities* of students to think, feel and act. It is another to pre-empt their right to choose which values they will *commit* themselves to.[4]

Stated in this form, the problem may seem abstract and even pedantic. But it bears heavily on the question of what views of human nature guide the teaching process. Christians must take very seriously the biblical view that God has given us powers of reason and will which enable us, potentially, to interrogate our cultural conditioning and arrive at our own value commitments. In the Scriptures we constantly see him challenging people to do just this.

The other side of this coin is that God will hold us accountable for the choices we make. But those who try to forestall the child's exercise of a potentially deviant choice in these matters – with the best of motives, no doubt – by using conditioning, indoctrination, or such other kinds of manipulation as were mentioned earlier, are stunting this capacity, and will themselves be held accountable by God for their presumption.

It is also important to appreciate that educational sites such as schools are far from value-neutral. Values govern decisions at every point, particularly about what shall be included in the curriculum and how it shall be taught. To put it more bluntly, sites of formal education inevitably control to some extent the access of students to the forms of discourse which characterize modern society, and by the way they do so are frequently guilty of subordinating the individual to the collective or the cause.

In general, schools do a good service to students in introducing them to many useful discourses. But once we rid ourselves of the notion that a select number of academic disciplines constitutes a neutral exposure to culture (whose culture? for whose benefit?), then we are better able to appreciate that curriculum selection and choice of teaching methods are political acts, and there is a great difference between studies which domesticate and studies which empower.

Jesus as model

How ought Christians to react to these ethical points of order? A first step is to review the model of teaching presented by Jesus. Significantly, he never taught within the schooling paradigm, and had nothing to say about it. But he did set an example of a teacher concerned for his student's best interests.

Consistent with this concern, he saw a need to inform people of the values of his kingdom through a variety of teaching strategies, ranging from parables and homilies to his own personal example. He also acknowledged the status and potential of children, and warned against violating their integrity (e.g. Mark 9:36–42). With enquirers, he was exceptionally scrupulous about ensuring that they understood their options and were not stampeded by his charisma into making commitments they had not thought through (see Hill 1985: 30–31). He actively discouraged 'impulse buying', and withdrew from situations where crowd psychology could have won him a swarm of followers (e.g. John 6:15).

The high value that Jesus set on raising people's consciousness and respecting their right and obligation to choose for themselves the way that they would go becomes our guiding beacon. It explains why the blunt social instrument of schooling so often encounters resistance in learners. Jesus' example restrains us from attempting to treat them as pawns in a greater game, whether played by modern society or by the faith community.

Many consequences flow from these observations. They provide reasons for Christian people to get involved in educational policy at all levels in our society, including participation on school councils and local education committees. They also provide criteria for judging the motives of those who espouse Christian schools. And they challenge us to re-evaluate our investment in the schooling paradigm for such purposes as the training of pastors and the nurture of the young in faith.

In regard to Christian schools, some writers give the impression that the Bible requires believers to espouse them. This often forestalls further debate about the validity of what goes on within them. But the Bible actually has nothing to say about schooling as such, and we are left to develop arguments that draw on more general biblical principles and cultural analyses.

I have sought to discuss these issues at length elsewhere (*e.g.* Hill 1985, chapter 4, and 1987). But to take one example: if, say, a Christian school is established primarily for evangelistic purposes, and the curriculum is heavily censored to exclude all discourse unfavourable to, or critical of, Christian values, then students will be ill equipped to understand the world in which they are expected to bear testimony, and their free choice of Christ's way will have been pre-empted. In both respects, the worst features of the schooling paradigm will have been exploited – that is, the control of access to educationally relevant discourses, and the manipulation of a 'captive audience'.

This is not to say that Christian schools cannot also be examples of the best features of the schooling paradigm, if the previous points of order have been taken. Some are in fact exemplary models of open education and pastoral care. Many biblical principles can guide us in humanizing the paradigm (as they also help Christians working in the state sector to moderate its theory and practice). My point is that we have to think these things through very carefully, because the schooling paradigm is not native to Scripture, and has the power to subvert our best intentions.

Looking inward, we are also obliged to ask ourselves whether the

Sunday-school idea adequately reflects the familial models of nurture in Scripture, and whether there may not in fact be evidence of that same phenomenon of alienation about which we spoke earlier in relation to schooling in general (see Westerhoff 1976 and Hill 1985: 45-48). In many churches, not only are Sunday-school classes getting smaller, but the drop-out rate in the adolescent years is almost total. By then they have had enough of the schooling paradigm, and they opt out as soon as possible.

Other educational paradigms

Having expressed so many reservations about the popular attachment to the schooling paradigm in church and society, it is appropriate at this point to go into a little more detail about some of the alternative teaching-learning paradigms which exist.

Modifications of the schooling paradigm

On a sliding scale it is useful to begin with strategies which are merely modifications of the schooling paradigm, rather than departures from it. In this category fall 'schools without walls' and home schooling.

The most notable example of 'school without walls' was the experiment by that name in Philadelphia (see Bremer 1971). Influenced by the 1960's debate about free schooling and deschooling, its proponents sought to reduce some of the institutionalism of the traditional model by having a minimal site for administrative purposes, while for most of the school day the students commuted between community and work sites offering a variety of learning experiences through observation and participation.

This pattern succeeded to some extent in breaking down the age-segregation of the traditional model, and achieving greater life-relatedness in learning because of the community sites chosen. Other features of the basic paradigm remained intact, however; notably compulsory attendance, curriculum and assessment. In addition, it was found over time that a more substantial central site was needed. The experiment served mostly to show how some of the isolation and segregationism of the traditional school can be usefully mitigated.

Home schooling has two histories, both emerging from the ferment of the 1960s. In the first case liberal intellectuals who deplored the regimentation and perceived poor standards of the state schools moved to develop resources for learning in the home, encouraged by critics like John Holt (*e.g.* 1971). In the second case, many conservative Christians who had left state schools to lend their support to the burgeoning number of Christian schools, became dissatisfied with them in turn, and elected to home-school, using Christian resources developed for this purpose, such as those of the 'Accelerated Christian Education' movement.[5]

In both cases, the expenditure of parental time, and the need for parents to have relatively high income and educational levels, suggest that this could never meet the needs of the poor. Proponents, however, make much of the fact that learning can proceed at the child's own pace, and the child is encouraged to become more self-reliant.

It is relevant to note that biblical admonitions concerning the direct nurturing responsibilities of parents did not relate to the range of studies associated today with general and vocational education, but specifically to moral and religious nurture, caught as much as taught through the common experiences (and parental commentary) shared by the family (*e.g.* Deuteronomy 6:4–9).

Workplace experience

A different paradigm is at work when learning occurs directly in the workplace. The centuries-old pattern of apprenticeship placed young people under master tradespeople to learn on the job, alternating specific skill instruction with observation and practice.

In the twentieth century, however, this kind of learning has been progressively relocated on educational sites, initially in state schools, then in technical colleges. More recently again, the need for experience in the workplace has been reasserted, on the grounds that school graduates, and lower achievers in particular, have not been adequately prepared to enter the workforce. This latter trend is worthy of Christian support, to the extent that it affirms the dignity of work, and can increase the individual's chances of employment if done well.

Voluntary contexts

Activities that are truly voluntary, in the sense that learners choose to enter into them, choose whether to remain, and are able to nominate the kinds of teaching they desire, create a totally different learning climate from the foregoing. The classic examples are interest groups run by volunteers. These range from sporting and hobby groups to groups with spiritual and community service orientations.

Some may even occur on school premises, in what is too often demeaningly referred to as 'extra-curricular time'. They are to be encouraged, though not if this means that the school is filling its students' free time with activities that are all school-based. It is desirable that the school also endorse, and encourage participation in, community-based activities. Nevertheless, the school is the first port of call for all youth in the community, and voluntary groups in the school can be a bridge to similar groups in the wider community.

The genius of the voluntary group is that it is free to commend the values for which it stands, and to invite the participants further into the kind of commitment it represents, in ways that would be a trespass in the compulsory curriculum. Its leaders cannot coerce, but that makes their influence all the greater, if their own personal commitment rings true. For these reasons, churches and parachurch organizations have much to offer, to the community as well as to their own young people, especially through Christian youth groups, task-forces and camps.

Learning exchanges – the internet

One of the concepts advocated in Illich's *Deschooling Society* was that of the 'learning exchange'. Illich's argument was that learners should be encouraged to identify for themselves what they needed to know, and then be given access to a network on which they could locate an expert willing to tutor them. In some countries this idea was taken up through community education centres catering for adults, but it was hardly a viable option for young children. The principle of encouraging self-reliant, self-nominated learning is commendable; the means of obtaining help is not practicable for everybody.

The idea takes on new life, however, with the emergence in recent times of the internet, available (for a fee) to anyone with a computer and modem. Although it is alarmingly easy to call up pornography or criminal data, the attempt to debar our children from access to the bulletin boards, texts and other documents now so numerous on the net would be like Canute trying to arrest the tide. In any case, these also include many superb resources for useful learning, including Christian resources. Moreover, great advances in interactive computer learning guarantee greater interest and engagement than can be found in many classrooms!

Some commentators have suggested that the development of the net will so transform the possibilities of computer-aided learning that schools will wither away. This is unlikely in the foreseeable future, if only because schooling serves a variety of legitimate purposes including social control and the enhancement of social skills as well as those functions which computer-aided learning might subsume. In any case, this is not likely to be a solution for schools in disadvantaged areas and countries because of the costs involved, raising issues of social justice that should concern Christians.

Another reason exists for maintaining the schooling paradigm. Schools continue to be ideal sites for the development of the critical faculties which will afford some protection against the wiles of the new technology. Computer awareness – or what we may call 'computeracy' – has become one of the basics, as essential to survival in the networked society as literacy. And like literacy, it requires that one should get beyond a basic skill level to a level of critical appropriation, so that one can resist users who have an interest in exploiting us.

The way forward

In sum, what is the way forward? Has the schooling paradigm a place? We have noted a wide range of educational benefits which schooling can make available to every child. But it cannot be assumed that any particular configuration utilizing the schooling paradigm – whether government, Christian or home-based – will have a monopoly on right answers. This, incidentally, is a reason for resisting legislation which would outlaw any one of these alternatives.

The moral of the story is neither to put all our educational eggs in this particular basket, nor to throw the basket away. That is, our theory of education should accommodate a range of complementary educational sites, including not only schools but those sites which encourage *voluntary* participation in worthy learning activities. It is encouraging, for example, to review the distinguished record of Christian involvement in the youth service. Such involvements must be woven more deliberately into our views of both education and Christian nurture.

NOTES

1 If the analogy were fully applied, the student would also have to be considered a consumer and a product. But the basic paradigm cancels out both possibilities by treating the student as a means to extrinsic ends. For example, the consumers who matter are those who will benefit from the student's competencies. Similarly, preoccupation with the stockpile of competencies emerging from the process results in a disregard for the integration of that developing self which is more than the sum of the competencies it can call on.

2 See, for instance, the summaries of research in Hurn (1978) and Musgrave (1988) esp. pp. 64-65.

3 A case forcefully argued by Musgrove (1966).

4 I have encountered opposition to this way of representing the issue. The ethical point is that we may reasonably lay down rules of behaviour which reflect values we desire to promote (and every school should make explicit the values charter within which it is operating), but we may neither assume that external behaviour equals internal commitment, nor include tests for such commitment in assessing students for grading purposes. That is a misuse of our power to compel.

5 I have discussed this further in Hill (1987: 26-29, 68).

BIBLIOGRAPHY

Blishen, Edward (1969), *The School that I'd Like* (Harmondsworth: Penguin).

Bremer, John (1971), *The School without Walls: Philadelphia's Parkway Program* (New York: Holt, Rinehart and Winston).

Collins, C. W., and Hughes, P. (1982), *Where Junior Secondary Schools are Heading* (Melbourne: Australian Council for Educational Research).

Connell, W. F. (1980), *A History of Education in the Twentieth Century World* (Canberra: Curriculum Development Centre).

Fensham, P., Power, C., Tripp, D., and Kemmis, S. (1986), *Alienation from Schooling* (London: Routledge and Kegan Paul).

Hill, Brian V. (1982), *Faith at the Blackboard* (Grand Rapids: Eerdmans).

—— (1985), *The Greening of Christian Education* (Sydney: Lancer).

—— (1987), *Choosing the Right School* (Sydney: ATCF Publishers).

—— (1990), *That They May Learn* (Exeter: Paternoster).

—— (1993), 'Quality Goods for the Clients of Schooling', *Journal of Christian Education* 36/1 (April): 23-38.

Holt, John (1971), *The Underachieving School* (Harmondsworth: Penguin).

Hukins, Austin (ed.) (1993), *Educating for Profit? People-Centred Education in a Market-Driven Age* (Sydney: ATCF Books).

Hurn, Christopher J. (1978), *The Limits and Possibilities of Schooling* (Boston, MA: Allyn and Bacon).

Husen, Torsten (1979), *The School in Question: A Comparative Study of the School and its Future in Western Societies* (Oxford: Oxford University Press).

Illich, Ivan (1970), *Deschooling Society* (New York: Harper and Row).

Judge, E. A. (1966), 'The Conflict of Educational Aims in New Testament Thought', *Journal of Christian Education* 9/1 (June): 32–45.

Kuhn, T. S. (1970), *The Structure of Scientific Revolutions* (Chicago: University of Chicago Press).

Marcuse, Herbert (1964), *One-Dimensional Man* (Boston, MA: Beacon).

Mavor, Ian *et al.* (1985), 'The Language of Religious Education Teachers', *Journal of Christian Education* Papers 83 (July): 5-12.

Musgrave, P. W. (1988), *Socializing Contexts* (London: Allen and Unwin).

Musgrove, Frank (1966), *The Family, Education and Society* (London: Routledge and Kegan Paul).

Sarup, Nadan (1979), *Marxism in Education* (London: Routledge and Kegan Paul).

Wardle, David (1974), *The Rise of the Schooled Society: The History of Formal Schooling in England* (London: Routledge and Kegan Paul).

Westerhoff III, John H. (1976), *Will our Children have Faith?* (New York: Seabury).

13

Harnessing the media

Ian Barns

The new media technologies are not merely powerful tools whose use or misuse have powerful impacts on society. They also arise out of and extend an existing cultural framework of liberal capitalist modernity. Despite the promise that the new media will enhance personal freedom, at a deeper level they are more likely to erode identity and community further. A Christian response to the new media should involve theological reflection on the Christian sources of modernity and a recovery of the vision of God as Trinity and the embodiment of this vision in the communicative practices of Christian community. Such practices provide a basis for re-framing media policies and technologies, particularly at the various levels of educational policy and practice: classrooms, schools and education systems.

For most people living in modern societies, the mass media have been an important, though largely taken-for-granted, part of everyday life, providing easy access to news and entertainment, and a sense of participating in the dramas of a wider world. Many of the images and icons of television and the cinema have framed our lives, subtly shaping our personal and collective visions of the world. Yet with the introduction of new information and communications technologies this familiar media world is undergoing a process of dramatic change. In just a short time we have become used to mobile phones, fax machines, computers, e-mail, bulletin boards, CD-ROMs, video conferencing, desktop publishing, telecommuting and interactive video games: devices which offer us greater creativity, productivity, access to information, and 'networking' opportunities.

These devices are, it seems, just a taste of what is to come. The promise is that over the next decade or so the process of 'digital convergence' will merge our television sets, our computers and our telephones to create interactive multimedia sets giving us easy access (via the electronic superhighway) to a wide variety of information, entertainment, education and opinion. A few taps on our keyboard (and not forgetting the passwords and a paid-up account) will take us, electronically speaking, just about anywhere we want to go: shopping, banking, a visit to the library, a browse through our favourite newspapers or magazines, viewing the latest movie releases, a few minutes in a video-game centre, or a chat with friends.

On the surface these new technologies will simply extend the capacities of our televisions, newspapers, telephones and computers. At a deeper level, however, they will transform the 'communication infrastructure' of modern societies by creating a single world of 'digital video communication' (Lennie 1993). Many commentators predict that the social changes brought about by this new information order will be as profound as those flowing from the introduction of the printing press in the fifteenth century.

The media, both the existing mass media as well as the emerging interactive media, have of course been the subject of much public discussion, particular with respect to how they should be regulated. While the new technologies open up exciting possibilities for greater information access and interactive communication, there are concerns about their potential regressive effects, such as the emergence of divisions between the 'information rich' and the 'information poor', the misuse of databases by governments and companies, and the exploitation of the information superhighway by criminals, drug pushers, paedophiles and the like.

The purpose of this chapter is to consider some of the implications for education of this changing media environment. In previous chapters various authors outlined a vision of education centred on the moral formation of 'persons in community', a vision much richer than that which currently applies in a secular liberal society. The media, both mass and interactive, are important contexts for the outworking of any educational vision. What challenges are posed by the emerging new information order? Will it create a more favourable environment for more explicitly value-based forms of education? Or will it make the formation of persons in community even more difficult than is presently the case?

A central theme of the chapter is that in responding to the challenges of the media we need to go beyond the instrumentalist understanding of media technologies assumed in most public debates. As Winner (1986) has argued, technologies are not just tools which expand our instrumental powers for good or for ill. They are also forms of life. As technologies diffuse through social life they reshape the practices that constitute us as persons and communities. We thus need to be able to 'read' as well as regulate our technologies, to interpret the ways in which they embody particular visions of nature, persons, society and God.

We also need to recognize that technologies do not simply emerge out of research laboratories and then have 'impacts' upon society. Technologies are developed within an existing 'cultural frame', which creates the needs and possibilities for innovation. In other words, technologies are cultural products. Yet they are also cultural experiments. As technologies diffuse through society, they are adapted in often quite unanticipated ways, enabling relatively novel forms of human community and personhood.

The specific task of this chapter is to develop an interpretation – a 'reading' – of media practices and the cultural frame they express in relation to the richer vision of education outlined earlier in this volume. In the first section, I discuss the ways in which media technologies re-shape the 'communicative practices' which are central to our formation as persons and communities. I argue that media technologies express the cultural frame of liberal capitalist modernity, a framework which is grounded in the secular Enlightenment vision of person, nature and society. Secondly, I argue that this crisis of modernity is fundamentally theological in nature, a consequence of the displacement of the (misrepresented) Christian God. In the final section, I briefly explore the implications of a trinitarian conception of human community for media-policy debates and media innovations in educational practice.

Media technologies and the cultural contradictions of liberal modernity

People in modern societies learn very quickly how to use and to 'read' novel technological devices. Yet as S. Hill (1988) has pointed out, the instrumental function and cultural meanings of such devices are by no means transparent. Observing their 'strangeness' in pre-modern societies shows how culturally well-equipped moderns are to make sense of new technologies. Hill describes this as a process of 'cultural alignment'. At the same time, as we incorporate them into our everyday lives (and perhaps more importantly, as they are applied to the wider infrastructure of society), these technologies also reshape our practices, and hence the kind of people we are.

Media technologies are especially important in shaping persons and communities because of the way they affect our forms of communication, including the forms of languages we use. Most people consider the developments of media technologies over the last 200 years to have been generally positive. Newspapers, magazines, radio and television have increased our abilities to participate (albeit vicariously) in a wider range of experiences. Through them we learn to see ourselves as part of larger regional, national and global communities. In particular, the mass media have been important in the emergence of a 'public sphere' which has done much to make the processes of government more democratic and accountable (Habermas 1989).

At the same time, media technologies have changed our communication practices in ways that have eroded human identity and community. The negative cultural effects of the mass media have of course been the subject of much scholarly discussion (Poster 1994). One influential argument has been that the mass media are vehicles for the imposition of the dominant ideology of a ruling élite upon a largely passive public. This thesis has, however, been challenged in recent years. An alternative analysis has focused on the active and often subversive ways in which audiences in domestic environments respond to what they read, see and hear in the media (Morley 1990).

Whatever we make of the content of the mass media, media technologies have significantly changed the nature of public discourse. Some analysts have identified the 'meta-discourse' of television as one of 'commodification' in which the diversity of messages is inscribed within an overall code of consumption. Postman (1985) has argued that television, by virtue of its emphasis on image rather than word, has resulted in the 'demoralization' of discourse. The imagistic nature of television discourse has been compounded by the economic imperatives of television programming (*i.e.* ratings and advertising revenue), resulting in the dominance of the scoop, the soundbite, the photo-opportunity, and the obsession with celebrities. Others have argued that television has created a 'secondary reality'. Meyrowitz (1985) argues that television-viewing leads to a loss of 'sense of place', as the preoccupation with a televisual world results in a disengagement from the local. Baudrillard (1988) goes further, arguing that television draws us into what he calls the hyper-real world of simulacra.

How the new interactive technologies will affect the communicative practices of the existing mass media is not yet clear. Poster (1994) notes that it is possible that they will be used to intensify the present arrangements of the uni-directional mass media. He believes, however, that it is more likely that fundamental changes in communicative practices will occur, exemplified by the phenomenal growth of the internet. If this happens, the present restrictiveness of the uni-directional mass media will be reduced, enabling interaction within various 'virtual communities' (Rheingold 1993; Hartley 1994).

Unfortunately, it is also probable that the emerging interactive media practices will undermine the modern self even further. First, the fragmentation of mass media practices will further erode the 'public sphere' (Murdock 1992, 1993). Instead of the existing broadcast newspapers, television and radio which make possible some sense of common public culture, the new technologies may lead to more fragmented and privatized media worlds. The gains in private freedom and interactivity (see Hartley 1994) would be offset by the decline of the mass media as a 'public watchdog', keeping governments and corporations publicly accountable. Secondly, an encompassing electronic environment would reinforce the tendencies toward disengagement and disembodiment evident in the present mass media. Thirdly, long periods at the 'interface' may blur the sense of difference between human and machine (see Haraway 1987; Emberley 1989). Finally, participation in electronic virtual worlds using multiple (disembodied) persona may further a sense of embodied selfhood (Poster 1994).

Despite the novelty of the new media technologies, in fact they continue the cultural trajectory of modern industrial societies. As noted earlier, our cultural receptivity to such apparently strange devices reflects a deeper cultural alignment. Media technologies express the cultural frame of liberal capitalist modernity. Liberalism, as Arblaster (1984) observes, is the taken-for-granted intellectual air we breathe. The discourse of liberalism governs political, economic and social life, providing the language in which we understand the relationships between individuals, society, markets, states and communities. It expresses the worldview of the Enlightenment: an individualistic and instrumentalist view of human agency, the primacy of scientific reason, a faith in human social and economic progress, and an instrumentalist view of nature.

Liberalism has been an optimistic creed, providing the ideological framework for continuing technological innovation ('You can't stop progress ...'). In the heyday of industrial progress, it expressed a confident belief in social and economic progress through scientific discovery and technological innovation. Although chastened by the growing problems of the twentieth century, the liberal vision is still a widely shared faith (see Lasch 1991).

The deepening contradictions of modern techno-science, however, bring to the surface the inherent moral incoherence of the Enlightenment vision. Ecological problems expose an objectivist ontology which reduces nature to the stuff of domination. The creation of a pervasive technological environment undermines the autonomy and dignity of the liberal self. This is evident in a number of areas: in the instrumentalizing of persons in the marketing strategies of commerce; in the forms of technological intervention in high-tech biomedicine and genetics; and in the managerialist approaches of many areas of professional expertise (MacIntyre 1985 and Lasch 1984).

The crisis of liberal modernity has prompted various writers to reappraise its deeper philosophical sources. Taylor (1989) locates the root of the problem in the Cartesian notion of the disengaged self, acting instrumentally in relation to others and to the natural world. The idea of the autonomous, disengaged self has in the past provided a firm foundation for the ideals of human freedom and dignity, and for technological control over nature. Yet its long-term effect has been to undermine the deeper communal and relational sources of human selfhood.

In this context, then, the media represent a particularly important site for the unfolding of the cultural contradictions of modernity.

They make visible a brave new world of even more pervasive instrumental control, a world which fragments the self through a process
of further disengagement from bodiliness and a 'placed' community.

The crisis of modernity and rediscovering the God who is Trinity

The critique of liberal modernity developed by Taylor, MacIntyre and
others has been taken further by Colin Gunton (1993) who argues that
the crisis of modernity is theological, resulting from the displacement
of the (misrepresented) God of western Christianity. Gunton claims
that modernity originates in reaction against a 'Parmenidian' concept
of God which emphasized the 'oneness' of God at the expense of
diversity and difference. Even as it sought to make room for difference
and individuality, however, modernity reproduced the Parmenidian
'oneness' of western Christianity in the 'sameness' of liberal individualism. Modernity still lacks an adequate basis for personhood,
particularity and temporality, a lack reflected in the incoherence of
postmodernism.

While Gunton criticizes the secularity of western culture, suggesting that its healing requires a return to its theological sources, he also
acknowledges the partial legitimacy of the reaction against the Parmenidian God of western Christianity. To address the problem of
modernity he argues that we need to recover a truly trinitarian
understanding of God. As we recover a vision of God whose nature
is relational and communal, we will be able to bring together unity
and difference and to respect the created particularity, temporality and
diversity of the world in which we live.

Recovering the relational God in the life of Christian community
Yet how are we to relate this to the world of the media? We do so by
considering the embodiment of the vision of a trinitarian God in the
communicative life of Christian community. Following Hauerwas
(1981, 1991) and Yoder (1992), I argue that focusing on the church
does not mean a 'sectarian' turning away from the world. Instead it
is the authentic way of making Christian claims with respect to the
world. The task of the church is to be a paradigm for the whole world,
demonstrating in its communal life God's ultimate purposes for the

whole of humanity. It is through the recovery of Christian (*i.e.* trinitarian and relational) 'communicative practices' in the life of the church that the concrete implications of a trinitarian vision of God for the world of the media might be displayed.

The church as a people who respond to the communicating God

The Christian God is a communicating God. The Christian church is a people who come together in response to the one who has revealed himself to humankind. God's revelation is in the form of a story which tells of God's actions in human history, reaching back to include the creation of the heavens and the earth, and pointing forward to the glorious resurrection of all things. God's communication addresses us as persons, calling us into the interpersonal life of Christian community and ultimately into the trinitarian life of God (Zizioulas 1985). We are called to live by the same love and unity in difference that is the quality of God himself.

Incarnating the good news: the communicative practices of the church

What God has revealed about himself should therefore shape the communicative practices of a Christian community. All these practices ought to be marked by a quality of worship, responsive to the word of God and the ministry of the Spirit. Similarly they should be characterized by mutual love, communal solidarity and the expression of the diversity of individual gifts. The total life of a church should also be a 'hermeneutic of the gospel' (Newbigin 1989, 1991) before the watching world.

As Yoder (1992) observes, a culture of dialogical openness is foundational to Christian community. Rather than being shaped by the unquestioned authority of dogma or priest, a church led by the Spirit is one that fosters peaceable dialogue in which all are able to participate in communal deliberation upon the preached word of God. Moreover, the various practices discussed by Yoder (the exercise of restitutive moral discipline; the sharing of economic resources; the exercise of the diversity of gifts in the life of the community; and the processes of community deliberation) are not esoteric, religious activities, but ordinary communal practices which have been transformed by the rule of Christ. Thus as we embody the relational life of God in the practices of Christian community we model God's intention for the whole of humanity.

A dialogical community of character

The formation of a dialogical community does not happen naturally. It requires active 'discipling', by pastors, teachers and the like, to school us in the virtues of Christian community (Hauerwas 1991), to enable us to 'see' ourselves and the world in terms of Jesus' story and thus to apply Christian principles to specific situations in appropriate ways (Hauerwas 1988).

It is in the context of the face-to-face situations of congregational life that we learn the skills and virtues of godly communication: to listen to and to be heard by others, to be able to speak truthfully about ourselves, to be able to work through misunderstandings and conflicts, to be able to 'judge' that which is false, misleading and evil, and to exercise moral judgment in ways that honour God and the community (Yoder 1992).

Christian informational practices

This kind of 'community of character' provides the resources to respond Christianly to the challenges of the media. It is impracticable to try to specify how members of the community should or should not use the media. The issue is one of moral and spiritual discernment. This should go beyond regulating the use of the devices themselves to reflecting upon the stories they embody for us. The magic box in the living-room exercises a seductive power over us because of the stories it tells. Attending to these stories – including the stories they embody as devices (Morley 1990) – offers a more constructive way of dealing with the dilemmas of media usage. Containing the amount of sex and violence on television might be better approached by 'decoding' the wider stories they tell about human identity and relationships. Similarly the problems of children (or professionals) spending too much time on their computers may best be related back to the implicit communal stories such usage embodies.

A communicative presence within an information society

How can this vision of the communicative life of Christian community be applied to media issues in a secular, pluralist society? I shall focus on three key issues. To what extent and in what way should we try to institutionalize a specifically Christian vision of persons-in-community (and of media issues) within a secular society? How may we intervene in ongoing media-policy debates? How should we approach the implications of new media technologies for educational practices?

Reconstituting public-ness: the gospel and the public sphere

In a liberal society the beliefs and practices of various religions, including Christianity, are expected to be largely confined to the private sphere. It is assumed that public life should be governed by a religiously neutral proceduralism. This exclusion, however, contradicts the claim of the Christian gospel to represent not just a private spirituality but 'public truth' (Newbigin 1991). Yet is it either possible or desirable for the Christian church to try to recover the public dominance it once enjoyed in western society, especially since the relegation of religious belief to the private sphere seems to have created a culture of religious tolerance?

Briefly, I suggest that while Christians should continue to participate in public life in terms of the dominant languages of secular politics, economics and science, we ought not to accept uncritically the ruling secular notions of 'public-ness', or what Hauerwas (1994) calls the 'democratic policing of Christianity'. 'Public-ness' is an essentially contested term. What counts as the 'public sphere' in terms of both its scope (the public/private division) and its agenda, depends upon some larger, generally accepted 'fiduciary framework' (Newbigin 1991). As noted earlier, the fiduciary framework of western democracies is secular liberalism. A necessary part of recovering a vision of the gospel as public truth therefore is to challenge the liberal vision of a secular public sphere and to develop an alternative explicitly Christian concept of public-ness.

A gospel vision of public-ness rejects a sectarian impulse to withdraw from the world as an evil place. It also rejects the desire to impose a Christian worldview through a restored Christendom. Rather, it expresses the creative tension between the church and the world implicit in the gospel. With this distinction the world is not negated as a fallen human order from which we seek to be saved. Rather, it is reconstituted under the rule of Christ as a free space of

221

gospel proclamation: a 'public domain' where the good news of the kingdom might be freely proclaimed, freely heard – and freely rejected. Because of its vision of history the church should not aim to 'Christianize' the world by seeking to impose conformity to Christian belief and practice through legislation and regulation. The task of the church is to seek to maintain the openness of the world, such that the gospel can be freely proclaimed and demonstrated.

It is beyond the scope of this chapter to discuss in any detail what this means in terms of Christian involvement in public policy-making. In brief, such involvement should not be constrained by the spurious notion of the secular autonomy and neutrality of the public sphere. It should be based on the conviction that a genuine, dialogically open public sphere ultimately depends upon the leavening influence of Christian belief in shaping the ethos of social and public life, and in particular the ideals of citizenship and 'common good' which sustain public practices and public policy.

Christian participation in media-policy and information-policy debate

In the context of rapid technological change, policy debates about the media are of vital importance. The new technologies have enabled the emergence of a truly global economy, a development which has far-reaching implications for the nature of political and economic life within nation states (Reich 1991). Of particular importance is the information and communications sector itself. Already we are seeing the emergence of a global telecommunications order and the formation of a small number of powerful global telecommunications companies.

In what ways should the structure of ownership within the communications industry be regulated? How can the concentration of media power in the hands of a few major companies be resisted? How should access to the developing information superhighway be regulated? How can the privacy of citizens be protected from intrusion by governments, private companies and criminals? How can access by children to pornographic material be restricted? How can the public life and local culture of nations, regions and communities be preserved against the global reach of the global networks?

One critical contribution Christians can make is at the level of the policy frameworks shaping the development of media technologies. At present media innovations are occurring with a policy framework of free-market or economic liberalism. Most developed countries have followed the example of the United States in deregulating, corporatizing and privatizing their telecommunications sectors (Hills 1986) primarily in order to facilitate private-sector economic development. Unfortunately, this free-market policy framework has increased the risks of the further erosion of the public culture of the western democracies and an increasing concentration of media ownership in fewer – and less publicly accountable – hands.

The need to develop an alternative policy framework has been recognized by writers such as Cunningham (1992) and Murdock (1992), who advocate a renewed social democratic framework in which the values of the public sphere and citizenship are guiding principles. Yet even this does not address the deeper cultural implications of the new media technologies: the fragmentation of social life and the emergence of a 'postmodern' or hyper-modern culture (Borgmann 1992). Christians can make a distinctive contribution by raising these fundamental questions of selfhood and community and seeking to maintain the 'free spaces' of civil society within which people are able to use and to resist the pressures of the new technologies.

Media technologies and educational change

Education is an important 'site' where the culturally corrosive effects of the wider culture of liberal modernity are particularly visible and yet where the new technologies can also be re-framed by a communicative ethos derived from a trinitarian faith. Against the background of the powerful negative effects of modern media practices, my discussion in this final section is focused on the positive possibilities opened up by the new media technologies.

Educational practices are already being significantly affected by the new media technologies (Riel 1993). The media enable changes at various levels: in classroom practices, in the nature of schools, and in public education systems. In the short term it is likely that the new technologies will consolidate managerial control over educational practice (Marginson 1993). In the longer term, however, they create new opportunities for a much greater diversity of teaching and learning practices, forms of educational institutions and organization of public education.

At the level of classroom practice, the new media enable easy access to a greater array of learning resources. This has the potential to change the nature of formal learning, enabling a move away from the present teacher-centred disciplinary oriented practices, to more flexible, interdisciplinary practices in which students are more able to direct their own learning. The role of the teacher may become that of a facilitator rather than that of an instructor. There are exciting possibilities for redesigning curricula and making use of the media for problem-focused learning projects.

The new media may also change the nature and purpose of schools. The development of electronically delivered 'open learning' courses makes it more feasible for people to learn at home. Home-based students will have ready access to world-class learning materials via the information superhighway. These opportunities may make it easier for families and neighbourhood associations to develop their own 'schools'. The local school may become more of a 'learning centre' providing information and advice. Schools may thus begin to converge with other educational providers, such as libraries, health-centres and business organizations.

Changes in public education systems are also being catalysed by the new media technologies. The neo-liberal policy direction adopted by many governments has meant that education departments, like other public agencies, are becoming less the providers of services and more the regulators or facilitators of provision by private agencies. Thus education departments have devolved a great deal of responsibility (though not necessarily commensurate resources) to local schools and regional offices. In part, this is a reflection of the more 'post-Fordist' (see Harvey 1989) temper of public life, in which the provision of a standardized mass education has become less appropriate for the needs of a more diverse and pluralistic society. These trends may enable the schooling system to deliver a greater diversity of educational resources. It might encourage greater participation in continuing education. Yet unless the state provides adequate resources for the schools of the future, there are likely to be serious problems with respect to distributional equity, something which has been one of the most positive features of public education systems in the past.

Changes in educational practices and institutional arrangements will never be determined by the technologies as such. What are always determinative are the institutional and cultural frameworks within which they take place. To reiterate the underlying theme of this chapter: contemporary developments in media technologies largely extend the cultural trajectory of a liberal capitalist modernity with its ultimately corrosive effects on identity and community. What is crucial, therefore, is that at each of these levels the various measures for educational change be framed as much as possible by a richer vision of person-in-community: a vision which keeps open the question of what is a good person and a good society. At each of these levels it is important that the catalytic effect of the media will not be to close off the possibilities for hearing the word of God.

It is particularly important that the spaces of public life are not closed off in a more fragmented and dualistic education system which embodies the cultural logic of late modernity. There needs to be a continuing commitment on the part of the state to provide adequate resources for public education. Yet if the necessary resources are provided, the devolution of responsibility for the provision of education to an associational level may open up a system whose secularity has effectively excluded God. A devolution of educational responsibility to communities, families and neighbourhoods might also have the positive effect of deprofessionalizing education (see Lasch 1991). As in many other areas of life, the dominance of professional experts has resulted in the disempowerment of ordinary people. Finally, changing teaching and learning practices may make it possible to rediscover a sense of the moral and spiritual purposes of education: the formation of persons-in-community who find their purpose in the trinitarian love of God.

BIBLIOGRAPHY

Arblaster, A. (1984), 'The Foundations of Liberal Individualism', in *The Rise and Decline of Western Liberalism* (London: Basil Blackwell).

Baudrillard, J. (1988), *Selected Writings*, ed. M. Poster (Stanford: Stanford University Press): 217.

Borgmann, A. (1992), *Crossing the Postmodern Divide* (Chicago: Chicago University Press).

Cunningham, S. (1992), *Framing Culture: Criticism and Policy in Australia* (Sydney: Allen and Unwin).

Emberley, P. (1989), 'Places and Stories: The Challenge of Technology', *Social Research* 56/3 (Autumn): 741–785.

Gunton, C. (1993), *The One, The Three and the Many: God, Creation and the Culture of Modernity* (Cambridge: Cambridge University Press).

Habermas, J. (1989), *The Structural Transformation of the Public Sphere*, trans.

T. Burger (Cambridge, MA: MIT Press).

Haraway, D. (1987), 'A Manifesto for Cyborgs: Science, Technology and Socialist Feminism in the 1980s', *Australian Feminist Studies* 4 (Autumn): 1-42.

Hartley, J. (1994), 'Citizens of Media, Technologies of Readership', *Arena Journal* 3 (1994): 93-112.

Harvey, D. (1989), *The Condition of Postmodernity* (Cambridge: Polity Press).

Hauerwas, S. (1981), *A Community of Character: Toward a Constructive Christian Social Ethics* (Notre Dame: University of Notre Dame Press).

―― (1988), 'Reconciling the Practice of Reason: Casuistry in a Christian Context', in *Christian Existence Today: Essays on Church, World and Living In Between* (Durham: Labyrinth): 67-88.

―― (1991), *After Christendom? How the Church is to Behave if Freedom, Justice, and a Christian Nation are Bad Ideas* (Nashville: Abingdon).

―― (1994), 'The Democratic Policing of Christianity', in *Dispatches from the Front: Theological Engagements with the Secular* (Durham: Duke University Press): 91-106.

Hill, S. (1988), *The Tragedy of Technology: Human Liberation vs Domination in the Late Twentieth Century* (London: Pluto).

Hills, J. (1986), *Deregulating Telecoms: Competition and Control in the United States, Japan and Britain* (Westport, CN: Greenwood).

Lasch, C. (1984), *The Minimal Self: Psychic Survival in Troubled Times* (New York: Norton).

―― (1991), *The True and Only Heaven: Progress and Its Critics* (New York: Norton).

Lennie, J. (1993), 'Digital Video Communications in Australia', *Media Information Australia*, 67.

MacIntyre, A. (1985), *After Virtue: A Study in Moral Theory* (London: Duckworth, 2nd edn).

Marginson, S. (1993), *Education and Public Policy in Australia* (Cambridge: Cambridge University Press).

Marvin, C. (1988), *When Old Technologies were New: Thinking about Electric Communication in the Late Nineteenth Century* (New York: Oxford University Press).

Meyrowitz, J. (1985), *No Sense of Place: The Impact of Electronic Media on Social Behaviour* (New York: Oxford University Press).

Morley, D. (1990), 'Domestic Communication - Technologies and Meanings', *Media, Culture and Society* 12: 31-55.

Murdock, G. (1990), 'Redrawing the Map of the Communications Industries: Concentration and Ownership in the Era of Privatisation', in Marjorie Ferguson (ed.), *Public Communication: The New Imperatives* (London: Sage).

―― (1992), 'Citizens, Consumers and Public Culture', in M. Skovmand

and Kim Christian Schroder (eds.), *Media Cultures: Re-appraising Trans-national Media* (London: Routledge): 17–41.

—— (1993), 'Communications and the Constitution of Modernity', *Media, Culture and Society* 15: 521–539.

Newbigin, L. (1989), *The Gospel in a Pluralist Society* (Grand Rapids: Eerdmans).

—— (1991), *Truth to Tell: The Gospel as Public Truth* (Grand Rapids: Eerdmans).

Poster, M. (1990), *The Mode of Information* (Chicago: University of Chicago Press).

—— (1994), 'A Second Media Age?' *Arena Journal* 3: 49–91.

Postman, N. (1985), *Amusing Ourselves to Death: Public Discourse in the Age of Show Business* (New York: Viking Press).

Reich, R. (1991), *The Work of Nations: Preparing Ourselves for 21st-Century Capitalism* (New York: Knopf).

Riel, M. (1993), 'Global Education Through Learning Circles', in L. Harasim (ed.), *Global Networks: Computers and International Communication* (Cambridge, MA: MIT Press).

Rheingold, N. (1993), 'A Slice of Life in My Virtual Community', in L. Harasim (ed.), *Global Networks: Computers and International Communication* (Cambridge, MA: MIT Press).

Schiller, H. (1993), 'The "Information Highway": Public Way or Private Road?' *The Nation* (12 July): 64–66.

Silverstone, R., and Hirsch, E. (eds.) (1992) *Consuming Technologies: Media and Information in Domestic Spaces* (London: Routledge).

Springer, C. (1991), 'The Pleasure of the Interface', *Screen* 32/3 (Autumn): 303–323.

Taylor, C. (1989), *Sources of the Self: The Taking of the Modern Identity* (Cambridge: Harvard University Press).

Winner, L. (1986), *The Whale and the Reactor: A Search for Limits in an Age of High Technology* (Chicago: University of Chicago Press).

Yoder, J. (1992), *Body Politics: Five Practices of the Christian Community Before the Watching World* (Nashville: Discipleship Resources).

Zizioulas, J. D., (1985), *Being as Communion: Studies in Personhood and the Church* (London: Darton, Longman and Todd).

PART 6

CONTINUING
THE DIALOGUE

COMMENTARY

For this part of the book we invited four scholars (and friends) to reflect on and respond to the foregoing thirteen chapters in the light of their own theological and philosophical perspectives. One of them shares the evangelical outlook of the contributors, and his brief was to comment on the contents in the light of the preface at the beginning. The other three represent, respectively, another Christian tradition, a non-religious perspective and a non-Christian religious perspective.

Colin Chapman, writing as an evangelical, comments on the good example of the 'hermeneutical spiral' that he finds in the book as a whole. (He did not see the other three contributions to this part.) The process is as follows: questions arise out of education as it is; they are reflected upon within a wider social and cultural context; underlying philosophical presuppositions are engaged with and criticized; Christian theology and history are reflected upon; and a transformationalist strategy of persuasion is commended. Colin Chapman also lists some omissions from among the issues tackled: school worship, religious education as a subject, and direct treatment of arguments for and against Christian schools and of the role of the state in education. Finally, he looks forward to a book on how, in detail, the vision expressed in this book can be translated into educational programmes. It seems that we aimed to offer practical ways forward and that we may not have achieved as much as we might have done in this respect.

Jeff Astley questions the professed distinctiveness of the evangelical perspective from which the book comes. The apparent emphasis on general revelation is not usually as strong in traditional evangelicalism, and some of the latter's usual emphases seem muted in this book. One of these is individualism, which seems to be losing out to communitarianism. Jeff Astley cautions against an imbalance here. He also finds some of the contributions unduly hard on relativism and its 'unruly sibling', postmodernism. Both deserve more sympathy and more serious attention. Liberalism, too, may deserve more positive treatment than it receives in some of the chapters. Jeff Astley ends his chapter with an argument for a form of spiritual education which can be, but is not necessarily, explicitly Christian. This is a plea for a form of 'evangelical' conversionism.

Monica Taylor raises a more fundamental question as she asks why there is all the concern at this time about being distinctively Christian and even distinctively evangelically Christian. As she sees it, Christianity already has a very privileged place in British society and in its educational system, and she goes on to provide evidence for this claim. Admittedly, this influence has been largely from Christians of a more liberal tradition, but then, she says, liberals share many of the concerns voiced by the evangelical contributors to this book.

She finds the 'real thrust' of the book in its concern to oppose variously secularism, secular liberalism or secular liberal humanism, and an absence of religious faith. But to be secular is not to be value-free, and Monica Taylor finds many of the values advocated by the contributors to be human rather than distinctively Christian. Indeed, the contributors to the book seem to her to be quite unclear on a definition of what would constitute distinctively evangelical Christian education. More concrete examples would have been helpful.

Monica Taylor ends with a plea for a more positive response to 'cultural pluralism' than that which she finds in this book. Diversity of worldview and dialogue between perspectives are to be celebrated rather than merely tolerated. For this, a transformed values education is of central importance. The common school, rather than a plurality of denominational or faith-based schools, should provide a conducive environment for such an education. What we value is of greater importance than the philosophical justification of these values.

Professor Syed Ali Ashraf is the final contributor to this section. He gives rather more of an outline of an Islamic approach than a response to the contributions (see p. 295). He expresses himself to be strongly opposed to the secularistic worldviews that, in his view, dominate western education, and he is supportive of the 'reassertion of the religious concept of knowledge' that he finds in this book. He suggests some common beliefs and values that are shared by religious people but not by secularists.

Professor Ashraf is also content to have common schools provided that they give a central place to a form of religious education which nurtures religious sensibility and religiously based moral sensibility. This requires that it be taught by teachers who have faith and an understanding of these sensibilities. Alongside common schools of this kind, there should also be separate faith-based schools which have financial support from the state. Foundational to the curriculum of Islamic schools are the three basic kinds of relationship: with God, with other human beings and with external nature.

These four chapters come from very different perspectives and this is reflected in their contents. There are interesting points of agreement and disagreement among them. Both Colin Chapman and Monica Taylor note the absence of much on school worship and religious education, and both also comment on the lack of concrete examples of how to work it all out in practice. Monica Taylor and Syed Ali Ashraf both discern a strong anti-secularist thrust to the contributions, but their reactions to this and to the place of faith-based schools are a long way apart! Jeff Astley and Monica Taylor both question the claimed distinctiveness of evangelical Christian education as it is presented, and both seem to display a greater sympathy for qualified liberalism and qualified relativism and pluralism than they find in the book as a whole.

Several of the comments expressed in this section merit some response, and I shall attempt to provide this, along with some additional reflections, in the closing chapter.

14

Applying the evangelical Christian mind: a concluding reflection

Colin Chapman

Two features of the essays in this collection are particularly noteworthy to this observer. The first is that these educationalists with Christian convictions write with a complete absence of dogmatism. The second is that their method of 'doing' theology involves reflecting in the light of Christian Scripture and theology on burning issues which arise out of the context in which they work. They all believe that Christian assumptions can be translated into viable and worthwhile educational programmes. The issues of collective worship in schools and of religious education are not addressed directly. We look forward to seeing the dreams translated into actual educational programmes.

When I began to read these chapters some weeks ago, I thought I would be listening in on a rather private conversation between Christian educationists. By the end of my second reading I had realized that they had been talking not only to each other, but also to people outside their number – educationists of every faith and ideology, school governors, politicians, and (even more uncomfortably) to me as a parent, citizen and fellow Christian.

In commenting on their work I want first to make some observations on the spirit and tone of their writing, and then secondly to reflect on the method of doing theology which they have adopted with remarkable consistency. Thirdly, as an outsider who is not a member of the 'trade union', I will then no doubt betray my ignorance and prejudices by pointing out what appear to me to be some significant omissions, and finally end with some suggestions on work that remains to be done.

The spirit and tone of their writing

I have been struck by the complete absence of dogmatism. Here are Christians with strong personal beliefs, thoroughly immersed in the world of education, who recognize that there may not always be one and only one Christian view on educational issues, but are prepared to commend what they see as *a* Christian view. Their language is commendably free of religious jargon, because they have mastered the language in which such debate has to take place in the public sphere. They are painfully aware of mistakes made by Christians in the past, and conscious of the extent to which they are influenced by 'faith commitments ... and cultural patterns' (Smith, p. 35).

While they are united in their evangelical convictions, there is nothing sectarian or divisive about their approach. They attach a great deal of importance to Scripture; but their method of handling it is extremely open. Although there is one reference to theological liberals who cut the gospel off from its scriptural foundations (Elsdon, p. 183), I suspect that few Christians of other traditions would want to distance themselves from the theology of these authors.

Their critique of views with which they disagree is offered 'humbly and lovingly' (Thiessen, p. 176), while their own views are presented 'tentatively', with 'humility and open-mindedness' (Thiessen, p. 173). They recognize that Christian thinking on these issues needs to be 'worked out with fear and trembling' (Smith, p. 29). And all of them have clearly turned their backs on any world-denying pietism which demands withdrawal from the world, since they enthusiastically embrace 'the authentic way of making Christian claims with respect to the world' (Barns, p. 218).

Their method

One might have expected evangelical Christians of an earlier generation to start with statements of biblical and theological principles, and
then attempt to apply these principles in the world of education. What
we find instead is a perfect example of what has been called 'the
hermeneutical spiral'. They begin with questions arising out of their
context, and then reflect on these in the light of Christian Scripture,
theology and tradition before going on to offer their own positive
contribution. Working with this kind of method, it does not matter
in a sense at which point of the spiral they begin. But the important
thing is that there is no simple progression which starts with the Bible
and ends with clear and agreed Christian policies. It may be worth
commenting on this process in greater detail.

1. The *questions* they raise all arise out of education as it is at
present: *e.g.* the rationale for the common school as opposed to the
denominational or sectarian school, plurality and pluralism, the
content of the curriculum, the extent to which any curriculum can be
'Christian', the purpose of education, assessment and education, and
the effects of developing technology.

2. They reflect on these issues within the *wider social and cultural
context* of western societies, aware for example, of the special dynamics
of youth culture, and the huge ethical questions related to the care of
the environment and the future of the human race. There are
occasional references to wider political and economic factors which
impinge on education.

3. Almost every writer in one way or another engages with the
philosophical presuppositions underlying the theory and practice of much
education today, because they recognize that 'the crisis of modernity
is theological' (Barns, p. 218). They are prepared to 'take on the
assumptions of a secular world ... *and do it on secular ground*' (Elsdon,
p. 192). They do this by mounting a sustained critique of the
dominant secular liberal humanism. As we are reminded so graphi-
cally, 'the Enlightenment party' is over, and what we suffer from is
'the continuing hangover' (Smith, p. 35). While postmodernism
exposes the obvious failures of scientific rationalism, it is unable to
offer anything beyond 'a culture of uncertainty' (Deakin, p. 93).

The authors are not content, however, with purely negative criticism. They have something very positive to offer, because they speak

235

of alternative 'metaphysical starting-points from which to construct theories' (Jones, p. 110). They want to bring the recognition of different worldviews out into the open, instead of relegating them to the private world of individuals, and to acknowledge freely the close relationship between knowledge and belief. One writer even speaks about the possibility of developing 'a pragmatic consensus ... in a pluralistic world after Babel' (Thiessen, p. 175).

4. When we see the writers turning to reflect on *Christian Scripture, theology and history*, the questions that they bring have arisen out of immediate educational issues, and from the total context and assumptions which inform them. Perhaps it is here that we see the hermeneutical spiral working at its best. There is no hint of any attempt to find prooftexts in the Bible. Instead they recognize that 'we are left to develop arguments that draw in more general biblical principles and cultural analysis' (Hill, p. 205). So, for example, there is frequent appeal to the creation narrative in Genesis to undergird the Christian understanding of the individual person, the value of work, and the need for responsible care of the environment. It is suggested that the 'principles behind Pentateuchal laws can be reapplied' (Elsdon, p. 190). We are reminded of the voices of the Old Testament prophets 'calling into question the established structures' (Bretherton, p. 123). The person of Jesus is appealed to as a model of creative teaching methods (Hill, p. 204), and as an example of 'strength in weakness' (Bretherton, p. 124).

This approach to Scripture, therefore, calls for 'creativity on the part of Christians in working out the implications of the biblical story in all spheres of life' (Thiessen, p. 172). They are 'invited to indwell the biblical narrative, allowing its "longings of possibility" to become ours and to shape the way we look at and live in the world' (Smith, p. 30).

The distinctives of the Christian worldview are presented in ways that are immediately relevant to the issues. For example, the confidence that there is such a thing as truth, and that it may be possible to find something approaching truth, is based on the conviction that there is a God who wants to reveal himself and the nature of the world. The dignity and value of the individual person, the affirmation of both individualism and communalism, the capacity for critical rationality, for personal relationships and for work, and diversities of gifts – all of these are rooted in the idea of human beings made in the image of the trinitarian God. The incarnation is seen to speak, among other things, of the goodness of creation (Elsdon, p. 191) and the need for 'intimate involvement in culture and life' (Bretherton, p. 124). There is nothing abstract or theoretical, therefore, about the way Christian doctrine is discussed.

There is one period of Christian history – the Constantinian experiment – which is no doubt present in the minds of many of the writers, but is referred to explicitly only by Jonathan Chaplin. He rejects the idea of Christians' ever using coercion, believing that 'all attempts in history to coerce people into accepting the Christian faith, from Constantine onwards, have been illegitimate', and that 'the "Christian capital" we have inherited in Britain and others may have inherited in their own countries ... is at best partly the result of illegitimate coercion by our Christian forebears' (Chaplin, p. 63). A lot will depend here on how much is read into the word 'partly'! But this represents a bold contemporary reflection on centuries of Christian tradition in the light of present-day ethical sensitivities.

5. Working through these various stages enables the writers to work out their *strategies of persuasion*. Here we find that there is a very evident consensus among them. All set their faces against both abdication and confrontation, and several speak of their commitment to a 'transformationalist' stance (*e.g.* Chaplin, Deakin, Thiessen), which 'works from within ... to transform' (Thiessen, p. 175), using 'the leavening influence of Christian belief' (Barns, p. 222). They are optimistic that their Christian alternatives can lead to educational programmes that will lead to greater well-being for the individual and society.

It is interesting that while they are not entirely in agreement about the wisdom of separate Christian schools, several writers do agree on the principle of allowing state-funded Muslim schools.

It remains to be seen whether this kind of Christian voice will be powerful enough in persuading others to chart a new course. But it is impressive to see the writers looking forward creatively to new possibilities, and not calling for the recipes of the past.

Some omissions

The authors want to show that a Christian worldview encompasses the whole of life, and not only activities that are regarded as 'religious'. I was surprised, however, to find no reference at all to the question of public worship in schools. Is this an area in which we could be enabled to explore the strengths and weaknesses of the British formula which has attempted to make some kind of public worship mandatory in schools, and the American formula which has banished it completely?

Similarly the desire to avoid identifying a Christian approach to education with 'religious education' is both understandable and commendable. It is good to see questions about truth, meaning and value being raised in the context of any and every discipline. And Trevor Cooling points out that religious education is often taught 'within a horizon which makes committed faith seem inherently implausible' (see Smith, p. 28). But does this do away with the need to have a subject or subjects in which these kinds of questions are worked into the syllabus and not left to the special interests of individual teachers?

Since the pragmatic British seem to have an aversion to philosophy, very few school-leavers in Britain have any idea of what existentialism or postmodernism is all about. Their counterparts on the Continent, however, will often have been exposed to Kant, Hegel, Kierkegaard and Sartre. So *how* are the big philosophical questions to be raised in the classroom? If it is not in a discipline in the curriculum called 'religious education', 'moral education' or something of the kind, where are the ultimate questions going to be raised?

I sense that more of the authors have serious doubts about Christian schools (*e.g.* Deakin and Hill), and only one reveals clear enthusiasm for them. But is there any reason why the issue is not given a chapter on its own? Did the editors feel that it would be going over old ground to rehearse the arguments for and against Christian schools? Even if this were the case, is there nothing to be learned from two or three decades of recent experience?

Another omission that may be more significant is the politics of education. There is a reference to the need for commitment on the part of the state to provide resources for public schooling (Barns). The mention of 'educational bureaucrats' (Deakin) reminds us that in western economies the accountants are probably as powerful in education as they are in business or the health services. And there is the sobering observation that in many cases 'parental choice ... becomes school choice of families' (Deakin, p. 96). These incidental comments in a number of essays may point to the need to look in a more focused way at the role of the state in education and the effects of different views on education.

Where do we go from here?

I am left at the end with one specific question and with one that is more general.

As someone with a special interest in Islam (and I happen to be writing this during a visit to a certain Arab country whose government has a clear policy of Islamization), I am specially eager to read the comments of my fellow respondent Prof. Syed Ali Ashraf. Will he compare the quest for a Christian curriculum with the programme for the 'Islamization of knowledge' proposed by the late Ismail al-Faruqi and others? I will also be intrigued to see what, if anything, he will make of the many ways in which different authors underline the significance of believing in a trinitarian God whose being combines both unity and diversity. And if Islam is wedded in principle much more strongly than Christianity now is to the public and corporate expression of religious faith in any society, how are Muslims coping with the very un-Islamic situation in which they live in the West? How are they coming to terms with secularism, pluralism and postmodernism? When Muslims strive to establish some kind of Islamic state as an ideal, is there any sense in which Christians can and should be saying, 'We have walked this way before ... and this is what we have learned from experience about the relationship between truth and power?'

The coming of Islam into the post-Christian western world is highly significant. On the one hand it challenges timorous Christians by its insistence on bringing faith into the public sphere. On the other hand it exposes the dogmatism of secular humanists who imply that the only truth that can be known is the truth of science. It may be that Christian–Muslim conversations in the context of education will open up more fruitful dialogue than some of the familiar controversies of the past over theology and law.

My final general comment is that I look forward to the next volume, or rather to specific programmes which will answer the question 'How?' *How* do you think 'moral religion' can be taught?

How can Christian assumptions be built into a curriculum so that they are evident even if individual teachers are not Christians? *How* is the integration you seek to be achieved? *How* are the different worldviews to be brought out into the open in a common market of ideas?

If Christian educationists see their task as one of persuasion, they need to be encouraged to go on to show in greater detail how their dreams and visions of change can be translated into educational programmes. The proof of an attractive pudding will then be in the eating.

15

An alternative Christian response

Jeff Astley

After a cautionary word about his own position and some positive comments on the evangelical perspective adopted in this book, the author muses on the question of the distinctiveness of the latter. He then goes on to offer apologias, from a more liberal and radical viewpoint, both for a qualified relativism and for a more positive approach to pluralism in education. The chapter ends with an attempt to shift the focus to spirituality, and to argue for a type of secular education that might be described as spiritual formation and transformation, at the core of which lies a commitment to the conversion of the heart.

I have been invited to respond to the arguments and insights presented in these essays, wearing the guise of 'a scholar from a non-evangelical Christian tradition'. Some may feel that this is a garb that does not quite fit me; others that its cut is too closely modelled on sheep's clothing. Certainly few would regard me as an evangelical. I am perhaps more of a *catholic* (in that odd, Anglican sense of the term – or at least one of those odd Anglican senses of it). Sometimes I am also to be numbered among the *liberals* – in theology at least, if not as a philosopher of education. Often, I fear, I sound like one of those dreadful *radicals*. In what I write here, some or all of these dimensions of my Christianity will show through, but none of them is simply or even accurately captured in the phrase 'non-evangelical'.

A positive word

I should say at the outset how very impressed I have been with the quality of these essays. 'Non-evangelicals' are likely to approach with caution books that claim to present an evangelical perspective on anything, but particularly perhaps on education. Such prejudice would be inappropriate here. There is much in these pages with which I heartily agree. To take just two themes that are to be found in many of these essays: the critique of the old liberal orthodoxy in the philosophy of education is particularly well done; as is the way that the bluff is called of the related, overblown claim to a value-free, context-less and individualistic perspective in education. I have also read here with great profit many insights on schooling (and 'common schooling'), assessment and the influence of the mass media; as well as a range of Christian perspectives on human nature, both individual and communal, and on other parts of the creation. Much of this material would be applauded even by people from religious traditions other than the Christian, and some of it indeed by readers of an entirely non-religious persuasion.

Agreement, however, is not usually very interesting. I will therefore strive in this chapter to locate some issues on which I take a rather different view, while leaving it to others to judge the extent to which these disagreements represent a 'Christian view' at all. But first I offer some less controversial comments.

On being distinctive

Evangelical theology, spirituality and ecclesiology all cover a wide spectrum. John Shortt's preface helpfully presents four features that define the particular region of evangelical Christianity in which this text is to be located. He goes on to acknowledge that a diversity of evangelical views exists on a number of other theological and educational topics. Nevertheless, the question may be raised of the distinctiveness of the theological presuppositions of this debate.

Traditional accounts of the difference between catholic and evangelical theology tend to separate the traditions over issues relating to the activity of God's grace and the status of human nature. On the whole, however, we have been provided here with a particular form of the evangelical tradition that lies close to the catholic tenet that God's grace perfects nature rather than destroying it. Thus Ruth Deakin writes of a sacramental world, and presents a strong case for recognizing the proper structuring of God's love in the ordering of society as one dimension of the order of creation. This view fits well with Elmer Thiessen's claim about a general revelation in nature that supplements the particular, special revelation captured in Scripture. All of this I welcome, believing that it does not matter that these themes do not particularly distinguish evangelicals from other Christians.

But some evangelical readers might expect more emphasis on a rather different attitude to the creation, especially to human nature, that acknowledges more explicitly the degree to which it is 'fallen' (as in the paper by Stanton Jones) and rejects anything that smacks of a natural theology. There are other classical evangelical themes in theology and education that are under-represented in this book. Examples include God's role as the supreme educator, intervening and counteracting human processes of growth, development and cultural socialization; more emphasis (*contra* Bretherton?) on didactic teaching of the propositional communication of a past revelation, rather than on an 'inductive' education focused on the learner's present experience; and a stress on a radical conversion as the only proper pedigree for the Christianly educated twice-born. These are more difficult and more controversial positions to justify, but they are also more distinctive of the traditional evangelical contribution to education.

A similar point might be made about the place of individualism in any evangelical perspective. On the evidence of these papers, evangelicalism is less individualistic than often it was; more (critically) affirming of a communitarian dimension (Deakin, Jones, Bretherton, Barns, *etc*). On this issue, we might say that evangelical Christianity has become more 'catholic', while recognizing that such an emphasis was commonplace among many of the Protestant Reformers. But individualism and the language of individualism – 'God and the soul; the soul and God'; 'what an individual does with his or her solitariness'; 'making my decision for Christ' – surely have a proper place in Christianity (on which see Hill), as they also have in liberal education. From my more catholic perspective, I still want to hear that individualistic voice; for I know that, uncorrected, the catholic position can end up with just too much community, and indeed too much church. Friends, beware!

On ruling out relativism and its relatives

But now for some more contentious issues. I expected to find some harsh words written in this text on the subject of relativism, and was not disappointed. It is fairly routine – and not just among Christians – both to reject relativism at a stroke with a succinct *reductio ad absurdum* argument, and to disparage postmodern perspectives on anything as unworthy of serious reflection. Elsewhere one often finds such reactions against the temper of the age couched in terms that are as embarrassingly naïve as the positions they denounce. Here the task is done much more intelligently, as befits an essentially 'critical realist' epistemology (see below). Nevertheless, I believe that relativism is not that easily dislodged. Having been sternly shown the door, it often slips back down the chimney.

A naïve relativism would contend that 'it doesn't matter what you believe because all truth is relative to the one who holds it'. This is easily, and properly, overthrown. But a more sophisticated and qualified relativism is less open to criticism, and has found support among a number of contemporary philosophers. Such a view *can* allow for genuine disagreement, argument and rational resolution of disputes, at least up to a point (*cf.* Elliott 1973: 55, 61; Runzo 1986; Astley 1994a, chapter 10). Alasdair MacIntyre has described relativism as 'one of those doctrines that have by now been refuted a number of times too often'. He adds: 'Nothing is perhaps a surer sign that a doctrine embodies some not-to-be-neglected truth than that ... it should have been refuted again and again. Genuinely refutable doctrines only need to be refuted once' (MacIntyre 1994: 463; *cf.*, from a different position, Margolis 1991, chapter 1). In MacIntyre's view, the problem essentially arises in the case of the bilingual speaker attempting to communicate both with his or her own culture and with the outside world, faced by a choice between sets of beliefs that are so structured that each has internal to it its own standards of truth and justification. Such a situation excludes an appeal to independent, neutral epistemological standards (we should recall the attack on liberal rationalism in education), but thereby it also supports a version of relativism that cannot be refuted. This can, however, be *transcended* if a community is critically open enough to recognize the possibility of a radical transformation - indeed 'defeat' - of the forms of theory and practice, including the criteria of truth and justification, embodied in its own tradition. Despite MacIntyre's critique of the liberal tradition, it has been argued that this transcending of relativism is possible only with the help of a form of liberal critical education (Markham 1994; *cf.* MacIntyre 1988).

In my view, part of the problem is that it seems natural to apply some high-level accounts of the logic of factual judgments and value-judgments, whether in science, ethics or theology, to lower-level operational understandings of scientific, ethical or theological facts or values themselves. This is natural, but inappropriate: for these meta-accounts about the nature of conceptual schemes as such cannot serve us as judgments *within* those conceptual schemes (*cf.* Arrington 1989, chapter 6). In any case, there is a danger in embracing, as the only alternative to an implausible unqualified relativism, an equally implausible extreme absolutism - whether theistic or Platonic. Elmer Thiessen and others recommend that one avoid either extreme; and they are right to do so. Clearly the naïve, unthought-through relativism of the adolescent (and of many adults - including many teachers) must be resisted. Perhaps it needs to be rooted out through education. But reflective, grown-up relativism (whose sophistication discourages many from recognizing it as 'relativism' at all) needs to be taken very seriously indeed both by educators and by Christians.

Interestingly, the critical realist position has itself been developed as a form of qualified relativism (see Runzo 1986; Hick 1989, chapter 14), although of course this development can be resisted. We are reminded in this book that critical realism must allow for *some* element of the relatedness of the perspective, thought-forms and other schemata of the knower in its analysis of that which the knower discovers (rather than entirely 'invents'). The claim that God's absolute Truth must be accommodated to our human - and especially our children's - limited outlooks (Wilkins) is also relevant here. Elmer Thiessen is especially helpful in hinting at the possibility of contrasting God's absolute and complete grasp of truth with our relative, incomplete and selective understanding, and of recognizing all interpretations of revelation as products of human construction, affected by our finitude and sin. It may be tempting to hear in this the echo of Ian Ramsey's battle-cry for liberal theology, that we may be 'sure in religion' – indeed sure of God – but must be 'ever tentative in our theology' (Ramsey 1963). Such a position would seem to offer us some certainty after all. But what sort of certainty is this, if it is untainted by corrigible descriptions and therefore essentially contentless (Astley 1984: 420–425)? Oddly enough, modern relativistic accounts may be able to give a better account of the notion of certainty in theology than can the older liberal position (cf. Runzo 1986: 155, 220–225).

What of postmodernism, relativism's unruly sibling? We must agree that this movement presents some severe intellectual problems. But, again, it can be *easily* dismissed only from within a framework and set of presuppositions that it explicitly denies; and what is the use of that? Some writers regard extreme postmodernists as retreating into private epistemic worlds, and argue against them both that we do manage to communicate with one another, and that we find it difficult not to talk about 'objective and universal truth in some sense' (Thiessen; cf. Putnam 1981: 124). But the question is: what sense? It should be accepted that this cannot be the old transcendent, independent, once-for-all-delivered-to-the-saints sense, for our conceptual scenery *has* changed.

There are elements underlying both relativism and postmodernism that contemporary education must take seriously because they capture, and to some extent arise from, powerful human insights and attitudes that need to be acknowledged. Perhaps sometimes we should acknowledge them only in order the more readily to change them, through education. But sometimes we may wish to encourage them. I am thinking of such things as a deeper intellectual humility; the recognition of the ineluctably human pole (biological as well as historical-cultural) of all knowledge; and an acknowledgment of the difficulties of comparing conceptual schemes and of the impossibility in the end of distinguishing the 'real world' from the 'intelligible world'. I would also add to the list that psychological shock that is delivered by our first discovery that different people think differently; an experience that has been described as the 'vertigo of relativity' (Berger 1967: 186; Taylor 1984: 176) and which some have identified as a significant step in the development of our way of 'finding' or 'making' meaning (Fowler 1981, chapter 19).

Postmodernism is more closely associated with cultural change and the 'logic' of rhetoric, and therefore less amenable to philosophical critique, than is relativism. As one commentator has put it, 'postmodernism is the aesthetic spilled over into the moral and cognitive' (Waugh 1992: 4). It is worth recalling, however, that its disciples share with the critics of liberal education a counter-Enlightenment standpoint, while capturing the cultural mood much more completely than do many more carefully considered analyses by philosophers of education. I believe that relativism and postmodernism will haunt Christian education for some time yet. Perhaps we will eventually find ourselves developing more sympathy for them.

Pluralism, liberalism and freedom

It is worth distinguishing plurality and pluralism along the following lines: *pluralism* marks a political/social or intellectual/theoretical unity that embraces the *plurality* (variety, a neutral descriptive term) of worldviews. One issue raised by this book is that of the justification for, and value of, educational practices that encourage and endorse a diversity of visions of the good life, and as a consequence the fundamental beliefs and practices that flow from them. Some of our authors offer a Christian defence of ('acceptance' of) this form of plurality as a function of tolerance, itself part of a Christian view of faith, while arguing that Christians should not encourage or promote the phenomenon (Chaplin, Cooling). I am not sure what to think about this position in the abstract. I would first like to see some fleshing-out of the different worldviews and value-systems that constitute these 'other faiths' that Christians must not encourage. There are, of course, a number of theologians and religious educationalists who are much more positive about pluralism (*cf.* Hick 1980; Thompson 1988).

I am sure, however, that education is essentially a practical and pragmatic matter and that it is undertaken for the sake of people who will have to live in an increasingly plural society, whether or not they (or their parents) desire this. The recognition of shared values and of the common ground between worldviews is essential in such a society, as Elmer Thiessen notes. My experience with humanists and others would indicate that this agreement can be closer than is often suspected.¯ But educators also bear the considerable responsibility of equipping learners with the skills to negotiate moral choices where people disagree in the arena of conflicting values (Kliever 1992). As Christians, we do have a clear duty to promote a community that encourages people to work and live together, despite their differences. This is a proper part of the Christian call to peacemaking.

Alan Peshkin, in his brilliant – though doubtless still flawed – study of an American fundamentalist Christian school, argues that in such tightly controlled institutions pupils cannot learn 'the habit of compromise nor grasp its necessity in a diverse, complex society' (Peshkin 1986: 296). In the present book, the dangers of isolation in schooling are recognized by both Trevor Cooling and Brian Hill, the latter arguing that the heavily censored and restrictive curriculum of some Christian schools results in 'students ... ill-equipped to understand the world' with 'their free choice ... pre-empted'. Yet, in another chapter, Paul Marshall argues persuasively against the notion that liberalism must necessarily encourage freedom and plurality (see also Allen 1982), while endorsing the view that community and freedom are uneasy bedfellows.

Whatever remains of my liberal instincts rebels against the results of many versions of 'Christian education' (in the sense either of Christian approaches to general education or of 'confessional' Christian education), especially from the other side of the Atlantic. I stand, however, with those who argue that all education, and certainly all Christian education, can begin only on a formation model and from a particular standpoint. I have also argued at length against the pretensions of many of the dogmas of liberal education. So do I have a problem? Well, at least it is an Anglican sort of problem: the problem of the person who wishes to tread a middle road, or to try to have it both ways! As Crowder (1996) has noted, we should not dismiss too quickly the liberal tradition in theology (and perhaps therefore in education?) in our eagerness to embrace the so-called postliberalism, with its stress on the community and the story-sustained tradition. Liberalism – and the individualistic, critical reflection it encourages – still has a role to play in the drama of any education that dares to call itself Christian. In part this is a developmental point – but only in part. Freedom must indeed have its limits; liberalism must learn its place. But it must still have a place.

Spirituality and conversion

In the opening chapter, David Smith has put his finger on the key issue of this book: 'the question of a Christian curriculum ... is the question of whether Christians are prepared to take responsibility for developing their vision for and understanding of the world'. Exactly. I would add that, in the end, all such debates return to the fundamental question of the nature of that Christian vision and understanding, and that question is very closely related to the theological question of what it is to *be* Christian.

In my view, the dimension of spirituality is central here; but I find myself wanting to hold two apparently contradictory positions about it. On the one hand, I aver that this Christian spirituality is not in essence the enemy of something less obviously 'Christian', or even non-religious. On the other hand, I recognize that Christian spirituality must be something distinctive: it is not just about having the 'right' attitudes. Hans Küng, as so often, puts the point well: '*Christian* does not mean everything that is true, good, beautiful, human ... But everything can be called Christian which in theory and practice has an explicit, positive reference to Jesus Christ' (Küng 1977: 125). We might argue, however, that Christian spirituality becomes explicitly Christian only when that reference becomes explicit, and that in advocating and 'educating for' spiritual formation and transformation *outside the church* there is no need for the reference to become explicit.

David Smith reminds us of the fundamental human questions about security, trust, power, purpose, and so on, that undergird all human living (and therefore all religious traditions). Our responses to these questions, he notes, are more than cognitive. This must be so if, as a reading of Stanton Jones suggests, our embodied nature comprises a balance of rational and non-rational dimensions. For my money the key domain that is relevant here is the *affective*, and the key category within it is that of *attitude* – a category that includes dispositions to experience and action, as well as virtues, values and 'stances for that living'. Spirituality, both 'human spirituality' and explicitly Christian spirituality, is primarily about attitudes.

I now find myself, curiously, arguing for *more* of an emphasis on conversion or transformation that many of my evangelical colleagues have offered. All education, at least in part, is an attempt to convert people to a different stance towards life. We may wish to call this a different 'moral vision' (McNaughton 1988), but I would contend that such language should be recognized as metaphorical. Embracing the metaphor, we might say that as educators we often – and quite properly – intend our students to shift their loyalties by trying to get them 'to look at the same things differently'. The significance of valuing is crucial here. Values must be taught (Jones), at least in the broadest sense of 'teaching'; and although I agree with those who argue that it is the home rather than the school that is the most effective cradle for them, yet the school has its part to play. And values cannot be rationally justified, or at least *intrinsic* values cannot; for on what grounds could such a justification possibly stand? Hence 'rational education' cannot be of much help to us here. Sometimes, as Barth would put it, you cannot argue with unbelief but needs must preach at it.

Jonathan Chaplin is therefore right: we do need an 'evangelical' proclamation of the truth, of the gospel.[1] But I would mean by this that we need, as educators who are Christian, to encourage people to adopt different attitudes to, and therefore to *feel differently* about, themselves, others and the world. To feel differently is to value differently, and valuing differently lies at the heart of human and religious formation and transformation (*cf.* Price 1969: 376–425; Blackburn 1984, chapter 6; Astley 1994a, chapter 9; Astley 1994b). At the very least, 'the preservation of ethical value lies in the reproduction of ethical dispositions' (Williams 1985: 51), and therefore of the attitudes and emotions that largely constitute the moral character.

The world being what it is, and human nature being what it is, all education that seeks the designation 'Christian' must at some point help people to look at life in a different way. That way, the Christian way, must involve some sort of overturning of values. That is the central concern of the Christian gospel. To educate for this is to educate for conversion. I am happy to sign up to the claim that ultimately *that* is the Christian's vocation, in each and every educational context.

NOTES

1   This is not, in my view, incompatible with a qualified Christian relativism.

BIBLIOGRAPHY

Allen, R. T. (1982), 'Rational Autonomy: The Destruction of Freedom', *Journal of Philosophy of Education* 16/2: 199-207.

Arrington, Robert L. (1989), *Rationalism, Realism and Relativism* (Ithaca: Cornell University Press).

Astley, J. (1984), 'Ian Ramsey and the Problem of Religious Knowledge', *Journal of Theological Studies* 35: 414-440.

—— (1994a), *The Philosophy of Christian Religious Education* (Birmingham, AL: Religious Education Press; London: SPCK).

—— (1994b), 'Communities, Feelings and Education', *Aspects of Education* 51: 46-52.

Astley, Jeff, and Francis, Leslie J. (eds.) (1994), *Critical Perspectives on Christian Education: A Reader on the Aims, Principles and Philosophy of Christian Education* (Leominster: Gracewing Fowler Wright).

—— (eds.) (1996), *Christian Theology and Religious Education: Connections and Contradictions* (London: SPCK).

Berger, Peter L. (1967), *The Social Reality of Religion* (Harmondsworth: Penguin).

Blackburn, Simon (1984), *Spreading the Word: Groundings in the Philosophy of Language* (Oxford: Oxford University Press).

Crowder, Colin (1996), 'Liberalism in Theology and Religious Education', in Astley and Francis (eds.) (1996): 105-113.

Elliott, John (1973), 'Neutrality, Rationality and the Role of the Teacher', *Proceedings of the Philosophy of Education Society of Great Britain* 7/1: 39-65.

Fowler, James W. (1981), *Stages of Faith: The Psychology of Human Development and the Quest for Meaning* (San Francisco: Harper and Row).

Hick, John (1980), *God Has Many Names: Britain's New Religious Pluralism* (London: Macmillan).

—— (1989), *An Interpretation of Religion: Human Responses to the Transcendent* (London: Macmillan).

Kliever, Lonnie D. (1992), 'Moral Education in a Pluralistic World', *Journal of the American Academy of Religion* 60: 117-135.

Küng, Hans (1977), *On Being a Christian* (London: Collins).

MacIntyre, Alasdair (1988), *Whose Justice? Which Rationality?* (London: Duckworth).

—— (1994), 'Relativism, Power and Philosophy', in Astley and Francis (eds.) (1994): 463-483, first published 1985.

Margolis, Joseph (1991), *The Truth about Relativism* (Oxford: Blackwell).

Markham, Ian (1994), 'Faith and Reason: Reflections on MacIntyre's "Tradition-Constituted Enquiry"', in Astley and Francis (eds.) (1994): 484-493, first published 1991.

McNaughton, David (1988), *Moral Vision: An Introduction to Ethics* (Oxford: Blackwell).

Peshkin, Alan (1986), *God's Choice: The Total World of a Fundamentalist Christian School* (Chicago: University of Chicago Press).

Price, H. H. (1969), *Belief* (London: Allen and Unwin).

Putnam, Hilary (1981), *Reason, Truth and History* (Cambridge: Cambridge University Press).

Ramsey, Ian T. (1963), *On Being Sure in Religion* (London: Athlone).

Runzo, Joseph (1986), *Reason, Relativism and God* (London: Macmillan).

Taylor, Mark C. (1984), *Erring: A Postmodern A/theology* (Chicago: University of Chicago Press).

Thompson, Norma H. (ed.) (1988), *Religious Pluralism and Religious Education* (Birmingham, AL: Religious Education Press).

Waugh, Patricia (ed.) (1992), *Postmodernism: A Reader* (London: Edward Arnold).

Williams, Bernard (1985). *Ethics and the Limits of Philosophy* (London: Collins).

16

A non-religious response: sharing in dialogue from diverse sources

Monica J. Taylor

If education is not value-free then whose and what values should inform it? This chapter reviews the case made for an evangelical Christian education in this collection from a sympathetic but non-religious perspective. In particular it considers the need for such a book, what is distinctively Christian and some challenges of cultural pluralism. It suggests that, especially in a school context, it is more important to offer opportunities to share in dialogue about beliefs and values despite the diversity of their sources.

Common ground?

If it is agreed – and it is taken as a premise of this book and reiterated by several contributors – that education is not value-free, then values in education and education in values become central issues for any formal education system, its institutions and curricula. Whose values? What values? These questions are all the more challenging in a pluralistic society with a dominant tradition which permeates its structures. Are there shared values, despite the diversity of their religious or secular sources? How is the need for commonality to be balanced with the claims for partiality from various religious perspectives within education? What structures and strategies can be developed for sharing in communicative dialogue in schools and society? Such questions seem to be implicit in any consideration of an agenda for educational change.

This book sets out to make a particular case, 'an academically serious and distinctively Christian contribution to discussions about the nature and purpose of education'. Each contribution aims to offer 'a clear evangelical Christian grounding. It should demonstrate how such a Christian theology makes a distinctive contribution to the subject matter.' In identifying fundamental issues and illustrating them from specific contexts, the book proposes to 'be influential in shaping education into the next millennium and to offer practical ways forward'. It is against these stated objectives that the contributions should be evaluated.

This contribution to the final part of the book, 'Continuing the Dialogue', is intended as a non-religious perspective, but from one who 'has sympathy with the religious quest' – indeed, with the quest itself, living with uncertainty – not wishing to deny the possibility of there being a God. As such, being invited to reflect on the book as a whole and to respond to it in the light of my own educational concerns and worldview is, I take it, a mark of the critical openness of the editors. This also applies with respect to the invited response from the Islamic scholar, Professor Ashraf. In the space available it is not possible to comment in detail on all of these wide-ranging papers and the complexity of some of their arguments. Neither am I qualified to comment on the theological perspectives. I intend, from a background in philosophy and empirical research, to point to matters of agreement, explore some areas of concern and tension, and mention one or two issues which might have received more attention. The context of my remarks is that of western Europe and primarily England.

There is much in these papers with which I can broadly agree. Conversely, Elmer Thiessen acknowledges that 'Christians do, to some extent, agree with those holding other worldviews', and suggests that 'it is possible to affirm, at one and the same time, that one's belief system is unique, and that it shares truths with other belief systems'.

The very fact that the editors have sought to compile a collection of papers which recognizes the significance of worldviews in educational policy and practices – to reject the myth that there can be neutral education – is welcome. Young people themselves are aware of the values implicitly conveyed in schools and the gaps between what is intended and what is experienced (Taylor 1996a, 1996b). There is much scope for articulation, interpretation and adoption of agreed values statements and their implementation in schools. But such goals in themselves need to be informed by a shared and coherent vision of the characteristics of young people and society which they seek to promote. This book begins to set out an evangelical Christian vision for education which includes the centrality of relationships, which again, to my mind, are central to learning endeavours (Taylor 1988). In turn, these have to be built on a sincere appreciation of what it means to be and to respect a person; Stanton L. Jones provides a helpful elucidation of different models of the person, features of a Christian vision of the person, and its educational implications. In respect of young people Luke Bretherton, too, talks of persons in relation, developing communication, and says that 'good learning is premised not just on good content but on good relationships, and this involves listening'. This is borne out from dialogue with young people themselves. It is also particularly important if schools them-selves are to be actively involved in the negotiation of values and working towards a framework of common values (see Haydon 1987).

Why the need to make the case for a Christian education?

What I find particularly interesting is the felt need for a book of this kind, attempting to set out a Christian education, at this time. Religious traditions continue to have a purchase in social institutions and to have an informal influence in many people's lives, even though, with the exception of rites of passage, individuals may not engage in religious practices. To me, in the UK at least, but also, and perhaps more so, elsewhere in western Europe (e.g. Norway), Christianity has a privileged place in society and in the educational system. For historical reasons (explored by Brian Hill), Christianity has continued to have a pervasive influence which does not necessarily facilitate the equal recognition of other religions or non-religious worldviews represented in an increasingly pluralistic society. England is more than nominally Christian. Public holidays are geared to the Christian calendar (Easter, not Ramadan). Christianity is enshrined in the structure of the educational system since denominational schools, which comprise over one quarter of state-aided schools, remain Christian (Church of England, Roman Catholic and Methodist), unlike, for example, in the Netherlands where there is a great diversity of religious and non-religious schools. Thus in the UK, and elsewhere in western Europe, Christianity benefits from the in-built power of the *status quo*. Indeed, Brian Hill acknowledges that 'many Christians fail to question the system because in each case [as one of the powerful groups in society and benefiting from denominational provision] they themselves are members of the most privileged groups'.

In education policy-making the church can be distinctively influential, as in the case of the Education Reform Act 1988. So, unless a school has sought an exempting determination, daily collective worship must be 'wholly or mainly of a broadly Christian character' (Great Britain Statutes 1988, 7[1]), and the local agreed syllabus for religious education in the basic curriculum must 'reflect the fact that the religious traditions in Great Britain are in the main Christian whilst taking account of the teaching and practices of other principal religions represented in Great Britain' (8[3]). Indeed, the structure of the local authority Standing Advisory Councils for Religious Education (SACREs) specifically advantages the Church of England, giving it one of the four main groups, alongside politicians, teachers and a group comprising other faiths in the area. In some localities where Christians are in a minority, such a structure serves only to perpetuate the marginalization of other faith and ethnic groups and may seem irrelevant to their needs (Taylor 1991 and n.d.).

The permeation of the assumption of a Christian influence and a religious foundation to spirituality and morality were evident from a recent influential conference on Education for Adult Life,[1] with particular reference to the spiritual and moral dimensions of the curriculum, initiated by the School Curriculum and Assessment Authority (SCAA) in England, as a result of which the Chief Executive's speech was dubbed by the media as calling for a school version of the Ten Commandments (Tate 1996; see also Dearing 1996). According to Nick Tate, 'the loss of the religious basis for morality has weakened its credibility', and religious education in the curriculum is 'vital' because 'children's spiritual development is so important, as the origin of the will to do what is right' (1996: 5). While it is heartening that the subsequently inaugurated National Forum on Values in Education and the Community includes among its twelve constituent groups (including parents, religious and other interest groups and teacher trainers) representatives of religions other than Christianity and humanism, the general cultural context of the debate to which this book contributes is nevertheless one in which Christianity (certainly as opposed to any other monotheistic or polytheistic religion) is deeply embedded. This is one sense in which education is not value-free. Thus, in discussion of a Christian involvement in public policy-making, Ian Barns's characterization of 'the spurious notion of the secular autonomy and neutrality of the public sphere' does not quite ring true for me, though I consider it essential that in a genuinely open public dialogue Christian arguments should be heard alongside others and be judged by their 'leavening influence'. Moreover, the fact that as a middle-aged white English female one has been socialized into a society with pervasive Christian traditions which infiltrate a non-religious worldview may also go some way to explaining why there is much in the papers in this book with which one can broadly sympathize. A British Asian Muslim perspective, for example, is unlikely to start from this frame of reference.

But in another sense it is less surprising that there should be a felt need with this book to give voice to a theoretical evangelical Christian position, at this time. Generally, with the exception of vocal minorities who have gained media attention, Christian influence in debates about the nature of education has come from within the liberal tradition. So the intention here is to produce a serious academic evangelical Christian contribution. The titles of parts of the book – 'Beyond the Liberal Society', 'Beyond the Domesticated Person', 'Beyond a Reductionist Curriculum', 'Beyond the Schooling Paradigm' and 'Continuing the Dialogue' – indicate, somewhat negatively, areas of dissatisfaction and the expressed need to be seen as seriously engaging with the challenges of both modern and postmodern educational thought and plural societies. But such implied dissatisfactions would also be widely felt by liberal educators, especially those with a concern for affective education (*e.g.* as David Smith seems to acknowledge about Paul Hirst's more recent writing). Moreover, although dissatisfaction with liberal education is expressed, I do not find a coherent argument in the book to suggest that a Christian education, such as is envisioned, would not take place within a liberal framework which respects religious freedom. Presumably a Christian education in a Marxist, neo-Marxist or Islamic society would be differently constrained.

It seems to me that there might be at least two motivations for the book. One is to do with the nature of evangelicalism – conversionism and the authority of the Bible being two central features. On the former, philosophically it can be argued that it is in the nature of strongly held belief that a believer thinks it is true and wants others to believe it too. So too, psychologically, there is a desire to change and include others. In terms of God-given biblical authority the position being argued for here seems to be that there is logically a truth to be uncovered through continuing critical dialogue between the text and the reader. This acknowledges the role of the reader's presuppositions and culture while rejecting relativism and subjectivism. Ironically, in terms of authority in teaching and learning, this might have parallels in a postmodern narrative approach to moral pedagogy. This seeks to develop an explicit critical dimension and to address the relationship between language and power by seeking ways in which teachers and students can engage in dialogue and exchange which do not grant all the authority to the teacher (Tappan and Brown 1996).

Secondly, a motivation to establish a theoretical evangelical Christian educational position might be to highlight the differences claimed between believers in the gospel and other religious believers and those of no faith. Considering that the book is an attempt to elaborate a specifically religious form of education it says, for me, curiously little about other world faiths (not to mention worldviews), or, for instance, the distinctive nature of a Jewish or Islamic education, and how an evangelical Christian education might be compared or contrasted. Indeed, there is a general acknowledgment that, for example, in the UK, the opportunity to establish faith-based schools should be open to members of faith communities other than Christianity and that world religions should be studied in the curriculum. So equal access to religious opportunities (if not equality) seems to be a main principle, perhaps above the specifics of faith. This appears to be the price for keeping religion in the public domain and giving it a special influence in education.

Rather, I think the real thrust of the book, detected from various passages, is a thorough-going concern with variously secularism,[2] secular liberalism or secular liberal humanism, and an absence of religious faith. For instance, Trevor Cooling argues against common schools 'imposing versions of humanism in the name of rationality'. Paul Marshall argues that 'liberalism tends to quash differences, especially in education, and pushes for a homogeneous secular society'. Ian Barns writes of 'the culturally corrosive effects of the wider culture of liberal modernity'. Such concerns may be shared by some Muslim and Sikh parents who prefer to send their children to Church of England primary schools rather than schools without a religious foundation.

But the alternative to religious beliefs and values is not a value-free vacuum, or necessarily the individualistic values of materialism, hedonism or relativism. Moreover, some who adhere to non-religious worldviews may have apparently similar objectives for the formal state educational system. The point is that the source and grounding of these objectives are different, not springing ultimately from the nature of the authority of God but, nevertheless, from a set of beliefs and values. These include beliefs about human nature and about the nature of morality, of the concept of persons and of the possibility of right action and goodness. From this follows a minimum set of core values for social life, based on respect for persons and life, such as protection of and caring for the young, truth-telling as the norm, and not killing people. These are not specific to context or culture, or particular to persons, but can claim some universality in common humanity. There were many times in reading these papers when I would have been happy to substitute 'human' for 'Christian'. Although such a 'secular' perspective needs a theoretical articulation in terms of implications for an education in values, it clearly overlaps with some, but by no means all, aspects of religious perspectives. To me it would commend honesty, openness, freedom of thought, a democratic spirit, the development of critical rationality, .equal opportunities and a valuing of pluralism. Those who wish to espouse secular worldviews have to learn how to make them clearer, coherent and more worthy of respect. Despite the confusions which still abound in discussions of moral and spiritual development, and contrary to some religious views ('Morality derives from the revealed character of the personal God and his declared will for his creatures', Richard Wilkins), it is possible to be moral without morality being grounded in religion or even necessarily in spirituality.

One of the problems of a liberal society and a secular worldview is the logical and psychological difficulty of articulating and standing up for the values to which they subscribe. There is also a downside to political correctness which can engender obfuscation, and the 'isms', such as feminism, can produce a polarization of beliefs and values. Such a climate may make for a retreat into subjectivism or relativism, rather than arguing for and applying moral principles. This probably also makes it more difficult to sell a vision of a common school than one which sets out to enhance a religiously inspired education.

A distinctively Christian education?

By comparison, despite textual differences of interpretation, is it possible to point to what is meant by Christianity, Christian beliefs and values, and being a Christian? In order to advocate a Christian education a case needs to be made for what is distinctively Christian and how this applies to education. So how do the contributions to this book define a distinctively Christian education? And what, moreover, is a distinctive *evangelical* Christian education? It seems to me that the case argued in this book is not clear. On a wider canvas there are significant differences between literal and evolutionary interpretations of creation. Here, too, there appears to be an at least implicit agreement that there is not necessarily just one account of *an* evangelical Christian perspective (let alone *a Christian* perspective) on education. For example, Trevor Cooling acknowledges: 'Clearly there are fundamental differences of great substance between Christians, so we cannot really talk about one Christian primary culture. Even if we talk about an evangelical Christian primary culture we still have problems.' It is also not particularly clear in this collection what values a distinctively Christian education would model. There are glimpses in discussion of 'God-given human rights' which also apply to children. Jonathan Chaplin refers to the Nolan Committee's 'seven key principles – selflessness, integrity, objectivity, acccountability, openness, honesty and leadership – to guide those in public life, the content (if not the detailed implementation) of which must surely command universal Christian endorsement'. Would these translate into the educational domain?

As Elmer Thiessen maintains, 'Christian scholars often find it difficult to provide concrete examples of conclusions that follow from biblical presuppositions for their discipline', and 'every attempt to develop a Christian curriculum is in the end a human construction, at least in part'. So it is usually easier to show differences when it comes to applying theoretical perspectives to practice. For example, in producing curriculum materials, whereas the Christian Schools Trust has started from a theoretical position and is concerned with materials for use in Christian schools, the approach of the Association for Christian Teachers' Charis Project is rooted in curricular relevance and pedagogic practices of the mainstream school, as the materials (to enhance spiritual and moral development through English, modern foreign languages, maths and science) also aim to be accessible to and used by non-Christian teachers.[3] There is a sensitivity as to the extent to which Christianity is to be explicitly mentioned, for instance in the form of quotations from the Bible, and a view that these should come in 'naturally', possibly alongside quotations from literary, scientific or other forms of knowledge, though not other religious sources. But, by contrast, Ron Elsdon argues that Christianity offers 'a worldview which can incorporate all the other disciplines that will be needed in order to care responsibly for creation'.

In another example from this book, Brian Hill accepts that there are difficulties in developing a Christian view of educational assessment. It is not clear whether there would be Christian criteria for academic achievement. The questions he put to social-studies teachers about their intentions (information-giving, conformity-seeking, developing enquiry skills, reformist critique or radical disruption of the *status quo*) aptly illustrate the different objectives which have to be taken into account in evaluating student learning outcomes. He rightly enters a caution about the ethics of assessment and the availability of character assessments. Yet, as he recognizes, it is often the personal qualities, such as empathy, taking initiative and exploring real-life dilemmas, which are valued by employers in the wider world. He suggests that certain qualities, such as the Christian respect for the dignity of each individual made in God's image, the enhancement of individual 'spiritual' gifts and development of critical rationality, as well as responsibility in relationships, could be assessed. Without the theistic reference and spiritual grounding, these seem to be qualities or capacities which would be widely acknowledged as of worth. To be effective, education has to be both academic and affective: an education which respects the learner as a whole person, one who thinks, feels and behaves.

Dialogue and diversity in the school

Another area of uncertainty is the view taken by contributors to this book about cultural pluralism. This seems to be seen as problematic rather than an enriching challenge. David Smith relates to 'today's problem of pluralism in beliefs and values which is itself shaped by specific commitments'. Jonathan Chaplin suggests that 'Christians should not celebrate or advocate such plurality as if it were a healthy, normative state of affairs. But where directional plurality exists as a social fact, they must respond to it in an authentically Christian way.' Trevor Cooling notes that many evangelical Christians accept the inevitability of pluralism 'in a fallen world', but that part of the evangelical credo is to proclaim the one gospel for all people irrespective of their primary culture.

Clearly cultural pluralism is a particular concern for state education – which must have some responsibility for promoting social cohesion and intercultural, if not global understanding – especially when it is openly recognized that education is not value-free. Pluralism is acknowledged as a fact of modern societies – indeed, it has a much longer history than is commonly recognized in terms of formal education, where multicultural anti-racist approaches have been developed only within the last thirty years. But pluralism does not entail relativism. To respond to cultural pluralism of all kinds is to begin to answer the question of what kind of society we want to live in. I take it that we do not want the kind of society I recently witnessed on a Saturday evening in London – a scene worthy of Breughel or Hogarth – with two young men, one white, the other black, knocking each other's heads against the walls of the Underground and then the skinhead setting about the foreigner who tried to separate them; drunken loudmouthed girls; men urinating in the street. But there is always the possibility of change and reform. One morning I was hailed by a thirteen-year-old boy, sitting in the sun with his girlfriend and a younger brother, waiting for friends to begin a game of football. He clearly remembered me and wanted to chat. About four years ago I had talked to him about teasing and frightening a cat and cycling on the playing fields. There are ways in which learning in and from the community needs to complement learning in formal education. In rebuilding society and empowering individuals and communities, it is important to develop effective personal relationships, enabling people to be responsible, caring and participative.

The response of some evangelical Christians to pluralism is to assert the traditional predominant position of Christianity in western societies through the public realm, including the law and educational policy-making (see the chapters by Jonathan Chaplin and Ian Barns). Ironically Barns points to a tension regarding whether to increase Christian church influence in public life, since the privatizing of religion has created a culture of religious tolerance. Other authors in this collection seem to argue for keeping religion in the public arena, repecting religious freedom and treating religions fairly, though the same respect is not necessarily to be accorded non-religious worldviews. It is the interpretation of the religious in education, in schooling provision and in the curriculum, that is so controversial and that exercises many contemporary philosophers of education (see, for example, Halstead 1986; McLaughlin 1987, 1992).

Trevor Cooling tackles this head-on in a clearly set out and clever justification of the common school as not inconsistent with the structural pluralist view of knowledge and concern for religious liberty, or, most importantly, evangelistic concerns. 'The common school is at least an institutional affirmation of the idea that there is ultimately one truth for all.' Although the theoretical ideal is a Christian education, the common school is preferable to admitting into the state system schools based on other belief frameworks (or imposing a Christian-only framework in state schools). This, however, means negotiating 'a framework of values that creates a learning institution with specific functions which are different from those carried out in a community of faith' and which is 'systematic nurture of a child's primary culture.' I can endorse Trevor Cooling's notion of the common school 'promoting reflective understanding of the relationship between belief and knowledge and promoting civic values'. But I think that he is wrong in saying that 'they are, in the final analysis, less important activities than faith formation', simply because to engage in this kind of development of appreciation and understanding is to sustain the kind of society which makes religious tolerance possible.

My own position with respect to denominational schools is that, in the short term, if they exist within the educational system, then, with appropriate safeguards about quality and standards, they should be equally open to religious groups other than Christian. If the argument about the importance of religion in prescribing a complete way of life is telling, this has even more force, for example, for Muslims living in a western, traditionally Christian society where the cultural context is not sympathetic to the incorporation of Islam into everyday practices. Such an argument for denominational schools would confirm that the predominant value-basis for education is religious and not any other values-vision, such as ecological, aesthetic or political. Rather, however, I would abolish denominational schools in favour of the common school because of the importance of learning together in community, and learning about the diversity of beliefs and values through shared experience, dialogue and common humanity. One is constantly struck by the different interpretations of critical and controversial events, and the expressed attitudes and actions even of those one knows well and with whom basic beliefs and values are shared. How much more important is it that we should come to have a wider and deeper appreciation, if not understanding, of those beliefs and values which act as mainsprings for others. Thus I would diminish the hegemony and partiality of religious influence in the structure of the education system, but take it seriously by strengthening religious education, together with moral education, in the common curriculum.

While acknowledging that this book sets out to make an academic contribution to the debate about Christian values in education, it clearly concentrates on structures rather than on the translation of vision and principle into educational practice. If the focus of formal state education is the development of the young person, preparation for adult life and lifelong.education, then these contributors often seem to have neglected to think about translating their aims to reach the young people themselves. In fact it says very little about the two key areas normally associated with religion in school, namely religious education and collective worship. I suspect that in terms of 'worship' *per se* (as opposed to assembly) there might again, but for different reasons, be some measure of agreement between evangelical Christians and my own position that this is an inappropriate activity in a common school.

In terms of the school curriculum I want to argue for making values education the core of education and, among other things, for a reconceptualization of the arena currently covered, often in an *ad hoc* and unstructured way, in religious education and personal, social and moral education. This would become, more commonly than now, a systematic study of beliefs and values, an initiation into a framework of moral and spiritual questions which can be asked of religious and other worldviews, and a study of their answers and of what these mean in relation to key moral, social and cultural issues of contemporary plural society. It seems to me at least arguable that there would be more chance of avoiding relativism if more were known about beliefs and values by engagement with those who are within the religious and other worldviews. The learner could discover which values are shared, without accentuating the commonalities or denying the differences. This would require a critical pedagogy, including developing the skills of intercultural discourse, with attention being paid to moral reasoning and the narratives of modern meaning-making.

Clearly, although they may have difficulty in articulating a moral issue, young people are very interested in questions of life and death, of right and wrong, in making sense of their lives and giving point to life (SCAA 1996). They are, however, cynical about the moral leadership of politicians and religious leaders and the honesty of the population at large. There is an increasing need for a focus on the moral in education so that, in a coherent, consistent, planned and relevant manner it can be addressed specifically as a form of knowledge, skill and understanding relating to attitude and action. Thus moral imagination might be best fired in English, drama or science; there might be opportunities for Aristotelian virtue ethics (becoming moral by doing moral acts) as a citizen of school and the wider community; and there might be opportunities for learning how to think and reason morally through attending to moral language, concepts and arguments in a specific timetabled time. As a focus we might ask what values, attitudes and personal qualities would we expect a young person leaving a school to have. The answers are unlikely to be value-free.

Of supreme importance to such an enterprise – and hardly touched upon here (see Ruth Deakin) – is the role of the teacher. Many teachers are professionally cautious about dealing with the moral, the spiritual and the religious because they have not been adequately inducted into ways of dealing with these forms of thought, and the complex controversial issues with which they deal, in their initial training, nor are they sustained by it in continuing professional development. Training should include experienced-based learning which involves working with ethnic minority and community groups as well as the development of ethical thinking. There is evidence to suggest that even those teachers and teacher trainers who have a Christian commitment need time and support for critical reflection on their pedagogy and the strategies by which they handle the implications of their subject for ultimate, temporal and spiritual questions, even though they may not lack the moral courage to do so.

Educational change?

So is the evangelical Christian agenda for educational change clear? Is there a prescribed path or only a sense of direction? What seems valuable in starting to articulate a distinctive evangelical Christian education is to begin to show the logical framework of critical beliefs and values and the accompanying psychological predispositions and orientations. Our visions of and for the world greatly influence whether we see things in religious, spiritual or moral terms, or a combination of these. Setting out what may be distinctive to evangelical Christianity contributes towards the mapping of whether there are shared values across diverse communities of believers, despite the differences of sources. It seems to me, however, that what we value, as evidenced by the way we try to live our lives, and actually do live, is of greater everyday significance than the philosophical justification of the source of these values and practices. This is not to deny the motivational thrust and the authoritative power of such grounding and its inspiration in conflicts of value. Indeed, it seems likely that as we approach the next millennium religious values will have greater influence on the global stage. Both locally and internationally, dialogue and having a language in which to begin the conversation become vital. Can an acceptance of and delight in diversity within the unity of creation be extended to an acceptance of, if not critical delight in, diverse accounts of 'truth' in terms of religious and other worldviews?

NOTES

1 The Education for Adult Life conference was motivated by 'deep concerns about the way our civilisation is going'. Sir Ron Dearing lamented the loss of a stable society and that 'the gradual erosion of the Christian religion, the decline of Sunday school as part of a child's Sunday, and the values they stood for, have further loosened the code that our society is based upon' (1996: 1, 2-3). Nick Tate pointed to the erstwhile traditional transmission, both in schools and in the home, of 'a set of rules, precepts and principles', including the Ten Commandments, and attributed the dominance of moral relativism to cultural relativism between and within cultures, the decline of religious faith, postmodernism and consumerism (1996: 3-6).

2 Secularism is defined in *The New Shorter Oxford Dictionary* (1993) as 'a system of belief based on the doctrine that morality should be determined solely with regard to the wellbeing of humankind in the present life, to the exclusion of all considerations drawn from belief in God or in a future existence' and 'the view that education, especially that which is publicly funded, should not promote religious belief or include religious instruction'.

3 The Association of Christian Teachers' Charis Project, sponsored by the Jerusalem Trust, is developing Christian materials for use by Christian and non-Christian teachers with students aged 14-16, addressing spiritual and moral dimensions in English, modern foreign languages (French and German), maths and science. The materials are available from ACT, Stapleford House, Wesley Place, Stapleford, Nottingham, NG9 8DP.

BIBLIOGRAPHY

Dearing, Sir Ron (1966), 'To Begin at the Beginning', speech introducing SCAA's conference on 'Education for Adult Life' (15 January).

Great Britain Statutes (1988), Educational Reform Act 1988, chapter 40 (London: HMSO).

Halstead, J. M. (1986), *The Case for Muslim Voluntary-aided Schools* (Cambridge: Islamic Academy).

Haydon, G. (1987), 'Towards "A Framework of Commonly Accepted Values"', in G. Haydon (ed.), *Education for a Pluralist Society*, Bedford Way Papers 30 (London: Institute of Education, University of London).

McLaughlin, T. H. (1987), '"Education for All" and Religious Schools,' in

G. Haydon (ed.), *Education for a Pluralist Society,* Bedford Way Papers 30 (London: Institute of Education, University of London).

—— (1992), 'The Ethics of Separate Schools', in M. Leicester and M. J. Taylor (eds.), *Ethics, Ethnicity and Education* (London: Kogan Page).

School Curriculum and Assessment Authority (1996), *Mori Poll on Moral Values* (London: SCAA).

Tappan, M., and Brown, L. M. (1996), 'Envisioning a Postmodern Moral Pedagogy', *Journal of Moral Education* 25/1: 101–109.

Tate, N. (1996), *Education for Adult Life: Spiritual and Moral Aspects of the Curriculum,* speech introducing SCAA's conference on 'Education for Adult Life' (15 January).

Taylor, M. J. (1988), *Relationships for Learning* (Slough: NFER).

—— (1991), *SACREs: Their Formation, Composition, Operation, and Role in RE and Collective Worship* (Slough: NFER).

—— (n.d.), 'SACREs: Current Controversies and Cultural Diversity' (unpublished paper).

—— (1996a), 'Voicing their Values: Pupils' Moral and Cultural Experience', in J. M. Halstead and M. J. Taylor (eds.), *Values in Education and Education in Values* (Lewes: Falmer).

—— (1996b), *Valuing their Values: A Plea for the Pupil,* paper for SCAA invitational conference on 'Education for Adult Life' with particular reference to the spiritual and moral dimensions of the curriculum (15 January).

17

The Islamic response: faith-based education in a multifaith multicultural country

Syed Ali Ashraf

In order to counteract the secularistic outlook that is promoted through education in the UK it is necessary for all religious groups to work together and promote the policy of faith-based education for all on the basis of three common beliefs and the concepts of knowledge and values based on those beliefs. The article discusses the need for an understanding of the religio-cultural background of the Muslims of this country by other faith groups, especially Christians. It also agrees with the idea of common schools for all, but it proposes fundamental change in concepts and teaching methods. At the same time it supports the need for Muslim schools and urges the authorities to give them voluntary-aided status.

Agenda for Educational Change is a scholarly attempt by evangelical Christian educationalists to propagate the need for faith-based education for the complete development of the human personality and to explore the methodology of achieving this goal in a multifaith multicultural country like Great Britain. It therefore presents from the Christian point of view the metaphysical concept of the human personality and its growth and development through education (Jones) and makes an attempt to assess the educational methods needed, including the structure of school, curriculum design and teaching methods.

These educationalists have assessed the way in which the Christian worldview has been replaced by the secularistic worldview (Marshall) and how the concept of a faith-centred human nature has been replaced by the concept of reason-governed human personality in which spiritual perceptions are not recognized and a human being is treated as a material being with some power of finding universal truths with the help of theories formulated logically out of sense perceptions (Smith, Cooling). They have indicated clearly that they can now reassert faith commitments and spiritual realization of truth because the Enlightenment foundation that considered reason as the only means of acquiring truth and universal knowledge has been eroded by developments in the theory of knowledge (Cooling).

Major differences between the backgrounds of Christians and Muslims

Muslims living in the UK feel themselves rooted in the traditions of the Islamic civilization in which there was no conflict between religious and secular knowledge. Christians on the other hand belong to the European tradition. The church itself created the dichotomy of the divine and the secular branches of knowledge, and natural scientists drifted away from the church. Universities were set up with a secular liberal outlook and philosophers and natural scientists drifted away from Christianity.

Thus a 'dissociation of sensibility' (Eliot, 1932) took place. This dissociation ultimately led to sceptical modernity, the dominance of reason as the only means of finding truth, and to the importance of freedom as the essence of individualism. Because of rapid changes in scientific paradigms, the Enlightenment foundation of reason has already been eroded and a reassertion of the religious concept of knowledge has become vocal among Christian educationalists. All this has been very ably presented in this book (Marshall, Cooling) and in other contemporary works (*e.g.* Hart 1995; MacIntyre 1988; Huston Smith 1989). This state of affairs is typically European and hence British educationalists have been going through this process for generations. Since the spread of the British Empire and the impact of western liberal education in Muslim majority countries, the Muslim mind has been reacting to liberal ideals in the following way.

Muslim society everywhere accepted this education as a necessity without bothering about its philosophical foundations or worldview. Authorities thought that by giving religious 'instruction' (not 'religious education' as we understand now in England), and by ignoring openly anti-religious theories such as the theory of evolution (Mabud 1991), they would be able to satisfy the public who are basically religious-minded. At the same time the public retained the tradition of theoretical 'madrasah' education. Even at the government level these two traditions are flourishing side by side. In England also several Muslim groups have established both types of schools, but these schools retain their separate identity. In other words the founders of these schools have not as yet understood the basic flaws in this liberal system of education. They are taking for granted that the modern system will always retain this secular character. To make pupils aware of faith and values, all that is necessary, they feel, is to grant them Islamic religious instruction.

At the same time it must be appreciated that there is a class of Muslim intellectuals educated in the West and even working as important academicians who have realized how Muslim minds are being secularized through the propagation of the secularistic worldview on which different branches of knowledge are based. After I had organized the first World Conference on Muslim Education (Makkah, 1977) and helped to organize four other conferences on curriculum design (Islamabad, 1980), textbook preparation (Dhaka, 1981), teacher education (Jakarta, 1982) and evaluation (Cairo, 1987), and after books and journals (Ashraf 1978–96; Abusulayman 1993; Faruqi 1982; Attas 1977) started to be published, a movement for the Islamization of education started in earnest. The criticism of the godless secularistic worldview at the roots of basic concepts on which textbooks are written has already been voiced by Faruqi (1982), Ashraf (1978, 1985), Attas (1977) and Nasr (1976). But instead of changing the existing curriculum, Muslim countries opted for the creation of Islamic universities, among which the Islamic University of Malaysia is the most forward-looking and active. Among the Muslim governments the Malaysian Ministry of Education under Mr Anwar Ibrahim went ahead and changed the existing school curricula, something worth investigating by Christian educationalists. The basic idea as proposed by me and accepted by all Muslim scholars is that the Islamic concept of human nature and knowledge should form the basis of all concepts for all branches of knowledge. In order to achieve this I have divided knowledge into three sectors on the basis of three kinds of human relationship: the relationship of the human being with God, with other human beings and with external nature. I call these 'religious sciences', 'human sciences' and 'natural sciences'. The first one provides the basic concepts, rules and regulations for the other two. That is how these kinds of knowledge are integrated into a unity. In order to implement this policy I have established a private university in Dhaka, Bangladesh, which is now recognized by the Government. The basic idea is that faith in and love for God and the Prophet of Islam must provide the only sustainable and permanent framework to hold unchanging values. Otherwise the evolutionary concept of values and the dependence of values on changing social scenes will destroy the basic framework and lead humanity to complete uncertainty about 'values' and the notion of the purification and improvement of the 'self'. Darul Ihsan University has already undertaken this task.

Common principles for faith-based education in a multifaith multicultural country

I strongly feel that to resist the corrosive influences of the secularistic worldviews that brainwash our children and create in them uncertainty about values, it is necessary for religious groups to stand together. I brought together senior educationalists belonging to Hindu, Buddhist, Judaic, Christian, Islamic and Sikh religious groups in 1990 after I had brought together Christian and Muslim educationalists in 1989. In spite of doctrinal differences they agreed that they share some common beliefs and values which could provide those groups and even our British society with a means of achieving unity in diversity in areas such as educational policy and practice. These include the following.
  1. Belief in a Transcendental Reality, *i.e.* Reality that transcends

all limitations that particular qualities impose upon an object. All except Buddhists believe this Reality to be the Essence of the Being whom they worship and whose name in English is 'God'. Buddhists do not deny the presence of God, yet neither do they affirm him. But they too believe in the transcendental character of truth.

2. Belief in the essence of the spiritual dimension in each human being.

3. Belief in eternal and fundamental values, such as truth, justice, righteousness, mercy, love, compassion and care towards all creation. These values are to be found reflected in the human self and need to be encouraged, nurtured, refined and developed in the conflict between selfishness and selflessness in each individual, a conflict that is also mirrored in societies, races, states and groups of people. Human beings, therefore, need some norms which transcend race, colour and groups. Human beings receive these norms from the Divine Source and through divinely inspired people (cf. Islamic Academy 1990).

These common beliefs indicate, as Trevor Cooling has rightly stated in his chapter, that 'there is ultimately one Truth for all'. Christians have one great advantage in working with Muslims. Muslims believe in Christ and consider themselves followers of Christ in the sense that he preached the same religion in essence as Prophet Muhammad. Therefore a common religious sensibility has to be cultivated and nurtured, and common principles have to be enunciated and followed.

Common schools *versus* separate schools

I agree with Trevor Cooling that 'common schools will be the major providers of education in the foreseeable future'. Most Muslim children will be studying in these common schools. Hence we should be seeking to reform them, 'to bring their rationale into line with developments in the theory of knowledge and to undermine those who wish to abuse them by imposing humanism in the name of rationality' (Cooling, p. 86). Just as common schools will not be able to offer a distinctively Christian education, so they will be unable to be Islamic in the true sense of the term. But these schools can do two things which the authorities and teachers will be deriving from religion.

First, the aim, content and method of teaching religious education

273

should be changed. Its primary aim should be to cultivate, nurture and strengthen the religious sensibility of pupils. By 'religious sensibility' I mean the innate sense of love and reverence for God generated by the innate hankering for worship which becomes strengthened as people strive for the 'good'. Examples should be drawn from Christianity, Islam and other religions. Thus the method of teaching will not be what it is in many cases today, namely, an objective account of different religions with some stress on the depiction of rituals. Only through this change in aim, content and method of teaching will this education in common schools fulfil the aim of the Education Reform Act 1988 to provide spiritual training for children.

The second thing that these common schools can do which will be highly acceptable to Muslims as well as to Christians is to uphold, and make pupils live in, an atmosphere of deep moral sensibility in which morality is based on religion. It is the integral relationship of the two and thus the appeal to the whole of a human being and not just to the person's reason that will help pupils grow up as good human beings. Here a close co-operation is possible between Christians and Muslims provided the Christians discard their antipathy to Prophet Muhammad bred by more than a thousand years of false propaganda. Just as love for Christ and God provides the essence for the incentive to love the 'good', love for Muhammad and God does the same for Muslims. Muslims at the same time love Christ with deep sincerity and the same intensity, because he is regarded by all Muslims as one of their prophets. There is not a single instance from the inception of Islam till today which can show that a single Muslim has ever uttered a single word of criticism against Christ. But just the reverse is the case with Christians. It is necessary for Christians to understand and appreciate that both these leaders represent the same 'Good' that God has given to us as the human norm. Only then will Christians be able to reciprocate with Muslims, and common schools will be able to generate a religious love for the good, leading to an emotionally sustaining and strengthening sense of morality common to all pupils and teachers.

The greatest problem facing anyone who wants religious sensibility, and morality based on this sensibility, to be cultivated in common schools is the presence in schools of teachers who do not have any faith and who do not uphold in their own lives the moral norm expected by religious-minded parents and teachers. This is the main reason many Muslim parents have got their children admitted to Anglican schools, thinking that in spite of doctrinal differences the teachers would have faith and moral values. The principal way to solve this problem, and to save children from a conflict between their primary culture and the culture of the surrounding society, is to insist that religious education is taught by teachers who have faith and hence an awareness of what religious sensibility means. Such a teacher, be he or she a Christian or a Muslim, must be trained to penetrate into the inner reality in which love for God becomes the mainspring of the incentive to moral consciousness in each child.

Another way is to let religious education play a significant role in curriculum design. This work has already been begun by Muslim scholars (Ashraf 1983-96) and evangelical Christian scholars. But none of this work can be effective unless political power in Britain becomes conscious of the basic problem. Along with Christians, Muslims were happy to see that the question of the relationship between curriculum design and spiritual and moral development was successfully raised in the House of Lords. Since then there has been intensive discussion of this relationship at various levels.

But there is always an attempt by liberal humanists to outbid the religious thinkers and intimidate them by saying that their attempt to lay stress on religion would lead to injustice to religious communities other than Christian. The answer to this challenge was given in the seminar already mentioned, where the representatives of six religions participated (Islamic Academy 1990). The suggestion made in that document regarding the method by which different branches of knowledge can be taught from a religious instead of a secularistic point of view, without at the same time interfering with the basic doctrines of each religion, is worth studying. In spite of the fact that both Muslim and Christian thinkers insist on the primary role of parents and religious communities in preserving their primary cultures, in instilling them into their children, and in training their children in them, in common schools it is impossible to evolve courses and teaching methodology that will enable students to study both human sciences and natural sciences with reference to the spiritual and moral perspective common to all religions (Islamic Academy 1990).

This does not mean that these courses will ultimately promote low-value education, because in most cases courses will depend not on the external profession of a doctrine but on basic concepts for each branch of knowledge as internally realized through faith in God and intellectually formulated for specific branches of knowledge (Ashraf 1985).

Is there a need for separate schools?

Common schools will have to persist, and may become the source of common understanding among Christian and Muslim scholars so that common texts and a common methodology may be produced as successful alternatives to the humanistic and secularistic texts and methodology at present available. Nevertheless, a feeling is common among British Muslims that separate schools controlled by Muslim educationalists should be set up in which the 'basics' will be determined by the Islamic concept of education, the Islamic concept of human nature, the Islamic concept of knowledge and the Islamic approach to life and values. In the Netherlands different religious communities are allowed to set up separate schools. The Dutch government gives equitable financial assistance to these schools. In Britain also, Anglicans, Roman Catholics and Jews are allowed to set up such schools and to have financial assistance from the state and thus have voluntary-aided status for their schools. But when a Muslim school approached the authorities, in spite of a certificate of competence by relevant inspectors, the Government has refused to give it voluntary-aided status. It is, I think, worth investigating in what way these Islamic basics are similar to or different from the Christian basics, and how in spite of common roots of common beliefs there are certain differences that compel a somewhat different teaching strategy and different framework. Just as Trevor Cooling and his colleagues think that the theoretical ideal for Christian students is that children receive a Christian education, similarly Muslim educationalists who met at the first World Conference on Muslim Education (Husain and Ashraf 1977, King Abdul Aziz University 1978) think that the theoretical ideal for Muslim children is that they receive 'Islamic education'. For Muslim majority countries the educationalists insisted on this Islamized education (Ashraf 1985) and proposed different methods of Islamizing all branches of knowledge (Faruqi 1982). Several Islamic universities have already been established, and different groups have tried to formulate Islamized curricula for school education in Malaysia and elsewhere. The steps taken by the Islamic Academy in Cambridge, UK, and by the International Institute of Islamic Thought in the USA, indicate this feeling. Already in England several schools have been set up for Muslim children in which theological education and secular education are imparted together to Muslim children without any integration of the two. I have, as stated earlier, established Darul Ihsan University in Dhaka, Bangladesh, where I am trying to achieve this integration by formulating concepts for each branch of knowledge from the point of view that Islam propagates (see p. 272).

An attempt has been made in Mr Yusuf Islam's school in Brent to design such an integrated curriculum. Attempts are being made by Farmington Institute and Oak Hill School and other such Christian organizations to achieve the same end. The Islamic Academy in Cambridge, in co-operation with the Department of Education of Cambridge University, has organized a series of lectures and seminars (Ashraf and Hirst 1994; Islamic Academy 1987, 1990) to establish a rapport between these two groups of religious thinkers. In spite of this co-operation and understanding, it has become obvious that Muslim parents consider common schools as something which cannot be avoided but not as something which is the best *modus operandi*. Just as the Christian educationalists would like to have a Christian atmosphere in the school, generated by teachers through references, quotations and instances from the Bible, Muslim educationalists similarly would like to maintain and deepen the Islamic character of the school not only through the character and conduct of the teachers but also, and mainly, through references, instances and principles derived from the Qur'an and the Sunnah. There would be religious instruction classes on Islam in addition to religious education classes for all pupils. Thus these schools will fulfil the need of parents who were accustomed in their previous tradition to have their children's faith nurtured in schools.

In spite of apparent limitations, one advantage of such an Islamic school is that in faith and morality it goes to the root of all religions. Secondly, so far as Christianity is concerned, a Muslim believes in Christ's miracles and purity and is always ready to show reverence to him. The school will therefore never be anti-Christian, and instances and references can always be drawn from Christ's life. As such, schools will have to remain open for the admission of non-Muslim children, and the lessons and the methods of teaching and moral atmosphere will be conducive to living together. Thus, the national government should encourage and support such schools and give them voluntary-aided status.

BIBLIOGRAPHY

Abusulayman, A. H. (1993), *Towards an Islamic Theory of International Relations* (Herndon, VA: International Institute of Islamic Thought).

Ashraf, S. A. (1978), *Crisis in Muslim Education* (London: Hodder and Stoughton).

—— (1985), *New Horizons in Muslim Education* (London: Hodder and Stoughton).

—— (ed.) (1983–96), *Muslim Education Quarterly* (see editorials).

—— and Hirst, Paul H. (1994), *Religion and Education* (Cambridge: Islamic Academy).

Attas, S. N. (1977), 'Preliminary Thoughts on the Nature of Knowledge and the Definition and Aims of Education', in S. N. Attas (ed.) (1979), *Aims and Objectives of Islamic Education* (London: Hodder and Stoughton).

Cooling, Trevor (1994), *A Christian Vision for State Education: Reflections on a Theology of Education* (London: SPCK).

Eliot, T. S. (1932), *Selected Essays* (London: Faber and Faber).

Faruqi, Ismail (1982), *Islamisation of Knowledge* (Herndon, VA: International Institute of Islamic Thought).

Halstead, J. Mark (1986), The *Case for Muslim Voluntary Aided Schools* (Cambridge: Islamic Academy).

Hart, Trevor (1995), *Faith Thinking: The Dynamics of Christian Theology* (London: SPCK).

Husain, S. S., and Ashraf, S. A. (1979), *Crisis in Muslim Education* (London: Hodder and Stoughton).

Islamic Academy and University of Cambridge Department of Education (1987), seminar on 'Education and the Muslim Community in Britain Today: Areas of Agreement', held in Cambridge.

—— (1990), *Faith-based Education in a Multi-faith Multicultural Country* (Cambridge: Islamic Academy).

King Abdul Aziz University (1978), *Report of the First World Conference on Muslim Education* (Jeddah: King Abdul Aziz University).

Mabud, Shaikh Abdul (1991), *The Theory of Evolution: An Assessment from the Islamic Point of View* (Cambridge: Islamic Academy and Kuala Lumpur: Islamic Academy of Science).

MacIntyre, Alasdair (1988), *Whose Justice? Which Rationality?* (Notre Dame, IN: University of Notre Dame Press).

Nasr, Seyyed Hosein (1968), *Science and Civilization in Islam* (New York: New American Library).

—— (1976), *Islamic Science: An Illustrated Study* (London: World of Islam Festival Publishing Limited).

Radhakrishnan, S. (1967), *Religion in a Changing World* (London: Allen and Unwin).

Smith, Huston (1989), *Beyond the Post-Modern Mind* (updated and revised edition, Wheaton, IL: Theosophical Publishing House).

PART 7

CONCLUSION:
TOWARDS TOMORROW

18

Postscript

John Shortt

This final chapter is a combination of summaries of insights from the chapters in Parts 1 to 5 on the key themes identified in the preface, responses to comments made by the scholars who contributed to Part 6, and some additional remarks on the way forward.

What *is* a 'worldview'?

A whole cluster of terms have been used in this book as different writers have sought to capture what is, for them, the essence of the notion of a worldview. Each term has its own limitations, and some have misleading connotations. The concept seems fuller than any of them can contain.

'Worldview' (German *Weltanschauung*) conveys notions of panoramic outlook and wholeness, but it can seem rather spectatorial and static. 'World-and-life-view' makes the scene, if not the viewer, more dynamic. 'Perspective' loses both the world and life. Visual words like these are common, and the same kind of thought is present in some of the accounts of how these 'worldviews' function. There is, for example, a reference in Elmer Thiessen's chapter to 'lenses through which we look at the world'. A slightly different idea is present in Michael Polanyi's (1967, esp. pp. 3–25) influential book *The Tacit Dimension,* where he speaks of this dimension of our knowing as being that which we view, or 'attend', *from*. Something of the 'lenses' idea seems to be present also in the usage of terms like 'framework' and 'cultural frame'.

'Ideology' sounds fairly comprehensive, but it also has a technical usage and some narrowly political overtones. 'Mindset' sounds very static indeed, but it does bring out the cognitive component. Views of the world can be both views of how it *is* and of how it *ought* to be – and sometimes, too easily, how it is can become accepted as being how it ought to be (as Brian Hill argues in relation to schooling). This idea of example or pattern is expressed in the usage of 'paradigm'. Another visual word, 'vision', occurs in phrases like 'moral vision' and Stanton Jones' 'vision of ultimacy' and, in such cases, a view of how the world and life ought to be takes precedence. There is also a more active, participatory, forward-looking sense to this, and these too are important ingredients of the notion.

One form of plurality and of pluralism is referred to by Jonathan Chaplin (quoting from Mouw and Griffioen's very helpful analysis, 1993) as 'directional' plurality or pluralism. This brings out the orienting and motivating sense of the notion.

A combination of all of these ideas is needed to express the nature and role of what many of us are trying to express in our usage of words from this family. Worldviews have to do with people's values and attitudes as well as their beliefs. As such, they may be more or less coherent and, to the extent that they are experienced as holding together, they integrate the understanding. (In the fragmented world of Luke Bretherton's 'Paradox Lane', he suggests that many young people seem to hold incompatible worldviews at the same time, and he goes on to say that they need something that will integrate their outlooks and lives.) Worldviews are related to the whole of reality, of the world seen and unseen, and of life in it. They direct, motivate and envision people and they provide points of reference for living.

What are presuppositions?

Worldviews are not simply sets of beliefs, but, I would suggest, beliefs are central to them. Are values central also? Values are, at their heart, beliefs, often passionately held, about what is regarded to be of value. And attitudes have cognitive cores, or so at least some of the psychologists tell us. These beliefs may be tacitly held – and we may not always find it easy to express them in words – but they operate at a deep level in our way of thinking and acting.

Nicholas Wolterstorff, in his *Reason within the Bounds of Religion* (1984: 67–70), writes of what he terms 'control beliefs', which have a function of shaping our views of what is important in devising and weighing theories (but the idea would seem capable of stretching to cover more than such scholarly activities). Here there is the idea that some of the cluster of beliefs in a worldview have a particularly central function. A more commonly used term for the idea of a belief that is central, basic and foundational to a worldview is that of 'presupposition', and it is used fairly freely by the contributors to this volume (maybe because it was used in their briefing paper!).

The idea of a presupposition is very important in the kind of discussion that has been taking place in the pages of this book. The word is sometimes misused, however, and needs to be handled with care. Paul Helm, in a relatively short but very careful study (1993), brings out several points of importance about presuppositions. Particularly relevant to our discussion are the following:

- Presuppositions are unavoidable.

- Presuppositions are general and basic.

- Presuppositions are premises that are *really* assumed – as opposed to those assumed for the sake of argument or merely entertained.

- Presuppositions are a matter of commitment. Only if they cease to function as presuppositions are they revisable.

- Presuppositions exercise control over enquiry (Helm refers here to Wolterstorff 1984, mentioned above).

- Presuppositions come in different strengths; some rule out certain conclusions while others require certain conclusions (as in the filter and pump models mentioned by Elmer Thiessen).

To this list, I should add two further points. First, the same conclusions can follow from different sets of premisses and, therefore, because presuppositions are a species of premiss, from different sets of presuppositions. This provides for the possibility of commonality in the beliefs of people with different worldviews (*cf.* Guinness 1991). In so far as the conclusions rest on the different sets of presuppositions, however, they are not neutral. Put briefly, common ground is not neutral ground.

The second additional point I should make is not unlike something else mentioned by Paul Helm, but I propose to develop it in a somewhat different way. Some presuppositions are, as we have seen, necessary for the truth of certain conclusions. There is another class of presupposition of importance to thinking about worldviews and their influence in thinking about education, the curriculum, or particular subject-areas: these presuppositions are necessary to the truth *or falsity* of other statements. Peter Strawson (1963: 176–179) points out that the statement 'Some of the books on the top shelf of my bookcase have green covers' presupposes that there *are* books on the top shelf, as does the statement 'None of the books on the top shelf ... has a green cover'. For these statements to be true or false, that is, for them to have meaning or point, we have to presuppose that there are books on the top shelf.

This suggests to me an important sense of 'presupposition' as an assumption that we find necessary for meaningfulness. They give *point* to whole groups of statements. Of course, the statement 'Some of the books on the top shelf have green covers' does have meaning: it is a perfectly grammatical statement and we can readily imagine the kind of situation to which it refers. Unless we *presuppose* that there are books on the top shelf, however, it is not meaningful to make this statement. It has no point. The presupposition *makes sense of the whole business.*

I suggest that this points to a way in which the presuppositions at the heart of worldviews can enable those to whom they are committed to make sense of something – a particular statement, a whole class of statements, an area of discourse, a particular theoretical approach and even life itself. The statements may have had meaning in English or whatever language they were expressed in, but the presuppositions throw them into a whole new light. There is a point to the whole business after all! It all makes sense! But note that it is not the *truth* of statements within the area that follows from, or depends upon, the presuppositions in question, but their truth *or falsity*, the *point* of it all.

This all suggests a way in which basic Christian beliefs, as presuppositions at the core of Christian worldviews, can serve not as premises from which certain conclusions follow by logical deduction, but as *foundations* which give a meaning to whole areas of thought or kinds of activity. I think this is a sense that at least some of the contributors to this book are using at least some of the time when they write of the role of presuppositions, worldviews and related terms.

Competing worldviews and pluralism ...

Two of the respondents in Part 6 felt that contributors to the earlier sections of the book were at times too dismissive of pluralism and relativism. Jeff Astley said that both a qualified relativism and pluralism deserved more positive treatment. Monica Taylor thought cultural pluralism should be celebrated.

On the subject of pluralism, Jonathan Chaplin outlined Mouw and Griffioen's distinctions between descriptive and normative senses of 'pluralism' and among 'associational', 'contextual' and 'directional' pluralism. The descriptive senses refer to the fact that there is in any modern differentiated society a plurality of institutions, associations or organizations (associational plurality); of customs, mores and cultural practices (contextual plurality), and of visions of the good life, and worldviews (directional plurality). These are facts and, in all three senses, western societies are, at least to a degree, plural or even pluralist (in a descriptive sense). It is one thing to describe the facts of the situation but it is quite another to favour the state of affairs. This is where the '-ism' of pluralism becomes more meaningful (and why 'plurality' for the factual sense, and 'pluralism' for the recommendatory sense, could help to reduce misunderstandings!). Diversity of associations is something to be celebrated by the Christian or anybody else who values variety in life. So also is diversity of culture.

Like a Christmas cake, the richer the mixture in our world, the better! The Christian vision is for a multicultural people of God – those from every people, every tribe, every tongue, every nation. So we should celebrate cultural diversity in the world and in the world of the classroom.

The real issue for Jeff Astley and, I think, for Monica Taylor (in spite of her use of the term 'cultural pluralism') is whether we should celebrate, or merely tolerate, directional plurality, that is, the plurality of worldviews and their sets of basic beliefs or presuppositions. 'Multifaith' and 'multicultural' tend to be used almost synonymously in discussions of educational issues, and this tends to muddy the waters. Admittedly, the relation between faith and culture is a big subject on its own (and the cultural implications of the gospel have long occupied the attention of missiologists and others). If we leave this to one side and focus on worldview differences, the question is more circumscribed.

As we have seen, some of the contributors have ascribed the plurality of worldviews to the fall rather than to creation. Assocational and contextual or cultural plurality are not the outcome of human sinfulness, but this directional one is. It, and not the other two, is an example of what I referred to in the preface as 'the noetic effects of sin'. It seems to me that it is another characteristic of evangelical Christianity to be committed to what may seem to many an exclusivist view. There are fundamental contradictions between worldviews as well as beliefs held in common among them. If two beliefs contradict one another, then at least one of them is false. Evangelical Christians hold strongly that their basic beliefs are true and, if they are, it follows that some of the basic beliefs of other worldviews are false. As Monica Taylor observes, it is in the nature of strongly held belief that a believer thinks it is true and wants others to believe it too – hence the conversionist characteristic of the evangelical and a general tendency in the media to confuse 'evangelical' and 'evangelistic'. But this exclusivism is true not only of evangelical Christians; it characterizes those of many other worldviews as well, often in spite of their protestations to the contrary. Paul Marshall points out in this book that it can be effectively true of liberalism, notwithstanding its advocacy of tolerance. Even the more thoroughgoing pluralists, such as John Hick, advocate a pluralism which, far from leaving everything as it is in regard to the many faiths and theologies, actually requires change in the basic beliefs of many faiths, if not of all (cf. Hick 1983: 98; 1984: 34). It is not simply that we all see and respond to the Real or the Ultimate in different ways, but, Hick effectively says, we have to change our theologies to come to see and respond in a new and different way, the way of pluralism. Hick's pluralism has its external limits too: it does not extend to include non-religious naturalists because they are not 'open to the transcendent' (Hick 1988: 367). The question seems to be not *whether* there are limits to our inclusiveness but *where* they are. For a very thoroughgoing study of pluralism from an evangelical standpoint, see Don Carson's recent book *The Gagging of God* (1996).

There are at least two ways in which this statement of Christian exclusivism needs to be qualified. First, Christians believe that the Bible is the Word of God, but it does not follow that their interpretation of the Bible has that status. Christians should always be prepared to submit their interpretations to the Scriptures for validation and, if necessary, for correction and improvement. The concern here should be to get the whole thrust of the Scriptures and not merely to find prooftexts. They should bear in mind that the noetic effects of sin affect everybody, Christian believers included. This interplay between interpretation and Scripture is an aspect of the critical realism referred to elsewhere in this book and of the hermeneutical spiral mentioned by Colin Chapman. Secondly, when we say that the basic beliefs of the Christian are true, it does not follow that all the basic beliefs of everybody else are false. The Christian doctrines of creation in the image of God and of the complementarity of general and special revelation both provide ample space for holding that truthful insights may be found everywhere.

... and relativism?

What then of relativism and its relatives, as Jeff Astley describes them? I found myself saying, 'Hear, hear!' to his quotations from MacIntyre. The fact, often pointed out, that a statement like 'All truth is relative' refers to itself, and therefore contradicts itself, readily makes nonsense of naïve relativism. But the philosophical sledgehammer of 'self-refuting incoherence' is much too blunt an instrument for more sophisticated versions of relativism. For a start, it is not so obvious that it destroys the statement 'All moral truth is relative', because this statement does not seem, on the surface at least, to refer to itself (see Astley's remarks about meta-accounts on p. 245). But perhaps, with more 'grown-up' versions of relativism, it is more helpful to replace the polarity of relative and absolute with a polarity of realist and non-realist, or realist and anti-realist? I suggest that the important thing about realism in all its forms is its commitment to a reality independent of our perceptions of it. Another basic belief of evangelical Christianity is, I suggest, that there is such a reality which includes God and that God makes himself and it known to us. We are finite, but we can know truly without knowing exhaustively: it is surely not necessary to know everything in order to know anything at all. We are fallen and our perceptions are distorted by our sinfulness, but that need not put us behind a veil of total ignorance. Fallenness and finiteness bring home to us the need for our realism to be critical rather than naïve. How critical? Not so much that the commitment of faith becomes meaningless, or so little that arrogance takes over. (I once heard of a headteacher who was reputed to have commenced his remarks after a Bible reading in assembly with the words, 'What God really meant to say was ...'!)

Perhaps the real concern here comes out in Jeff Astley's remark that postmodernism 'can only be *easily* dismissed from within a framework and set of presuppositions that it explicitly denies: and what is the use of that?' The problem is the epistemological gap between worldviews that leaves us talking past one another. Here I find helpful the approach of what has come to be termed 'Reformed epistemology', which many of my friends think makes too much of faith-commitment and too little of reason and evidences (see references in Elmer Thiessen's chapter, and Shortt 1991). The gap between worldviews may be such that it is impossible to bring somebody across by rational argument or 'positive apologetics'. But there is still room for the negative kind which consists in discussing with others on the basis of their own presuppositions in an attempt to show their internal coherence or other defects. There is also room for pointing to features of our own worldview and 'evidences for belief', as to those of a work of art, in the hope that others will come to see them for themselves, to see the point and find it all meaningful. Here we often talk about 'illumination by the Holy Spirit'. Perhaps this is why the New Testament has a greater emphasis on 'proclaiming' and 'incarnating' the gospel than on rational apologetics (not that they are entirely absent).

One *and* many, not one *or* many

And so to the anthropological. I will not rehearse again here all that has been said about the Christian view of the person, of human nature and of persons-in-relation that Stanton Jones and the other contributors have brought out in their chapters. Instead I will add just a few comments.

Paul Hirst in the seventies, and others in the approach to philosophy known as conceptual analysis, made much of the distinctions between 'knowing how', 'knowing that' and knowing with a direct object, for instance knowing a person or a place. The philosophy of education of the time seemed to give precedence to 'knowing that' over 'knowing how', and did not really seem at all comfortable with personal knowledge (or, where it was, it was more in terms of 'respect for persons' than love). A Christian theory of education, in the light of the central beliefs that God is personal and loving and that he is three and one, must give the highest place to personal knowledge. It is not that knowing that something is the case is not important, or that it is even partly constitutive of personal knowledge. No accumulation of factual knowledge about a person is sufficient in itself to enable us to claim that we know the person if there has not at some time been some immediate awareness between us and the person. At the same time, it would be strange indeed if I claimed to know Murphy or to know Dublin, although I was unable to state a single fact about either.

Knowing and loving are very closely related in the Bible. This seems a long way removed from the cold, dispassionate, detached knowledge that our education system seems to value so highly. Wisdom is also a key scriptural concept. It has to do with, among other things, 'knowing how'. But it is rather more than a set of skills; it has a whole-person, whole-of-life emphasis. The wisdom literature of the Old Testament says so much about knowing God and ourselves, and relating with others as a central 'life skill'.

Individualism or communitarianism? Not one or the other, but both! Jeff Astley suggests that the contributions to this book may be too much on the communitarian side and in danger of losing something that was good about the more typically evangelical stress on the individual and his or her personal response to the gospel. What can we say? Balance is hard to keep, and thank you, Jeff, for your friendly advice!

Jeff Astley also said he thought the evangelical emphasis on sinfulness was muted in these contributions. Having re-read them in the light of his comment, I am not personally sure that I agree. It may be expressed differently from what might be expected of the stereotypical evangelical, but it is there, not least in the recurring theme of the effects of sinfulness on our reasoning and knowing. This is perhaps different from some evangelical views of the past, which have tended to leave the person's reasoning and choosing faculties outside of the scope of the fall. But it is not, I think, a muting of the emphasis on sinfulness.

Monica Taylor pointed out that a central emphasis on relationships in education is not something by any means distinctive of the evangelical Christian. You do not have to believe in a personal trinitarian God to value the relational. This is certainly the case, but perhaps this illustrates some of the things said above about worldviews and presuppositions. People may come to the same conclusions from different sets of premises. Values may be shared without being neutral in relation to the worldviews in which they are grounded. But perhaps there is something else here. Christians find the idea of a personal God a very 'powerful' underpinning for their valuing of the relational. Is it not plausible to argue that worldviews can be compared for their 'power', or for the adequacy of their explanations of things? Again, this comparison may be rather more like comparing two works of art than producing rational arguments for one and against the other.

Monica Taylor, near the end of her chapter, wrote this: 'It seems to me that what we value, as evidenced by the way we try to live our lives and actually do live, is of greater everyday significance than the philosophical justification of the source of these values and practices.' The suggestion seems to be here that *why* we believe or do something is not as important as *what* we believe or do. I hesitate to draw this conclusion from the words of such a distinguished editor of the *Journal of Moral Education* because, on the face of it, it does seem to run counter to what I am sure she believes is of central importance to moral education.

Worldviews and education theory

This takes us to the subject of the relationship between worldviews and education theory or curriculum or particular subject-areas. Here I do not have a lot to add to what Elmer Thiessen and others in the book have said, namely, that it is not always, or even often, simply a matter of logical deduction from premises to consequences. Filtering out that which is not consistent with presuppositions, or does not comport well with them, is a very important aspect of the whole business. The creativity required by having to act out the final scene with only the script of the earlier parts, and the diversity for which this provides, make it all rather more open-ended. This is not least because the actors have not only the script (the Scriptures) to work from. Christians working in education draw not only from their theology but also from other areas of knowledge, such as psychology, sociology, philosophy, and what we call 'common sense' – although of course the same filtering, creating and transforming process is called for with them as well.

The relationship between religion and morality could provide a good example of what is involved in integrating worldview and area of knowledge. Talk of 'Christian ethics' is often objected to on the grounds that it denies the logical autonomy of the ethical form of understanding and makes it, in some way, dependent on religious belief. Morality does not require religious underpinning, it is said, and anyway non-religious people are often very moral, sometimes more so than some religious people. In response to the second part of this, I would agree wholeheartedly. But it does not follow from this that I must also accept the first part. Moral philosophers are still, after centuries of debate, very far from agreement on the foundations of ethics. It would therefore seem at least slightly premature to rule out the possibility of a Christian foundation.

At this point, two major counter-arguments come into play. First, moral terms cannot be deduced from premises which come from outside the moral domain because, it is said, one cannot logically deduce an 'ought statement' from an 'is statement', even if it is a theological 'is statement'. Secondly, moral terms cannot be defined by reference to non-moral terms. Attempts to define the morally good in terms of what God is, or what he wills or commands, have to reckon with what is known as the 'open-question argument'. This says that 'good' cannot be defined in terms of what God is or wills or commands because it is open to question whether what God is or wills or commands is really good. The purported definitions can, it is claimed, be denied without self-contradiction.

This latter objection seems to me easier to respond to than the former. It is also of greater interest in considering non-strictly-logical relations between worldviews and education, curriculum or subject-areas. I would ask whether it is so clear that it 'makes sense' to ask whether what God is or wills or commands is really good. It seems that it does for some, but does not for others. From a particular whole perspective on reality, it may not make sense to ask whether God is good, but from another whole perspective it may.

It seems that some approaches to morality are rooted in worldviews which recommend definitions of ethical terms, while others are rooted in those which reject all such definitions and insist on the autonomy of ethics. Viewed in this light, the 'open-question argument' itself may express nothing more than a recommendation from within a particular kind of worldview. Iris Murdoch, in an article called 'Vision and Choice in Morality', writes:

> If we do not accept the current view of moral concepts as commendations of neutral areas, and consider rather the way in which a moral outlook is shown in ramifications of more specified concepts which themselves determine a vision of the world, then a prohibition on defining value in terms of fact loses much of its point (1966: 214).

The link between an ethical or meta-ethical position and a worldview – or, in Murdoch's term, a 'vision of the world' – may not be strictly a matter of logical deduction. It could still be that it is reasonable for a person of a particular worldview outlook to recommend a particular ethical or meta-ethical position. Donald Evans has what I find a helpful approach here when he talks of 'onlooks' or 'ways of understanding situations', which are typically expressed by 'I look on x as y'. For instance, 'I look on the body as the prison of the spirit', or 'I look on human beings as clever apes'. In his essay 'Does Religious Faith Conflict with Moral Freedom?' he writes:

> An onlook applied to a situation will affect the selection of

293

relevant facts and will provide within itself the move
from 'is' to 'ought', though the precise specification of the
'ought' will also be linked with the particular facts of the
situation, and require further judgement and decision by
the agent (1973: 378).

William Frankena writes of definitions of moral terms in a somewhat
similar way:

Underlying one's acceptance of the definitions there is or
should be an attitude, interest or point of view already
taken - i.e., that the definition is really a crystallisation
in a certain mode (formal or material) of an attitude,
interest, or point of view ... What would then really
mediate the inference from Is to Ought or from Fact to
Value would not be the definition but the underlying
commitment (1973: 146)

What these writers seem to be suggesting is that our worldviews
(visions of the world, or 'onlooks') have at their heart a cluster of basic
beliefs which may be religious and moral, factual and evaluative.
Moral vision is therefore something basic. It does not have to be
religious, and plainly often is not, but it can be. In particular, it can,
I think, be claimed that a Christian moral vision gives point to life.
In reply to the open-question argument, it can be argued that it does
not make sense to ask if God or his will is really good in that, although
it may be semantically meaningful, it is nevertheless the case that from
within such a worldview there is no point in asking such a question.
    If I am right, this is an example of how it can be meaningful to
talk of Christian ethics. May there not be something analogous to
this in talk of Christian art or a Christian approach to any other
subject-area or a Christian view of education? Granted, the outcome
- the particular moral principles or whatever - may not always differ
from one worldview to another. But their grounding certainly does.
And those who ask 'Why?' as they go through life need to find adequate
groundings.

Distinctively evangelical?

There is more than one point to respond to from the comments in the chapters in Part 6. First, Jeff Astley questions whether the theological position underlying the contributions to this book is always distinctively evangelical. Secondly, even if it is, both he and Monica Taylor ask whether the view of education that we seem to be coming up with is distinctively evangelical or distinctively Christian, or even distinctively religious. Furthermore, Ali Ashraf finds quite a lot in common between this approach to education and that which he takes as a Muslim.

I think I have partly responded to the first of these points already. I would add only that a part of the problem may be that in Britain the distinctions between 'evangelical', 'fundamentalist' and 'Reformed' are not as clear-cut as they are, say, in North America. This means that some characteristics which are more fundamentalist in the North American sense can be misapplied to a more broadly evangelical outlook in Britain. In terms of those particular characteristics, the contributions to this book may well be less distinctively evangelical than might be expected. But, as I have suggested earlier, I think there is enough left to mark out the theological position as quite distinctive.

On the second point, I have also suggested that there are commonalities (and I have tried to account for their existence). I would reiterate the need, the importance and the distinctiveness of the vision. One of the educational concerns is for wholeness, for integration in place of compartmentalization in the young person's worldview, and I think that there is evidence here that a Christian worldview and approach to education are capable of providing this. Although elements on their own may not always seem very different, it is their presence in the whole vision or way of thinking and living that makes the difference. In that whole, different elements may occupy more or less central places and be seen and emphasized in rather different ways.

Syed Ali Ashraf provides us with more an outline of an Islamic view of education than a response to the contents of Parts 1 to 5 of this volume. This outline gives evidence of commonalities with the kind of Christian approach which is generally advocated by the contributors to the earlier parts. There is also evidence of how the differences between the basic underlying Islamic and Christian worldviews mean that what may appear to be common is in fact seen differently.

Taking the apparent commonalities and differences in the order in which they appear, there is first a common opposition to a dualism of the sacred and the secular. Ali Ashraf suggests that this has become a problem in Islamic education only because it was the Christian church that first introduced a 'dichotomy of the divine and the secular branches of knowledge' (p. 270), a dichotomy which paved the way to Enlightenment rationalism and which is only comparatively recently having an impact in the Islamic world. In like manner, some Christian scholars have talked of a dualism of nature and grace in some forms of Christianity, which eventually gave birth to the Enlightenment. Ali Ashraf suggests that many Muslims have come to accept this dualism unthinkingly and to take as normal the existence of secular educational institutions whose influence is countered by the existence alongside them of 'madrasah' education. Have not many Christians adopted this dominant paradigm just as unthinkingly, assuming that Christian nurture in home and church (for 'madrasah' read 'Sunday school'), combined with secular education, is all that is needed? The approach to education advocated in this book questions this paradigm and calls for a holistic approach based on a Christian view of reality, human nature and knowledge. Ali Ashraf wants one based on an Islamic view and has apparently found a ready acceptance by 'all Muslim scholars' (p. 272). The Christian academic world is certainly more plural than this!

Ali Ashraf goes on to suggest that religious groups need to stand together to resist secularism and that, in spite of doctrinal differences, they can do this on the basis of common beliefs and values (p. 272). He instances common beliefs in a transcendental Reality, in 'the essence of the spiritual dimension in each human being' and in certain 'eternal and fundamental values'. I doubt that it is possible to separate doctrinal differences so easily from common beliefs and values. At times, Ali Ashraf seems to suggest that the doctrinal differences are secondary and that what matters most are common beliefs and values, 'religious sensibility' (p. 273), 'the same religion in essence' (p. 273) and 'the root of all religions' (p. 277). But study of the suggested common beliefs and values quickly reveals that they are at the same time matters of deep disagreement and that these disagreements are matters of doctrinal belief. For a start, there is disagreement as to whether or not the transcendent Reality is personal. Then there is disagreement on what he terms the 'norms received from the Divine Source and through divinely inspired people' (p. 273). Agreement that there is divine revelation is one thing, but agreement on how and through whom God reveals his truth is quite another!

Ali Ashraf assures us that 'Muslims love Christ with deep sincerity and the same intensity, because he is regarded by all Muslims as one of their prophets' (p. 274). I would strongly question whether Christ generally occupies the same place in the thinking and lives of Muslims as he does in those of Christians. If he does not, I do not see how it can be claimed that Muslims love him with the same intensity.

I suggest that what all this shows is that, although there are certain commonalities between worldviews, these common elements are themselves viewed differently from within different worldviews. The overall vision transforms everything to a greater or lesser degree.

Nor is it simply a matter of classifying some of these worldviews as religious as opposed to those which are secularist, and concentrating on what is common to many or all religious worldviews. Christians and Muslims may agree on certain matters which are unaccceptable to secularists but Christians and secular humanists may well agree on others that they do not share with Muslims. For example, Christians and Muslims may agree that morality is in some way rooted in religion (as Ali Ashraf suggests on p. 273), but Christian moral principles and humanist moral principles may have more in common with each other than either has with Islamic moral principles.

Educational practice

Both Colin Chapman and Monica Taylor write of the need of concrete practical examples of the outworking of evangelical Christian thinking about education. He suggests that it should be the subject of the next book, and she mentions the Charis Project (in which I have to declare a vested interest!).

We did intend this book to have something practical to offer, although its major concern was more theoretical from the outset. Perhaps we have not delivered in this regard as well as might have been expected. I do, however, think there is a lot here of almost immediate practical relevance. I would add that this book is sponsored by the Stapleford Project which has published over thirty books of resources for the teaching of Christianity in schools (mainly for religious education and assemblies). The Charis Project is a newer curriculum project, and its first four books have appeared only more recently. I suggest that the whole process has something to say about the relation between educational theory and practice. Educational theory is a practical theory; it is embedded in practice. Teachers are, or should be, reflective practitioners. It is not a case of going up the mountain at the start to obtain the formula from the philosopher-kings, and then coming down to 'apply' it in practice. Rather, there is a dynamic interplay, a to-ing and fro-ing between action and reflection. Theory may be largely tacit or intuitive at the outset, becoming more explicitly formulated only as we go along. Part of what this book represents is an attempt to stand back from the practice and take time to do a bit more of that explicit formulation and reformulation of theory. From this, we return to the practice with, hopefully, a better understanding of what we are doing and a clearer grounding for it. This in turn will help to refine the practice, to improve and develop it and perhaps to take some lateral moves; for instance, to construct educational institutions less dominated by the schooling paradigm.

Talking of religious education and assemblies, Colin Chapman mentioned his surprise at their omission along with the arguments for and against Christian schools. In response, I would say that we wanted to keep to more general and more basic issues about the whole of education. In Britain at least, much has been said and written elsewhere about school worship and religious education. The deeper issues about structural pluralism were seen as being more basic than the particular arguments about Christian schools, not that the latter are unimportant.

Finally, back to transformationalism

Was there a suggestion of reconstructionalism in that final remark of the paragraph before last? If so, it should not be surprising, for, as has been suggested, the different strategies for integrating faith and learning are spaces along a continuum rather than different and widely separated points on it. I have referred elsewhere (Shortt 1991, chapter

5) to transformationalism and reconstructionalism as, respectively, 'soft-presuppositionalism' and 'hard-presuppositionalism', to bring out the fact that the difference is one of degree rather than of kind.

The strategy recommended has been transformationalist. The contributions should themselves provide examples of that strategy in operation. The tone should be appropriate, and the favourable things that Colin Chapman and the other respondents say about the manner of the discussion seem to suggest that the contributors have had some success in that regard.

Distinctives and commonalities are put together into the arena of discussion. Otherwise, dialogue will not get very far. Part 6 was entitled 'Continuing the Dialogue'. Amen! Let it continue so that education, schools, and what we do with our children and young people may continue to be transformed into something more and more pleasing to God! Did I hear an answering 'Amen'?

BIBLIOGRAPHY

Carson, D. A. (1996), *The Gagging of God* (Leicester: Apollos).

Evans, Donald (1973), 'Does Religious Faith Conflict with Moral Freedom?' in Gene Outka and John P. Reeder (eds.), *Religion and Morality* (New York: Anchor).

Frankena, William (1973), 'Ought and Is Once More', in Gene Outka and John P. Reeder (eds.), *Religion and Morality* (New York: Anchor).

Guinness, Os (1991), 'Tribespeople, Idiots or Citizens? Religious Liberty and the Reforging of the American Public Philosophy', *Spectrum* 23/1 (Spring): 29-50.

Helm, Paul (1993), 'Understanding Scholarly Presuppositions: A Crucial Tool for Research?' *Tyndale Bulletin* 44/1: 143-154, reprinted in *Spectrum* 27/1 (Spring 1995): 25-34.

Hick, John (1983), 'On Conflicting Religious Truth-Claims', *Religious Studies* XIX, reprinted in John Hick, *Problems of Religious Pluralism* (London: Macmillan, 1985).

—— (1984), 'A Philosophy of Religious Pluralism', in Frank Whaling (ed.), *The World's Religious Traditions: Essays in Honour of Wilfred Cantwell Smith* (Edinburgh: T. and T. Clark), reprinted in John Hick, *Problems of Religious Pluralism* (London: Macmillan, 1985).

—— (1988), 'Religious Pluralism and Salvation', *Faith and Philosophy* 5/4 (October).

Mouw, R. J., and Griffioen, S. (1993), *Pluralisms and Horizons: An Essay in Christian Public Philosophy* (Grand Rapids: Eerdmans).

Murdoch, Iris (1966), 'Vision and Choice in Morality', in Ian T. Ramsey (ed.), *Christian Ethics and Contemporary Philosophy* (London: SCM).

Polanyi, Michael (1967), *The Tacit Dimension* (London: Routledge and Kegan Paul).

Shortt, John G. (1991), *Towards a Reformed Epistemology and its Educational Significance* (PhD thesis, University of London Institute of Education).

Strawson, Peter (1963), *Introduction to Logical Theory* (London: Methuen).

Wolterstorff, Nicholas (1984), *Reason within the Bounds of Religion* (Grand Rapids: Eerdmans).

INDEX